Beyond Smart Beta

Index Investment Strategies for Active Portfolio Management

GÖKHAN KULA
MARTIN RAAB
SEBASTIAN STAHN

WILEY

This edition first published 2017
© 2017 Gökhan Kula, Martin Raab and Sebastian Stahn

Registered office

John Wiley & Sons Ltd, The Atrium, Southern Gate, Chichester, West Sussex, PO19 8SQ, United Kingdom

For details of our global editorial offices, for customer services and for information about how to apply for permission to reuse the copyright material in this book please see our website at www.wiley.com.

Wiley publishes in a variety of print and electronic formats and by print-on-demand. Some material included with standard print versions of this book may not be included in e-books or in print-on-demand. If this book refers to media such as a CD or DVD that is not included in the version you purchased, you may download this material at http://booksupport.wiley.com. For more information about Wiley products, visit www.wiley.com.

Designations used by companies to distinguish their products are often claimed as trademarks. All brand names and product names used in this book are trade names, service marks, trademarks or registered trademarks of their respective owners. The publisher is not associated with any product or vendor mentioned in this book.

Limit of Liability/Disclaimer of Warranty: While the publisher and author have used their best efforts in preparing this book, they make no representations or warranties with respect to the accuracy or completeness of the contents of this book and specifically disclaim any implied warranties of merchantability or fitness for a particular purpose. It is sold on the understanding that the publisher is not engaged in rendering professional services and neither the publisher nor the author shall be liable for damages arising herefrom. If professional advice or other expert assistance is required, the services of a competent professional should be sought.

Library of Congress Cataloging-in-Publication Data is Available

ISBN 9781119315247 (hardback)   ISBN 9781119315278 (epub)
ISBN 9781119315285 (epdf)   ISBN 9781119395263 (o-bk)

Cover Design: Wiley
Cover Images: Market Quotes image: © crystal51/ Shutterstock;
Sky Background image: © deepadesigns/Shutterstock

Contents

Preface

Exchange-traded funds (ETFs) and index-linked investment products have enjoyed more than two decades of massive growth. They emerged from quirky no-name products to become rock stars. Institutional investors along with retail investors use passive instruments more and more as important building bricks for their portfolios.

Thanks to their compelling benefits for all kinds of investors and the growing demand for liquid, cost-effective exchange-traded products (ETPs), global assets under management in ETFs/ETPs grew jointly to over US$3.408 trillion at the end of Q3 2016[1]. Among financial professionals, ETFs are meanwhile very well known. But not all professionals have already realized that they should not only understand the product wrapper, which is the ETF, but also the index, which the ETF tracks effectively. Also, there are some developments in the indexing space which will enrich investors' possibilities.

As always, more choice leads potentially to greater confusion. Nowadays, more than 4,400 ETFs are available globally and this number is increasing every day. Even more explosive growth happened in the index sector itself. Meanwhile there are more than one million indices calculated daily – a dizzying range of asset classes, strategies and exposures.

With this book, we want to provide a clear picture about what ETFs/ETPs are able to offer the investor (and what not), how to use them for specific investment needs and advanced portfolio strategies. In addition, we have packed many practice examples into the index evolution chapter in order to shed some light on facts which are sometimes overlooked. Also, we put a strong emphasis on the latest developments in indexing and how investors could benefit most from blending active management with passive products.

Despite all the transparency initiatives, we witnessed that it could be hard for investors to research current data and details about various indices. Some index providers lack transparency. In some cases, investors could bypass the black boxes that index providers created artificially by directly looking into holdings and weightings of the ETF. Anyway, we collected the essential data in this publication – and saved you valuable time. Time you could use to consider active index investment strategies for your portfolio.

We wish you successful active decisions and long-lasting outperformance while using index investments!

NOTE

1. ETFGI as of October 19, 2016

Acknowledgments

This book is a synergistic product of three friends who have been active in the financial industry since the mid-1990s, blessed with domain expertise and still enthusiastic about investments, portfolio management and financial products.

For the development and production of this book we want to express our gratitude to:

- **Gemma Valler**, our Commissioning Editor, and Jeremy Chia, Content Development Specialist, at John Wiley & Sons for their outstanding support and mentoring through all stages of this publication.
- **Thomas Merz**, Managing Director, UBS Global Asset Management, for his contribution about using ETFs for Environmental, Social and Governance (ESG) Based Investments.
- **David Lichtblau**, former Chief Executive Officer, ETF.com, for his permission to support this book with selected data.
- **Linda York**, Senior Vice President, Syndicated Research and Consulting at Market Strategies International, and **Anne Denz**, Director at Market Strategies International, for their survey data.
- **Markus Schuller**, Managing Partner Panthera Solutions, for the continued joint research cooperation and the always enriching input.
- **Dwijen Gandhi**, Managing Director, New York Stock Exchange, for the support concerning the NYSE Dynamic US Allocation Index.

Finally, this project was only possible with the patience and support of our wonderful families and wives: **Ayse, Christina and Kathrin**.

About the Authors

Gökhan Kula, Chartered Financial Analyst™, Financial Risk Manager™
Gökhan is Managing Partner and Chief Investment Officer of MYRA Capital, an investment management company specialized in systematic investment strategies and advanced indexing solutions. He is a proven capital markets expert with over fourteen years of experience in the European investment industry with relevant track record and awards. Following various management positions in the asset management of the Walser Privatbank AG, he was appointed as the Managing Director of the Walser Privatbank Invest S.A., which was established in January 2011. In addition, he was board member to several Luxembourg investment companies. He has gained his MA at the University of Innsbruck and University of Bradford. He is a regular interviewee in various financial media from Germany, Austria and Switzerland.

Martin Raab, Chartered Alternative Investment Analyst™
Martin has extensive experience in financial products, including derivatives and ETFs as well as cross-asset portfolio management and holistic client advisory. Over the years, he became an internationally recognized investment expert and publisher (quoted in business publications including Politico, Bloomberg Brief, Handelsblatt and Finanz und Wirtschaft). He started his career in finance in 1996 with a bank apprenticeship. After positions in institutional asset management, Martin became part of a newly formed joint venture between a large U.S. bank and the world's largest bond manager, with offices in Munich, London and Newport Beach. His responsibility was for flagship funds, investing into structured bonds and complex derivatives. Afterwards, he continued his career working for five years with a German Landesbank as New Products/New Markets Executive. Since 2010, Martin has managed Switzerland's leading investor magazine as Executive Director. As regards his exchange-traded funds and indexing capabilities, Martin has been appointed Senior Advisor to the Board of MYRA Capital AG, Salzburg/Frankfurt, mainly responsible for cross-border index projects, together with the New York Stock Exchange. As Founding Partner of two U.S. financial companies, Martin has been actively involved in the transatlantic business for seven years. His profile is completed by

a Bachelor in Business Administration (Faculty Degree, TU Munich) and a diploma as a Chartered Alternative Investment Analyst (CAIA).

Sebastian Stahn, Chartered Financial Analyst™
After his education as a banking specialist, Sebastian studied business administration at the University of Applied Sciences Landshut and Anglia Ruskin University Cambridge. He is a CFA charterholder and dedicated his education and research focus particularly to the areas of ETFs and indexing. After his studies he worked as a fund manager and advisor to institutional clients at Walser Privatbank and MYRA Capital, an investment management boutique with a strong focus on efficient and rules-based investment strategies. In 2017 he joined Wüstenrot Group as Treasury & Investment Manager. Stahn specializes in absolute-return and portfolio insurance concepts and is a renowned expert on efficient, forecast-free and rules-based investment strategies.

CHAPTER 1

The Beauty of Simplicity – The Rise of Passive Investments

In the old days, asset management was a pretty straightforward business: A fund manager, skilled and equipped with the ability to find attractive deals and investments in the financial markets, took care of the investor's money and got in exchange a decent fee and tried to increase profit. The majority of fund providers or portfolio managers in the asset management industry tried to pick attractive stocks, bonds or other securities, to decide when to move into or out of markets or market sectors, and to place leveraged bets on the future direction of securities and markets with options, futures and other derivatives. Their objective over the year was to make a nice profit, and, sometimes by chance, to do better than they would have done if they simply accepted average market returns.

In pursuing their objectives, active managers searched out information they believed to be valuable, employed legions of research analysts in all parts of the world, and often developed complex or proprietary selection and trading systems. Active management encompasses hundreds of different methods, and includes fundamental analysis, technical analysis (interpreting charts) and macroeconomic analysis, and all of these have in common an attempt to determine profitable future investment trends. But don't be too impressed: if one looks behind the curtain, in some cases a "proprietary selection" is often nothing more than a simple play with Bloomberg's equity screening and its back-testing tools or one of replicating the investment strategy of a competitor firm.

OUTPERFORMANCE – A TOUGH CHALLENGE

In the mid-1970s, change came to the active asset management world. Not radical change, but the active world faced some competition for the first time from the pure, minimalistic approach of passive investing, namely the index fund. As described in detail in the next chapters, at this time the first generation of passive investments was born. An index fund provides investors with a return and performance equaling the underlying market. The market is effectively a well-known benchmark index like the S&P 500®, Euro STOXX 50®, FTSE100® or the DAX®. While the idea of consistent, market-beating returns that transform a smaller initial investment into greater wealth was and is still attractive to millions of investors, the reality over the last decade shows clear evidence that outperforming broad markets over longer periods of time has become more and more challenging. A matrix of the best-performing asset classes in each year or the hot stocks of one year will often become poor performers in the following year.

As a result, settling for achieving, rather than exceeding, market return is an increasingly popular option. Rather than trying to guess which investments will outperform in the future, index fund managers try simply to replicate the gains in a particular market, sector or, nowadays, factor. This means that they invest in all or most of the securities in the index – a technique called "indexing". Also, increasingly volatile markets, shifting correlations and the most recent disruptive interventions of many central banks have made it even more challenging for active managers to correctly predict the winning stocks or assets and to outperform the market or a sector. Therefore, many investors who are looking for exposure to broad markets and low costs switch to passive investment products.

INSTITUTIONAL INVESTORS: A SMALL CHANGE IN ALLOCATIONS, A BIG STEP FOR PASSIVE INVESTMENTS

Despite the massive rise of passive investments, active managers will probably not become the dinosaurs of the financial industry as smart investment ideas always stay in fashion. Particularly in some exotic investment spaces like Frontier Markets, Small Caps or Alternative Investments, skilled active managers have good chances to generate extraordinary returns. However, the broader the market, the more rapidly the chances of delivering returns that outpace market returns are diminishing. Also, buy-side investors are more and more sensitive with regard to costs and outperformance over time. Thrifty retail investors, with no sizeable amount of assets that would justify hiring a smart investment advisor, stick more and more to passive products like ETFs for their core investments. Sophisticated institutional clients like pension trusts, endowments and other "big dollar investors" are increasingly reviewing their investment mandates to decide whether their external managers effectively run a truly active managed portfolio – and therefore are justified to charge higher management fees compared with a passive mandate – or merely replicate an ordinary index.

Although the majority of fund assets are still actively managed, there has been some decrease in allocation to active funds over the past three or four years, according to the ETF sell-side. Mostly after the financial turmoil in 2008, the institutional world became more receptive to passive investments – though they did not switch every single one of their assets into ETFs. Of course, that is a story that the ETF industry often tends to tell a bit differently. According to the latest issue of the US Institutional Investor Brandscape® report, one of the most detailed surveys of institutional ETF usage, published by Cogent Research in spring 2016, the vast majority of pension investors, over 95%, still incorporate actively managed strategies in their institutional portfolios. There is a similar picture in Europe. In the 2016 edition of Mercer's European Asset Allocation Survey, which reflects data and feedback from nearly 1,100 institutional investors across 14 countries representing assets of around €930 billion, only 3% of participants in the survey reported any direct exposure to ETFs. This means that €28 billion from these institutional market participants is invested in ETFs already.

NOT ALL "BIG GUYS" LOVE ETFS

A detailed picture of the current state of active vs. passive investment styles can be painted based on the US Institutional Investor Brandscape®[1]: Figures 1.1 to 1.4, which show the results of the 405 investors managing $20 million or more in institutional investable assets, show that the use of active management varies little by asset size, ranging from 93% among pensions managing between $250 million and $1 billion in assets to 100% of the $1 billion-plus pensions. Interestingly, when questioned about their current usage of passively managed strategies, only 68% of the pension plans in 2016 report that they are using them, down from 81% in 2014. Notably, the use of passive investments is lowest among the cohort of smallest pensions, as just 54% of pensions managing less than $100 million in assets invest in passive instruments. Conversely, pension plans managing larger assets are much more likely to allocate at least a portion of their assets into passive products or to devote some portion of their assets to passive strategies (90% of pensions managing between $250 million and $1 billion in assets and 82% of $1 billion-plus pensions). Corporate pensions appear to be driving the decrease in use of passive investments. Some experts assume this might be a reflection of the reliance on liability-driven investment strategies among this cohort of the pension market.

In the non-profit world, where 89% of organizations utilize actively managed strategies, the picture seems similar as regards a decreased usage of passive strategies, and this decrease appears to be driven by the smaller

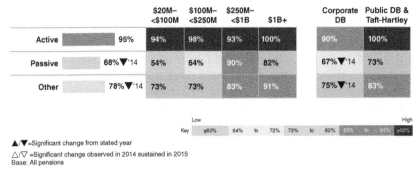

		$20M–<$100M	$100M–<$250M	$250M–<$1B	$1B+		Corporate DB	Public DB & Taft-Hartley
Active	95%	94%	98%	93%	100%		90%	100%
Passive	68%▼'14	54%	64%	90%	82%		67%▼'14	73%
Other	78%▼'14	73%	73%	83%	91%		75%▼'14	83%

Low   High
Key   ≤63%   64% to 72%   73% to 82%   83% to 91%   ≥92%

▲/▼=Significant change from stated year
△/▽ =Significant change observed in 2014 sustained in 2015
Base: All pensions

FIGURE 1.1   Usage of Active vs. Passive Strategies – Pension Assets
Source: Market Strategies International, "The Pull of Active Management – Examining the Use of Active vs. Passive Strategies in the Institutional Marketplace", April 2016

		$20M–<$100M	$100M–<$250M	$250M–<$1B	$1B+	Endowment	Foundation	TEO
Active	89%	85%	95%	99%	100%	93%	86%	89%
Passive	59%▼'14	56%▼'14	63%▼'14	66%	67%	63%	75%▲'13	48%
Other	88%▼'14	88%	84%	90%	97%	85%▼'13	95%	85%

Low   High
Key   ≤58%   59% to 69%   70% to 79%   80% to 90%   ≥91%

▲/▼ = Significant change from stated year
△/▽ = Significant change observed in 2014 sustained in 2015
Base: All non-profits

FIGURE 1.2   Usage of Active vs. Passive Strategies – Non-Profits
Source: Market Strategies International, "The Pull of Active Management – Examining the Use of Active vs. Passive Strategies in the Institutional Marketplace", April 2016

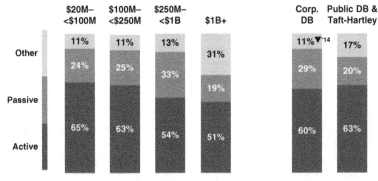

	$20M–<$100M	$100M–<$250M	$250M–<$1B	$1B+	Corp. DB	Public DB & Taft-Hartley
Other	11%	11%	13%	31%	11%▼'14	17%
Passive	24%	25%	33%	19%	29%	20%
Active	65%	63%	54%	51%	60%	63%

▲/▼ = Significant change from stated year
△/▽ = Significant change observed in 2014 sustained in 2015
Base: All pensions

FIGURE 1.3   Proportion of Active vs. Passive – Pension Assets
Source: Market Strategies International, "The Pull of Active Management – Examining the Use of Active vs. Passive Strategies in the Institutional Marketplace", April 2016

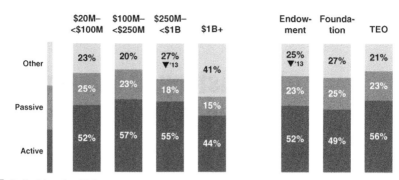

▲/▼ = Significant change from stated year
△/▽ = Significant change observed in 2014 sustained in 2015
Base: All non-profits

FIGURE 1.4　Proportion of Active vs. Passive – Non-Profits
Source: Market Strategies International, "The Pull of Active Management –
Examining the Use of Active vs. Passive Strategies in the Institutional
Marketplace", April 2016

institutions which manage less than $250 million in assets. However, there
is a growing fan base among the non-profits: foundations report an increase
in their use of passive strategies compared with 2013, and are the only segment of the non-profit market to have boosted their use of passive management over the past three years. The use of other asset classes is more prevalent
among non-profits (88%) than among pensions (78%) and is noticeably
higher among the $1 billion-plus segment. In addition, 95% of foundations
incorporate these asset classes in their portfolios – that is higher than any
other type of institution.

One aspect that has not changed is what drives asset allocation changes.
Institutional investors continue to follow two divergent paths: the focus of
pensions is very clearly on de-risking, while non-profits seek higher returns
and further diversification. Thus asset managers serving the institutional
market need to employ dramatically different strategies, with distinct product offerings to retain and cultivate existing relationships and position
themselves effectively for consideration for future mandates.

NOTE

1.　Market Strategies International, 2016

CHAPTER 2

The History of Indexing and Exchange-Traded Products

In today's world, there are a lot of indices – some of them are directly investable and some not. Often cited in the media and closely monitored by investors are consumer price indices, indices reflecting home prices and indices reflecting asset prices of stocks, bonds or commodities. However, indexing is nothing new really. Frequent price quotations of certain goods or values have been recorded since the 18th century. Whether it was the price of tea from shiploads in the Boston harbor or wheat quotations of the historic Hanse merchants in Hamburg, traders and wholesalers have been always interested in price patterns. Particularly in the commodities sector, seasonal effects are still an important factor which drives prices up and down.

FREQUENT PRICING THANKS TO COPPER AND FEATHER

Price recordings of certain goods become more valuable as the speed of getting a fresh, updated price increases. In this way, the trader is able to react more quickly and can try to anticipate future price changes. Paul Julius Reuter recognized this when he arrived in the year 1851 in the British empire's capital from Aachen in Germany, where he had been running a news and financial media company using a combination of the then high-end IT equipment called telegraph cables and a fleet of carrier pigeons. This smart combination of copper and feather helped Reuter to establish an enviable reputation for speed, accuracy and impartiality. Reuter's office at 1 Royal Exchange Building in London's financial district quickly became the place where continuous price quotations of stocks were available. Technically, he utilized the then new Dover-Calais submarine telegraph cable for this newly invented "data stream".

JOURNALIST TRIO PICTURES THE MARKET

With the continuous evolution of capital markets in Europe and the emerging United States, in the late 1800s a financial journalist named Charles Dow co-founded a company called Dow Jones & Company with his two press mates Edward Jones and Charles Bergstresser. The trio published the *Wall Street Journal* and worked in New York City's financial district out of a basement office. Wall Street of 1882 was a vibrant place, crammed with established high-society investors, distinguished bankers with top hats, ambitious immigrants from all over the world, wannabe-rich-fast brokers and bribed stock reports (perhaps some Wall Street critics would argue that parts of this "cocktail of interests" survived the last 130 years). Dow was the one who found a good solution for calculating the daily price moves of 12 large Wall Street stocks – mostly railways and heavy industrials then – on a frequent basis and simultaneously including corporate actions such as dividends and splits. The Dow Jones Industrial Average™ Index has become the oldest existing stock market barometer in the world. The index was increased to 20 constituents in 1916 and finally to 30 stocks in 1928. This index became the picture of the ups and downs in the American stock market. Despite all the respectable pioneer work that has given the Dow its reputation, this index has some flaws that investors should be aware of.

INDEXATION ACROSS THE GLOBE

With the computerization of the financial industry in the 1970s and 80s, more and more indices were launched. Surprisingly, the first notable index launch happened in Far East. On November 24, 1969 the Hang Seng Index was calculated the very first time by its Hong Kong-based sponsor, the Hang Seng Bank. It is Hong Kong's globally recognized equity index. Two years later, on America's east coast, the Nasdaq Composite Index® was launched. Since February 5, 1971, with a starting value of 100, this index has represented all domestic and international common stocks listed on the Nasdaq Stock Market. Much older is the S&P 500 Index, which was initially introduced in 1923. The S&P 500 index in its present form started originally on March 4, 1957. This index is the most commonly used benchmark for stocks. In 1984, the Russell 2000 Index® was created and back-tested until 1978. In the same year, the British equity barometer FTSE 100 index was launched. On January 3, 1984 the index was calculated with a starting value of 1,000 points (and back-tested until 1969). A latecomer was the meanwhile well-known DAX® index. The major index representing German large-cap equities including companies like BMW, Daimler or Siemens was a joint project of the German regional exchanges, the Frankfurt exchange and the financial newspaper *Börsen-Zeitung*. The DAX® index continued a precursor index calculated by *Börsen-Zeitung* since 1959 that measured the performance of the German equity market. The DAX® was officially launched on July 1, 1988 with 1,000 points. One of the latest launches of a broadly recognized equity index happened in 1998. On February 26, the EURO STOXX 50® Index was introduced by index provider STOXX. The start level was 1,000 points – like most European index peers. This index quickly became the widely used reference for performance of Pan-European (Eurozone) stocks.

CUSTOMIZED INDEXING AKA SMART BETA

With the rise of passive investment products like ETFs, index providers have been pushed into a battle over technology, speed and smart methodologies used to create new, advanced indices. Also, the indexing business began more and more to acquire a certain tailored flair. Hence five or six years ago, so-called "customized indices" became more and more popular. Unlike predefined benchmarks, which have been created more or less solely by major index providers together with a couple of large banks or exchange providers to represent a general market gauge for the public, customized indices are designed based on the highly individual needs of certain investors. These tailored indices are available across a variety of asset classes, including but not limited to equities, fixed-income, commodities, alternative strategies and even combinations of asset classes – so-called "multi-asset indices". In this context, the financial industry created the well-known and often-cited names "smart beta", "strategic beta" or "alternative beta" – but not each customized index is a smart beta strategy. This topic will be introduced in a couple of pages.

The rise of customized indices is also associated with declining costs for launching one's "own index". For example, in 2005 a customized index was affordable for institutional investors only. A small asset manager was not in a position to create an index based on its own proprietary allocation model, because of the costs for such a venture. On average a high five-figure amount was necessary to start a "build-your-own-index" project. In the interim, custom indices have become a kind of standard offering – for almost each index provider globally. And more new players are entering the market. The new wave for tailored, unconventional (and often sold as smart beta) indices also influenced the acquisition strategies of various established exchanges. For example, in 2015, Deutsche Börse paid nearly $700 million for the takeover of index provider STOXX and its accompanying IT and indexing platform. A year earlier, London Stock Exchange Group paid $2.7 billion for Russell Investments, an index provider and asset manager, which was put up for sale by its parent company Northwestern Mutual. In 2016, LSE Group sold the asset management business of Russell Investments to TA Associates and Reverence Capital Partners for $1.15 billion and kept the indices business, which became FTSE Russell. But there are also a number of smaller emerging index providers (like the Frankfurt-based Solactive or ERI Scientific Beta, with their customized index factory based on specific optimized index strategies), more or less fully focused on customized indices, which are enjoying increasing business activity. The driver for their soaring business is often an aggressive pricing model compared to large index providers. However, the journey is far from over. The latest trend in indexing leads to a blending of active and passive investment strategies, with the incorporation of existing capital markets models and advanced academic research. Before we shed light on the world of exchange-traded products and then on advanced index strategies in portfolio management, we have first compiled a comprehensive summary of the most notable and relevant milestones in the history of index investing (Table 2.1).

TABLE 2.1   Key milestones in the still-young history of exchange-traded funds and index investing.

1969–1973	**Experimental index labs:** The U.S. bank Wells Fargo, before it took over rival Wachovia, utilized various academic models to develop index investing. This project was led by John McQuown. Accordingly, Wells Fargo became a pioneer of index investing, launching the first index fund in 1971 with a $6 million investment from Samsonite Luggage Corporation's pension fund. This mandate should reflect the performance of 1,500 NYSE-listed stocks. From an operational point of view, it turned out to be very difficult to manage. In particular, the portfolio's equal-weight approach turned out to be "mission impossible" because of heavy trading costs in an era where US$5 flat-fee commissions were unknown. Also, Wells Fargo developed the Stagecoach Fund, a portfolio of low-beta stocks leveraged up so the beta of the portfolio was 1.0. The fund was set up as a closed-end mutual fund to be marketed to pension funds and other institutions. After almost two years of marketing, only $30 million had been committed, so the fund was dropped in November 1973[1]. About the same time, the American National Bank of Chicago got convinced by its then employee Rex Sinquefield to create a trust based on the US S&P 500 Index, minimum investment US$100,000. The fund was only available to institutions, and the New York Telephone Company became its first major investor. Also, no-load funds were introduced, a new way to attract investors for mutual funds while slashing fee layers.

(Continued)

TABLE 2.1   (*Continued*)

1973–74	**Index investing "manifesto" published:** The well-known book *A Random Walk Down Wall Street* is published by Princeton University professor Burton Malkiel. He calls for the establishment of a low-cost fund that reflected the market index, a laughable idea to most coevals in the fund industry.
1974–76	**Vanguard launches first index mutual fund:** One year after its foundation, The Vanguard Group – under the leadership of the well-known John C. Bogle – launched the first index fund for retail investors, the Vanguard® 500 Index Fund. It started with US$11 million assets under management. Today, this is the world's largest managed fund of any type, with assets of about US$250 billion[2].
1990	**World premiere of today's ETFs:** The world's first exchange-traded, index-linked fund was launched on the Toronto Stock Exchange (TSX). This product was labeled as the Toronto 35 Index® Participation Units. Eventually, this product structure became the precursor of today's ETF. In the same year, Vanguard created the first international share index funds available for U.S. investors.
1992	**The factor model:** Eugene F. Fama and Kenneth R. French, both University of Chicago professors, published their legendary article "Common Risk Factors in Returns on Stocks and Bonds". Fama and French's model compares a portfolio to three distinct risks found in the equity market to assist in decomposing returns. Prior to their findings, the Capital Asset Pricing Model (CAPM) was predominantly used as a "single factor" way to explain portfolio returns. Their findings are important for the evolution of indexing. Both gentlemen in 2013 received the Nobel Prize in Economic Sciences.
1993	**The birth of America's first ETF:** Three years after the launch of an ETF in Canada, the American Stock Exchange (AMEX) together with State Street Global Advisors (SSgA) launched the first authorized stand-alone index-based exchange-traded fund in U.S. history: the S&P Depository Receipts Trust Series 1, better known for its nickname "SPDRs". The SPDR ETF is benchmarked to the S&P 500® Index. It quickly gained acceptance in the marketplace and became one of the most successful ETFs in the U.S.
1996	**ETFs go international:** In March 1996, U.S. investment bank Morgan Stanley launched the first ETF containing non-U.S. securities under the name WEBS, an acronym for "World Equity Benchmark Shares". WEBS were 17 separate series of single-country-index-based ETFs listed on the AMEX. It was later renamed by Barclays Global Investors as iShares MSCI (Morgan Stanley Capital International indices) series. This product introduced another important structural variation; it had an asset manager (as these ETFs were mutual funds), not a trustee. Barclays Global Investors (BGI) was the WEBS's manager.

TABLE 2.1 (*Continued*)

1999	**New sector-tracking approach – without an index:** Merrill Lynch's Holding Company Depositary Receipts or HOLDRS introduced a new concept in tracking: portfolios of securities designed to cover various market sectors. These do not track an index. Instead, the stocks are selected at the time the HOLDRS is established, based on particular selection criteria such as company size and liquidity. A HOLDR is a fixed selection of stocks with a very specific selection. This selection does not change, and HOLDRs are not managed. As a result, they do not have the dynamic sector-tracking aspect of an ETF. Stock selection represents a particular and narrow view of an industry or sector. If a company included in a HOLDR is acquired, or if it goes off the market, its shares are not replaced. HOLDRs are seen by those who favor them as offering a more specific type of market approach than ETFs. For example, with a HOLDR, an investor can follow a theme like "broadband" or "Internet security". The AMEX has developed indexes based on types of HOLDRs. **Repack it – debut of Hong Kong's first ETF:** After the motto "virtue out of necessity", the Hong Kong SAR Government was initiator of Hong Kong's first ETF. The Government acquired a substantial amount of Hong Kong-listed stocks to sustain the exchange rate during the Asian Financial Crisis two years earlier. To prevent disruption to the domestic stock market, the Government decided to repack the equities portfolio into an exchange-traded fund, called the Tracker Fund of Hong Kong.
2000	**ETFs arrived in Europe:** In April 2000, Frankfurt-based Deutsche Börse launched the so-called "XTF" segment, where two exchange-traded funds got listed: a EURO STOXX 50® ETF and a STOXX® Europe 50 ETF. The issuer for both was Merrill Lynch International with the LDRS product suite. The trading segment Xetra was Europe's first trading venue for ETFs and has since been one of the market leaders. Also in April, exactly 17 days after its then rivals in Frankfurt, the London Stock Exchange celebrated the listing of the UK's very first ETF, tracking the FTSE 100 index. In September 2000, ETFs hit the Alps: SIX Swiss Exchange introduced an ETF trading segment too. A few months later, German lender HypoVereinsbank (today Unicredit Bank) launched Indexchange, the first European ETF issuer. **First smart beta ETF was launched:** With its inception on May 22, 2000, the iShares Russell 1000 Value ETF (IWD) was the first smart beta ETF.

(Continued)

TABLE 2.1 (*Continued*)

2001	**Europe's first swap-based ETF, made in France:** Lyxor, a fully-owned subsidiary of French banking giant Société Générale, rolled out Europe's first swap-based ETF in 2001. The performance of this synthetic-replicated ETF was not generated by the underlying index portfolio but from a swap agreement with a counterparty. Swaps are nothing unusual or suspicious, but it was simply the first time that an ETF collateral basket (for example Japanese Government bonds) did not necessarily reflect the market or index an ETF is tracking (European Large-Caps).
2002	**ETF debut in Singapore:** Singapore's first ETF, the streetTRACKS Straits Times Index Fund, was listed on 17 April. ETF sponsor State Street Global Advisors attracted primarily a couple of large local institutional investors to subscribe for the product initially. Singapore retail investors spurned the "new thing" for a while because there was no leverage build-in.
2003	**World's first ETC launched down under:** In March 2003, Gold Bullion Securities – the world's first physically-backed gold exchange-traded commodity (ETC) – began trading on the Australian Stock Exchange. The ETC was developed by Gold Bullion Limited (a predecessor to the London-headquartered investment product provider ETF Securities) in association with the World Gold Council over a nine-month process.[3]
2004	**China's first ETF and the Gold ETF launched:** In January 2004, China Asset Management was approved to cooperate with the Shanghai Stock Exchange in developing the first ETF in mainland China[4]. After months of intense work, on December 30, 2004, the China 50 ETF was launched. A month before, in November 2004, State Street Global Advisors' streetTRACKS Gold Shares was listed on the New York Stock Exchange with the sponsorship and endorsement of the World Gold Council. After a name change in May 2008, the world's first physically-backed Gold ETF trades as SPDR Gold Shares (Symbol GLD).
2005	**World's first crude oil ETC:** In July 2005, ETF Securities listed ETFS Brent Oil, the world's first oil ETC.
2006	**Premiere of Europe's physically-backed gold ETF:** In March 2006, Zurich Cantonal Bank and Barclays Global Investors launched physically-backed commodities ETFs: The Swiss-based bank introduced its legendary Gold ETF (Symbol ZGLD) and Barclays launched the world's first silver-backed ETF, iShares Silver Trust (Symbol SLV). The silver ETF raised great concerns over supply and demand among various commercial silver users.

TABLE 2.1 *(Continued)*

2008	**Launch of world's first leveraged commodity ETFs:** In January, the Canadian investment provider BetaPro Management, came up with new Horizons BetaPro ETFs, covering gold bullion and global mining companies. This was the first time that through an investment in an ETF investors were able to participate twice on the daily performance or the inverse daily performance of the underlying benchmark. Lucky was the man who bought the right leveraged ETFs the month before the implosion of the world's financial markets. At the end of November 2008, almost exactly two months after the spectacular default of Lehman Brothers, Maryland-based ProFunds Group, one of the world's largest managers of short and leveraged funds, announced that it was launching the first exchange-traded funds in the United States to provide short exposure or to provide leveraged exposure to commodities. ProShares benchmarked to broad commodities and crude oil indexes. **World's first active ETFs launched – and closed months later:** 2008 was unquestionably the worst year in modern history to launch a financial product. It was the year of record numbers of defaults, including General Motors' $1 billion default on its bonds, all-time lows in many sectors and ultimately the time when then investment giant Lehman Brothers collapsed. In mid-March 2008, a day after J.P. Morgan Chase raised its takeover bid, distressed Bear Stearns' asset management arm moved forward with a notable milestone in the ETF history: they launched the first actively managed exchange-traded fund. Due to the shocking headlines about Bear Stearns' dramatic fall, the Bear Stearns Current Yield Fund started trading almost unnoticed by the financial community. On March 16, 2008, the Bear Stearns executives signed the merger agreement with J.P. Morgan Chase. The deal was structured as stock swap in which Bear Stearns' shares were worth US$2 each. This represented an eye-popping loss as Bear Stearns traded early 2007 at US$172 per share. A few months later, in September 2008, the trustees of the active ETF decided to close it by October 1, 2008. At the same time, rival Invesco PowerShares started its Active Low Duration Portfolio ETF (Symbol PLK). The PowerShares ETF survived the financial market crisis but holds currently only a small amount of assets (approx. US$7 million).
2009	**Commission-free ETF brokerage:** The well-known U.S. brokerage company Charles Schwab, which became a national brand through its discount offer, brought cost competition to a whole new level when it debuted four exchange-traded funds that could be traded entirely commission-free on its platform. Today, there are several hundred ETFs that can be traded commission-free on a number of different trading platforms, the so-called "Schwab effect".

(Continued)

TABLE 2.1 (*Continued*)

2010	The ETF-blamed "Flash Crash": It is no surprise to hear that stock prices are volatile, but what happened on May 6, 2010 was more than just a rollercoaster ride. Roughly a quarter of all Russell 3000 Index constituents dropped within minutes by more than 10%. Well-known large-cap stocks also collapsed suddenly. Within five minutes, the Dow Jones Industrial Average lost 1,000 points or 9%. Over 20,000 trades across more than 300 securities were executed at prices more than 60% away from their values just moments before. Hence mostly all market-making pricing models began to struggle in seconds. ETFs were heavily affected by the market makers' inability to accurately assess the value of ETFs' underlying holdings. The media quickly blamed ETFs for causing this market shock. In reality, the pressure was built up by a large mutual fund which initiated a sell program to sell a total of 75,000 E-Mini contracts (valued at approximately US$4.1 billion) as a hedge to an existing equity position[5]. To make a long story short, this event triggered actions from the Securities and Exchange Commission and other market regulators to install circuit breakers and other measures to protect markets from a repeat performance. But it would not remain the last "flash crash" for long.
	US$1 trillion invested into U.S.-listed ETFs/ETPs: In December of 2010, days before the holiday season, assets in U.S.-listed ETFs and ETPs broke through an historic milestone, reaching US$1.027 trillion. In these days, in the U.S., there were 894 ETFs with assets of US$887.2 billion from 28 providers on two exchanges.
2012	Largest Active Fund Manager goes ETF: To some market observers it was as though the devil had started to sell holy water: Active funds giant PIMCO announced an active exchange-traded fund based on the asset manager's flagship Total Return fund. "Here is an opportunity for the small investor to get into a PIMCO product," then CIO Bill Gross told Reuters in an interview in January 2012. "The Total Return fund is the largest in the world. We expect the Total Return ETF to be the biggest as well." In retrospect, the fund launch itself was a great achievement. The expectation of becoming the biggest bond ETF in the world will take some time. Currently the product (Ticker: BOND) has roughly US$2.6 billion assets under management. Products of BlackRock (Ticker: AGG) and Vanguard (Ticker: BND) lead the bond ETFs league table by far.

TABLE 2.1 (*Continued*)

	First RMB ETF Debuts in Hong Kong: In Asia, ETFs also became more and more popular – mostly among institutional investors. In February 2012 the launch of the Hang Seng RMB Gold ETF marked a new milestone in the development of renminbi (RMB) products at Hong Kong Stock Exchange, with the listing of the Stock Exchange's first ETF traded in Chinese currency RMB.
2014	**ETF assets in the U.S. hit US$2 trillion:** A new landmark for the ETF industry was reached by year end 2014: The consolidated assets in the U.S. reached more than US$2 trillion.
2015	**"Alpine Peak" – 1,000th ETF listed on the Swiss Exchange:** The Swiss stock exchange is recognized as a pioneer in ETF trading in Europe, having launched this product segment in 2000 with two ETFs on STOXX indices. Since then, the number of products has continued to grow from year to year. In February 2015 the continually growing selection of ETFs on SIX Swiss Exchange has reached an historic peak: with five ETFs listed by UBS, the number of exchange-traded index funds on the Swiss Exchange jumped to 1,000. Currently, the small country hosts 1,225[6], one of the broadest ETF offerings in Europe.
2016	**Global ETF assets well above US$3 trillion:** The inflows into ETFs reached a new record level in fall 2016. According to data from ETFGI, a leading data aggregator, the assets invested into ETFs listed peaked at US$3.408 trillion at the end of Q3/2016. These vertiginous asset numbers of US$3.4 trillion break down to US$2.415 trillion ETF AuM in the United States, US$566.74 billion in Europe and US$131.88 billion in Asia-Pacific ex-Japan.

EXCHANGE-TRADED FUNDS – A UNIQUE ALL-ROUNDER

More than two decades ago, ETFs as we knew them were born. Since then they have increasingly become part of the modern financial portfolio as transparent, attractive and flexible investment products. Today, ETFs are important building bricks for active portfolio management.

An executive of a large mutual fund company recently stated that "Americans own more cats than ETFs and this will continue for a while" during a presentation. Although there are no serious statistics about cat ownership (or, more accurately, cat care, as cats do not have owners but servants), we know relatively precisely that in mid-2015, nearly 54 million, or 43% of U.S. households, owned mutual funds[7]. Roughly 5.2 million of these households owned ETFs, according to the Investment Company Institute study published in spring 2016. These numbers are encouraging for all persons engaged in educating investors about the benefits of this product, as they mean that nearly 10% of U.S. households use and benefit from ETFs. Probably the fund guy is wrong with his statement – the ETF ownership percentage will soon double from 10% to 20% in the coming years – but it does express that ETFs are still a niche investment of a sort, compared to stocks or mutual funds.

The latest milestone figures in the still-fresh history of ETFs are encouraging. In December 2015, the global ETFs/ETPs industry celebrated a record level of US$372.0 billion in net new assets. This represented a 10% increase over the previous record of US$338.3 billion of net new assets gathered in 2014. Today, sophisticated investors – in the U.S. and Europe – benefit from the extremely broad choice of ETFs and are perfectly prepared to use them for active portfolio management. We strongly believe that we can help through this book to increase the understanding of technicalities and raise the awareness of indexing strategies among all readers.

An earlier accolade for ETFs, connected with the popular tag "active management" was bestowed in March 2012. Investment legend Bill Gross, the then Co-CIO and former founder of famous bond manager PIMCO, announced to the press the launch of the PIMCO Total Return ETF. With that move, one of the most important active fund managers in the world launched a passive investment vehicle – exchange-listed and liquid on a daily basis, instead of tradable only once per day. Market observers compared his decision to replicate his flagship fund as an ETF to the Devil himself deciding to sell holy water. Meanwhile, this is not the only example of an active mutual fund company that launched its own ETF series. The U.S. financial group John Hancock started with "Multifactor ETFs", sub-advised by Dimensional Fund Advisors, and Goldman Sachs recently launched a suite of "Active Beta" ETFs designed to capitalize on a diversified basket of stocks with specific factors that differentiate them from traditional passive indexes.

But ETFs and the soaring asset inflows into this dynamic product are not something that is exclusive to U.S. financial institutions. For a while now, Chinese asset managers have discovered the advantages of ETFs and (not surprisingly) ETF issuers from China have appeared on the landscape. In March 2015, CSOP Asset Management debuted with its CSOP FTSE China A50 ETF on the New York Stock Exchange. This was the first ETF offered by a Chinese asset manager to American investors. The Chinese financial conglomerate seeded this ETF with a mind-boggling $237 million. European stock exchanges attract Far East newcomers too. In June 2016, the first Chinese asset manager listed an ETF on the London Stock Exchange: Fullgoal FTSE China Onshore Sovereign and Policy Bank Bond 1-10 Year Index ETF. This is the first ETF by an independent Chinese issuer ever listed in Europe. Also, there are some first joint ventures between Western and Eastern investment companies. The latest example involves the ETF provider

WisdomTree and Hong Kong-based asset manager ICBC Credit Suisse. Both financial companies have joined forces to launch a new China-focused equity ETF on the London Stock Exchange in summer 2016.

QUICK REFERENCE: MOST-USED ETF AND INDEXING JARGON AT A GLANCE

Authorized Participant (AP)

An AP is typically a broker/dealer or market maker with a proprietary ETF trading desk that has entered into a legal contract with the ETF issuer to be able to create and redeem shares of the fund officially. APs do not receive compensation for their work from the ETF issuer. Rather, APs pay fees for any order submitted to the ETF issuer. APs derive their compensation from commissions and fees paid by clients for creating and redeeming ETF shares and from arbitrage between an ETF's NAV and its market price.

Bid-ask Spread (Spread)

The spread represents the difference between the bid and the ask prices of an ETF. Competition increasingly forces market makers to set the narrowest margins possible. However, in most cases, this does not apply to niche markets. In general, the following applies: the spread reflects the quality of the market-making and is also dependent on the assets under management of the ETF – the larger the ETF, the lower in general the bid-ask spread.

Custodian

Usually, a trust company, bank or similar financial institution that is responsible for administration and safeguarding the securities owned by an ETF or ETF structure. The custodian is also responsible for calculating the net asset value, net income and realized capital gains and losses.

Equal-Weighted

Equal weight is a type of index calculation that gives each stock in the index or portfolio the same weight. In this way, all index constituents are equally important for the index performance. A regular rebalancing schedule is enforced to secure that the individual weightings are set to equal.

Market Cap Weighted

Capitalization weight is another type of index calculation, in which individual components are weighted according to their market capitalization. Larger market value components carry a larger percentage weighting; smaller components play a smaller role in the overall index performance.

Market Maker

A market maker quotes bid and ask prices for securities. Unlike an authorized participant, theoretically each broker or trading firm can act as market maker for ETFs/ETCs and quote prices. Unlike APs, market makers do not have any legal contract with the fund's issuer/ sponsor. In most cases, market makers derive their compensation from the bid-ask-spread or arbitrage solely.

Net Asset Value (NAV)

The NAV represents a fund's per share market value on a daily basis (end of day) and is calculated by the fund's custodian. This is the price at which investors buy ("bid price") fund shares from a fund company and sell them ("redemption price") to the fund issuer. It is derived by dividing the total value of all the cash and securities in a fund's portfolio, less any liabilities, by the number of shares outstanding.

Total Expense Ratio (TER)

The total expense ratio of active funds/ETFs includes administration costs and operating costs, as well as expenses for fulfilling legal requirements. The issuers set the TER on an annual basis, but deduct it regularly from the fund's assets. Investors should be aware that transaction costs and performance fees are not part of the TER.

Tracking Difference

This measures how well an ETF is likely to perform in relation to the underlying index. The tracking difference is calculated over time (ex-post) comparing the performance of the ETF with the performance of the index it tracks. This should not be confused with tracking error (see below), which measures the volatility of the tracking difference over time. For investors, the tracking difference is an important factor to use to monitor the true cost of holding a specific ETF.

Tracking Error

This figure indicates the standard deviation of the daily return difference between the ETF and the replicated index. A low tracking error, however, does not necessarily mean that the passive fund is following its benchmark particularly closely.

Estimated Tracking Difference

Deutsche Bank introduced in 2013 a new figure called "estimated tracking difference". This is the estimated difference between the returns of the index being tracked and the returns of the ETF based on past performance. Specifically, it takes account of the negative impact on performance of the all-in fee, or TER, the negative impact on performance of any OTC swap transaction costs, if applicable, and the positive impact on performance of OTC swap enhancements or securities lending. The ETD is calculated using the latest annual figures.

Physical Replication (Full Replication)

When using the full replication approach, the ETF buys all securities (shares) of the underlying index. This approach, also known as full replication, works well when used for blue chip indices with liquid underlyings and a smaller number of index constituents. With small-caps and mid-caps, this method becomes difficult and costly to implement.

Optimized Replication

ETFs using an optimized replication method invest in a representative sample of index constituents. This technique uses quantitative models (optimized sampling vs. representative sampling). The tracking error differs here according to the model's individual quality and covered market.

Synthetic Replication

This method is implemented using derivatives. The ETF invests in a broad, diversified basket of securities that may vary dramatically with regard to the underlying index (collateral). Additionally, the ETF enters into a swap deal with a bank. By doing this, the ETF exchanges the performance of the fund (basket) with the return from the reference index. Using synthetic replication, the tracking error of the ETF is (theoretically) the smallest compared to the other methods.

Underlying

The underlying is simply the index or benchmark that the exchange-traded product (ETF, ETC etc.) is linked to. For example, the S&P 500 ETF's underlying is the Standard & Poor's 500 Index, a capitalization-weighted index of 500 American stocks. Movements in the index (i.e. 1% price increase) will reflect nearly 1:1 in the ETFs performance (1% price increase).

Rising Bars, Soaring Product Launches: The Global ETF Market at a Glance

As ETF assets are growing and product launches soaring, there are major differences between the global ETF market and its sub-markets like Europe or Asia-Pacific. iShares, for instance, is the market leader globally and in Europe, with market shares of 37% and 46.4%. In Asia-Pacific they are just ranked number 8, with 3.5% market share. Here Nomura leads with 25.3%. Figures 2.1 to 2.4 and Tables 2.2 to 2.4 give interesting insights into the global ETF market.

A New Kind of Financial Product   The concept of an ETF was based on that of index-based funds at the start. What the two had in common was that stocks in the fund were selected on the basis of type, grouped and traded like a

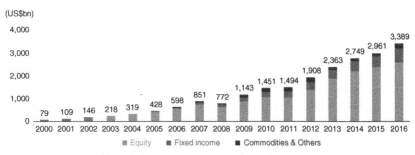

FIGURE 2.1   Global ETF Assets
Source: Bloomberg, Markit, and BlackRock

TABLE 2.2   Global ETP Providers Ranked by Assets (US$bn)

	Assets under Management	Market Share in %
BlackRock/iShares	1,253.70	37.00
Vanguard	611.8	18.10
State Street	494.8	14.60
Invesco PowerShares	111.2	3.34
Deutsche AWM db x-trackers	80.7	2.40
Nomura Group	78.9	2.30
Charles Schwab	53.8	1.60
SocGen/Lyxor	53.3	1.60
First Trust Portfolios	40.3	1.20
WisdomTree Investments	38.9	1.10
Other Providers	571.3	16.80

Source: Bloomberg, Markit, and BlackRock
Note: as of September 30, 2016

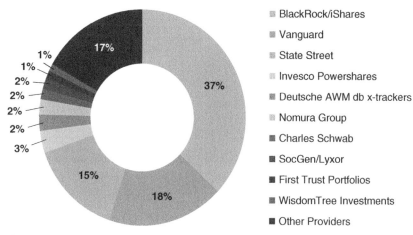

FIGURE 2.2   Global ETP Providers Ranked by Assets
Source: Bloomberg, Markit, and BlackRock

TABLE 2.3   Europe ETP Providers Ranked by Assets (US$bn)

	Assets under Management	Market Share in %
BlackRock/iShares	263.3	46.40
Deutsche AWM db x-trackers	65.8	11.60
SocGen/Lyxor	53.3	9.40
UBS	31.5	5.50
Credit Agricole	23.1	4.10
Vanguard	23	4.10
Source Holdings	21.9	3.90
ETF Securities	19.5	3.40
State Street	17.5	3.10
Commerzbank	8.6	1.50
Other Providers	40.4	7.00

Source: Bloomberg, Markit, and BlackRock
Note: as of September 30, 2016

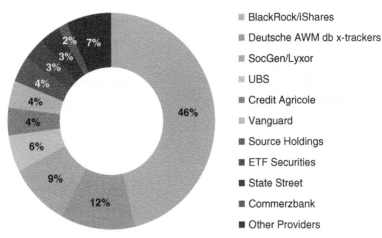

FIGURE 2.3   Europe ETP Providers Ranked by Assets (US$bn)
Source: Bloomberg, Markit, and BlackRock

TABLE 2.4 Asia-Pacific ETP Providers Ranked by Assets (US$bn)

	Assets under Management	Market Share in %
Nomura Group	78.8	25.30
Nikko Asset Management	34.6	11.10
Daiwa Securities Group	33.3	10.70
State Street	18.6	6.00
Mitsubishi Group	15.4	4.90
Fortune SG Fund Management	15.2	4.90
HSBC	12.4	4.00
BlackRock/iShares	11	3.50
Samsung Asset Management	10.7	3.40
China Asset Management	8.8	2.80
Other Providers	73	23.40

Source: Bloomberg, Markit, and BlackRock
Note: as of September 30, 2016

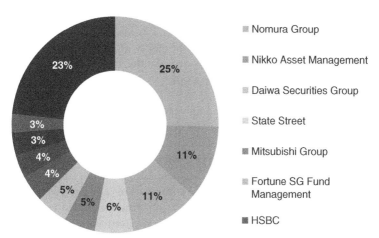

FIGURE 2.4 Asia-Pacific ETP Providers Ranked by Assets (US$bn)
Source: Bloomberg, Markit, and BlackRock

single stock on equity markets. What we know today as ETFs originated with the idea of portfolio trading, also called program trading. This was the then-new ability for large investors to trade an entire portfolio – in most cases all the S&P 500 stocks – with just one order ticket.

In March 1990, the first ETF was listed on the Toronto Exchange, based on the idea previously adumbrated by the Los Angeles-based investment firm Leland, O'Brian and Rubinstein. The company tried to launch a portfolio insurance product based on the S&P 500 Index called "SuperShares", but not a single "SuperShare" ever hit the market. Quite the contrary happened in Canada: investors could, for the first time, participate in the performance of the TSE 35 Index without actually having to purchase all 35 stocks. This was a revolutionary concept and it worked very well in practice.

And it soon attracted attention. Nathan Most and Steven Bloom, who worked for the American Stock Exchange (AMEX) in New York City, developed a listed fund (in the form of a unit trust) that tracked the entire Standard & Poor's 500 Index. The new index fund was shortened to the four letters "SPDR" – for S&P Depositary Receipts, commonly referred to today as "spiders". At first, the SPY (SPDR S&P 500 ETF Trust) was used mostly by major asset managers and banks, but private investors soon perceived its advantages. The SPY has become the largest ETF in the world, and has a market capitalization of more than US$137 billion. ETFs have established themselves in just over ten years as a critical component of asset management. Worldwide, there were 269 ETFs in 2003, in which US$205 billion was invested; ten years later, the assets globally invested in ETFs reached US$3.408 trillion, a new record. At the end of September 2016, investors had 6,526 ETFs to choose from.

Solid Product Advantages   The exchange-traded fund performed just like the index and tracked it like a shadow. Investments of this type are referred to as "passive investments". Using them, an investor does not miss out on a market movement in the index just because they did not include one or two shares in their share account, or because they did not otherwise have the means to track the index. The composition and in particular the management – in the context of the operational administration – of an ETF are clearly simpler and more economical compared with classical investment funds, because the exclusive goal of the ETF manager is to track the performance of a reference index. Another advantage is that, with ETFs, the investor pays considerably less in fees than they would for classical investment funds. These innovative characteristics continue to define ETFs to this day. However, particularly with regard to short- to medium-term trading with these products, there are some important things to pay attention to. Specifically, the "hidden" costs, particularly in complex and hence complicated index and ETF structures, are important. We explain the relevant dos and don'ts in the following pages.

ETF's Legal Structures at a Glance

Even if the name "exchange-traded fund" is used globally, there are some differences in how ETFs are legally structured. In the European Union, most ETFs are governed by laws regulating collective investment schemes, known as "Undertakings for The Collective Investment of Transferable Securities" or UCITS for short. This regulatory framework provides a number of important safeguards for ETF investors.

- **Segregated assets**: ETFs are bankruptcy-remote in the event of the insolvency of the ETF issuer. The assets of a UCITS fund must be entrusted to an independent custodian for safekeeping, segregated from the assets of that custodian and the company that issued the ETF. These assets cannot be used in any case to discharge the liabilities of either the custodian or the ETF issuer.
- **Diversification limits**: This fact should ensure that investors are not exposed to concentrated risks by investing into a single asset. To be UCITS-compliant, the index an ETF tracks must be sufficiently diversified. Under UCITS V, an UCITS based on replicating an index may invest up to 20% of net assets in shares and/or debt securities issued by the same body, with the 20% limit raised up to 35% in the case of a single issuer where justified by exceptional market conditions. This flexibility is permitted where the relevant index is recognized by the Financial Regulator on the basis that it is sufficiently diversified, it represents an adequate benchmark for the market to which it refers and it is published in an appropriate manner.[8]
- **Collateral**: If an ETF uses derivatives, such as swaps, forwards or futures, UCITS compliance requires an ETF to limit the amount of its exposure to a single counterparty. The amount exposed through a derivative contract must not exceed 5% or 10% of NAV, depending on the type of counterparty. Furthermore, UCITS regulations oblige the fund to reduce its exposure to any counterparties in case such counterparties default on their obligations under the derivative contracts. One way of doing this is to post collateral, which is usually a tradable security. Also, the collateral must be valued on at least a daily basis and assets that exhibit high price volatility should not be accepted unless suitably conservative "haircuts" have been applied.

Accordingly, exchange-traded commodities (ETCs) and exchange-traded notes (ETNs) – both are covered in the next chapters – are not collective investment schemes for the purpose of the UCITS directive, and are therefore not governed by the UCITS regulations.

In the United States, still the most vibrant place in the global ETF business, there are various legal structures used to establish ETFs.

- **Open-end Funds:** The vast majority of U.S. ETFs are structured in this way, regulated under the Investment Company Act of 1940. The open-end structure is used by ETFs whose primary objective is to provide exposure to stock baskets, equity indices or fixed-income assets. Dividends and interest received by an open-end ETF can be immediately reinvested, and derivatives, portfolio sampling and securities lending can be used in the portfolio. Open-end ETFs that meet certain Internal Revenue Service standards are treated for tax purposes as pass-through entities, with income and capital gains distributed to shareholders and taxed at the shareholder level.[9]

- **Unit Investment Trust (UIT):** This is an investment company that holds a generally static investment portfolio ("one-time offer") and is used by a few ETFs that track broad asset classes. A prominent example of a UIT is the SPDR S&P 500® ETF, the oldest, largest and most-traded ETF in the world. With no board of directors or investment advisors managing the portfolio, UITs have less investment flexibility than open-end ETFs. For example, UITs do not reinvest dividends and instead hold them until they are paid to shareholders, usually quarterly. During rising markets, this can create a disadvantage known as cash drag. In addition, UITs are not permitted to lend securities in the portfolios or use derivatives, and they must fully replicate the indexes they track. However, like an open-end fund, UITs are registered investment companies regulated under the 1940 Act and therefore offer the same level of investor protections as open-end funds. Also, UIT ETFs that meet certain Internal Revenue Service standards are treated for tax purposes as pass-through entities.[10]

- **Grantor trusts:** This form of trust is typically used by ETFs that invest solely in physical commodities or currencies. A well-known example is the SPDR Gold Shares ETF. Grantor trusts are required to hold a fixed portfolio, as opposed to a variable one, making the structure ideally suited for physical commodities and currencies. Because the nature of the underlying investments prevents grantor trusts from being classified as investment companies under the 1940 Act, grantor trust ETFs are regulated only by the 1933 and 1934 Acts. Therefore, while grantor trust ETFs must disclose regular financial information, they provide none of the additional investor protections laid out in the 1940 Act. Grantor trust ETFs also do not qualify for regulation by the Commodity

Futures Trading Commission (CFTC), unlike partnership ETFs. ETFs that use the grantor trust structure consider investors direct shareholders in the underlying basket of investments. As such, investors are taxed as if they directly owned the underlying assets.[11]

- **Limited Partnerships:** A niche structure, mostly used for offerings exposed to commodities or energy infrastructure, are ETFs organized as Limited Partnerships (LP). Partnership ETFs are considered publicly traded partnerships because they trade on a stock exchange. They generally are treated as partnerships for tax purposes, which avoids double taxation at both the entity and the investor level. The income and realized gains and losses from a partnership ETF flow through directly to investors, who then pay taxes on their share. However, depending on what they invest in, partnership ETFs could be taxed as corporations. Partnership ETFs can accommodate many different types of investments, including futures that provide exposure to certain types of commodities that are hard to store physically. For example, while grantor trust ETFs can be used to invest in gold or silver (commodities that do not deteriorate over time and can be stored at relatively low cost), partnership ETFs generally track commodities such as natural gas and oil (which are difficult to store and lose their value over time). So instead of holding these items physically, partnership ETFs access these products through the futures market. Partnership ETFs are usually regulated as commodity pools by the CFTC. While regulations by the CFTC include disclosure and reporting requirements, they are not as stringent as those required by the Securities and Exchange Commission under the 1940 Act.[12]

Replication Methods

Even if two exchange-traded funds refer to the same index, the way in which they track the index performance can be different.

- **Physical Replication:** The simplest method is called "physical replication". Physical replication is a derivatives-free product design – what the investor sees is what he gets. Assume that an investor purchases into an equity index ETF with 50 constituents. The issuer/asset manager of the physically replicated ETF buys all 50 different shares into the ETF portfolio and the ETF investor (unit holder) effectively holds these securities pro-rata. This is how almost all U.S. ETFs are set up, except those which track future contracts.
- **Synthetic Replication:** Another method to track the underlying index is through synthetic replication. These methods are often used by some of the European ETF issuers. Synthetic replication often leads to lower

transaction costs and lower tracking difference of indices with many constituents or lower liquidity compared to physical replication. As a result, in synthetically replicated funds, the tracking error between the ETF itself and the reference index (underlying) is nearly non-existent.

The **unfunded swap model** is the oldest method of synthetically tracking an index. Under this model, the ETF issuer purchases with the cash of the ETF buyers a basket of securities from a swap counterparty (collateral) and agrees to deliver the basket's performance to the swap counterparty. In exchange, the swap counterparty delivers the performance of the specific ETF underlying (for example, the EURO STOXX 50® Index) to the ETF issuer. Important fact: The basket of securities usually does not correspond with the ETF's underlying index itself. Hence a synthetic replicated EURO STOXX 50® Index ETF which is operated with an unfunded swap model does not necessarily hold shares of the EURO STOXX 50® Index universe but could instead contain liquid U.S. or Asian stocks or Government bonds. The exact collateral is at the sole discretion of the ETF issuer, which can be usually found on the ETF issuer's website, updated daily. As the swap counterpart is often the investment banking arm of the ETF issuer's parent company, the fund holdings (securities basket) origin is mostly out of the bank's securities inventory. However, all fund holdings are in a segregated account, administered and reconciled by an independent custodian. In an advanced version of the unfunded swap model, the ETF issuer has swap agreements with different swap counterparties in order to decrease the counterparty risk. Counterparty risk arises if there is a substantial difference between the ETF's NAV linked to the swapped reference index performance and the value of the substitute securities basket. According to the European financial markets regulation (UCITS rules), the exposure to the swap counterparty should not exceed 10% of the ETF's NAV. This means in turn that the daily value (at the end of trading day) of the securities basket should amount to at least 90% of the ETF's NAV. In cases where the ETF's exposure to the swap counterparty exceeds 10% at the end of a trading day, the swap counterparty will make a cash payment to the ETF issuer in order to bring the net exposure of the ETF to the counterparty back within the allowed limits (Figure 2.5).

A second variation is the **funded swap model**. This model was introduced in 2009 in Europe. Unlike the unfunded swap model, the funded swap model does not use the investors' cash to purchase a basket of securities. Instead, the cash is used to enter a swap agreement and paid to the swap counterpart in exchange for the performance of the specific index (less swap fees), for example the EURO STOXX 50® Index. The swap counterparty is obliged to put a diversified basket of securities into a collateral account which is administered by an independent custodian. Usually, the value of the

Day[1]	Index	Basket Value	Swap Value[2]	ETF NAV[3]	Counterparty Exposure[4]	
Day 1	100	100	0	100	0/100=0%	Initial investment of 100, starting level of the index 100, swap value is 0.
Day 2	105	100	5	105	5/105=4.76%	The index rises whereas the basket remains flat; swap value is 5.
Day 3	110	108	2	110	2/110=1.82%	Both the index and the basket rise: swap value is 2.
Day 4: Before Resetting	115	103	12	115	12/115=10.43%	Under UCITS III, counterparty exposure is limited to a maximum of +– 10%, so the swap is
Day 4: After Resetting	115	115	0	115	0/115=0%	reset. Resetting to zero[5] involves a payment of 12 from the swap counterparty to the ETF (reinvestment in the substitute basket).
Day 5: Before Resetting	102	113	–11	102	–11/102=–10.78%	The swap value falls below –10%, so the swap is reset[6]. Resetting involves a payment of 11
Day 5: After Resetting	102	102	0	102	0/102=0%	from the ETF to the counterparty (securities from the substitute basket are sold).

[1]End of business day. No Intraday reset; [2]Swap Value = Index Value – Substitute Basket Value; [3]ETF NAV = Substitute Basket Value + Swap Value; [4]Counterparty Exposure = Swap Value/ETF NAV; [5]Not all ETF provider reset swaps to zero; [6]Not all ETF providers reset swaps based on the fund owing the swap counterparty money.

FIGURE 2.5   Counterparty Exposure of an ETF
Source: © 2016 Morningstar, Inc. All Rights Reserved. Reproduced with permission.

collateral basket is equal to or greater than the ETF's NAV. On trading days, when the exposure of the ETF to the swap counterparty becomes positive, the ETF provider requests additional funds at the swap counterparty – to reset the counterparty risk back to zero. The swap collateral, often liquid stocks, bonds or money market instruments, is used in the case of the default of the swap counterparty.

In the aftermath of the financial crisis of 2007/2008, synthetic replication techniques have been frequently questioned by regulators, investors and the financial media because of their sometimes complex interconnections between various counterparties, especially in times of extraordinary market movements. Influenced by the public debate, large European ETF issuers like Deutsche Asset Management, which switched its flagship funds in 2014 to physical replication, focus more and more on physical replication rather than swap-based (synthetic) replication.

Trading ETFs

Over the years, ETFs have been held for shorter periods in the securities accounts of investors – like the average holding period of stocks. In some cases, like hedge funds or similar tactically-oriented traders, these types of investors keep ETFs just a few days or even a few hours in their portfolios. But the shorter the time held, the more important the bid-offer (buy-sell) spread becomes as a cost factor. Let's assume, for instance, that an investor buys an ETF in the morning, holds it until shortly before the end of trading on an exchange, and then sells it at a profit of 50 basis points (0.50%). A difference in the ETF's bid-ask spread of five basis points (0.05%) is more important than it would be for a long-term investor. Spreads widen and narrow in the market for various reasons. Popular ETFs with deep liquidity (large volumes), tend to have narrower spreads under normal market circumstances. Thinly traded ETFs or such with illiquid, exotic underlyings in most cases have wide spreads. As a rule of thumb, the following also holds true: The tighter the spread, the more attractive it is to use the instrument for tactical positions. Especially for frequently rebalanced portfolios (sector rotation, momentum etc.), ETFs with narrow spreads should be selected. Depending on the underlying asset, the average spread (five-day) could fluctuate between 0.15% and 0.50%.

Liquid Benchmarks, Mostly Low Spreads As mentioned, an important influencing factor of the spread is liquidity, and the following applies: The more liquid the market, the lower will be the implicit transaction costs and the tighter will be the spread. The daily trading volume provides information on the effective depth of liquidity. Looking at the NYSE-traded volume, for example, the SPY, which had a daily trading volume of circa US$140,000,000 in October 2016, was the strongest index fund in terms of volume. For that product, the time-weighted average spread was an extremely low 0.01%[13]. In this case, high-order flow – in the benchmark and also in the fund – played a role. For less-liquid products, close spreads of that kind are hardly possible. In particular, the more esoteric the ETF's underlying index is, the more likely are wide spreads. For example, Janus' Obesity ETF, a fund focused on healthcare and the treatment of complications associated with obesity, has an average spread of 2.23%. A wide spread does not necessarily mean that the ETF is less attractive with respect to the investment opportunities, it just reduces the performance when trading in and out of the fund. Hence investors should take a look at websites such as ETF.com, Morningstar, regional web platforms or professional market data applications like Bloomberg or Thomson Reuters to review the quoted ETF "spreads".

Silent Commitments Another factor that has an influence on the level of the spread is often overlooked: The commitments made by the market maker. The market maker is the market interface between seller and buyer. The market maker makes binding quotes on sales and purchase prices for ETFs in order to ensure that trading functions smoothly. The spread is a commercial incentive to act and thus to create liquidity. What is important is the will and eventually the ability of the market maker to quote competitive buy and sell prices. Along with the high trading volume, the competition among various market makers is also a factor that helps to keep the spreads tight. But market makers do not generally have a comprehensive contract with the issuers on pricing; rather, they act as purchasers and sellers of previously-owned securities. That kind of "authorized dealer" is an authorized participant. The dealer is authorized to trade baskets of shares directly with the issuer – as described further on – in the context of a creation/redemption process.

Local Time and News Headlines   An important criterion for trading with ETFs is also local market hours, or the period of time in which the ETF is traded. Markets in different geographic areas trade at different times during the 24-hour day. For example, a U.S. investor enters a trade in a Chinese Index ETF at 9 AM in New York City. While the American ETF buyer is sipping his morning coffee in his Manhattan office, the Chinese stock market has been closed for hours as it is 9 PM in Hong Kong or Shanghai. In trading times during which the market maker does not have the chance to buy or sell foreign shares on his own home exchange, because it has closed, the bid-offer spreads are usually a bit wider, because they have an increased security risk for the market maker. For the investor, this specifically means: Anyone trading with benchmarks not traded in one's time zone (such as the US S&P 500® Index for Europe-based investors or the Hang Seng Index for US-based investors) will have to take into account higher spreads in the calculation. Certainly, the surcharges for important benchmarks like the S&P 500® Index, EURO STOXX 50® Index or the German DAX® Index are kept in tight limits. The reference exchanges such as futures markets offer mostly sufficient liquidity even for a closed underlying market, so that the market maker can continuously quote on the ETF exchange. Along with the issue of the differing time zones, there are other factors that influence hedging costs for the market maker and lead to the bid-offer spread widening. Thus, for the market maker, it is more difficult and more expensive to hedge against risk when a passive product involves exotic or highly-regulated markets such as Indian shares. Sharply rising volatility can also lead to the bid-offer spread widening. A prominent example is the famous (or merely infamous) shutting down of the Greek market in the middle of 2015. The Greek government decided to close the country's banks as well as the Athens stock exchange to avert the collapse of its banking system. Owners of the Global X FTSE Greece 20 ETF and the Lyxor ETF FTSE Athex 20 found themselves held captive. The above-mentioned market makers priced the ETFs on the information they had in front of them. This information was very limited. Hence the price of both ETFs went south. As another example, after the nuclear catastrophe in Fukushima, Japan, the bid and offer prices for ETFs on the MSCI Japan exchange went to the moon. Some market makers even stopped quoting prices due to the high level of uncertainty.

The Creation/Redemption Process While secondary market takes place on the exchange, the primary market operates using a complex creation/redemption process (Figure 2.6). For physically replicated ETFs, an authorized market maker, the AP, puts together a basket that mirrors what the index contains. For delivering this basket, he receives as compensation from the ETF issuer fund shares in the same value as the basket – the "creation" is thereby carried out. In the context of a "redemption", the AP gives ETF shares back to the issuer. He receives shares in compensation. For swap-based ETFs, cash is exchanged for new share certificates. With the inflow of funds, the ETF firm receives a basket of securities from a counterparty that does not correspond to the index. The issuer uses a swap to exchange the performance resulting from that for the price development of the index. Independently of the type of replication, for the issuance/redemption, a fee applies, which is billed by the ETF firm to the market maker in the context of the primary market transaction and that the market maker includes in its calculation in the secondary market – i.e. ultimately, in the spread. The creation/redemption process keeps the price of the ETF – for the most part – very close to the NAV. However, a passive fund can be traded with a mark-up or discount to its NAV.

This discrepancy is possible, for example, when relatively new developments move the markets, but the underlying stock exchange has already closed. However, larger deviations only rarely continue for long periods of time. Ultimately, that would spur the interest of arbitrageurs, who would attempt to exploit the price differences for profit. At the latest, when that "species" of market participant becomes active, the ETF price again approaches the NAV. In the end, the following can be said: For tactical

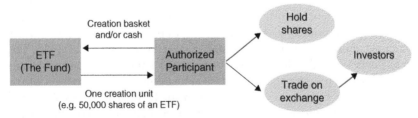

FIGURE 2.6 The Creation and Redemption Process
Source: Bloomberg, Markit, and BlackRock

investments with ETFs (including tracker certificates), investors should primarily pay attention to low spreads and the bid-offer volumes. This depends, in particular, on the liquidity of the market and on the competency of the market maker. However, larger fluctuations in the bid-offer spread can occur. Therefore, it is a good idea to work with bid and offer limits, because even with the most liquid products, due to short-term events, a sub-optimal execution of the order can occur.

Tracking Difference vs. Tracking Error As briefly described in the "Quick Reference", two additionally important quality measurements for ETF investors are tracking error and tracking difference. Through these, the investor gains a true sense of how well its ETF is likely to perform in relation to the index it aims to track. Tracking difference is defined as the difference over time of the performance of the ETF versus the performance of the underlying index.

The second well-cited measurement is the so-called tracking error. This is the volatility of the tracking difference over time. The calculation of this figure is somewhat complex: It measures the volatility of the difference (standard deviation) in returns between the ETF and its designated benchmark index. If an ETF's returns are more volatile than its benchmark index returns, it will have a higher tracking error and vice versa.

A Return Source Called Securities Lending As we all know, investors who own securities in their portfolio are entitled to receive the dividends (stocks) and interests (bonds). But there is another way to generate income through one's portfolio holdings: securities lending. For decades now, it has been a well-established practice among institutional investors and banks to offer short-term loans of stocks or bonds to other market participants. Thanks to securities lending fees, the portfolio manager could generate a partial increase in its total returns. On average, securities lending may contribute between 5 and 30 basis points (0.05% to 0.30%) per year to the overall return of a portfolio. An academic research study found, that "under plausible assumptions, ETFs make 23–28 bps per year from securities lending." The study also showed that by actively screening the most profitable-to-lend securities within the portfolio and consequently lending these securities out, the revenues can be as high as 55–114 bps per year.[14]

However, it depends on the stocks or bonds you lend out. Securities that are highly in demand in the lending market generate higher premiums than others broadly available. ETFs that hold these highly desired securities will earn a hefty premium lending out this part of its fund portfolio, but securities lending fees usually fluctuate as certain industry sectors, regions or single stocks fall in and out of favor with hedgers, short-sellers and other market participants. It is not only pension trusts, endowments or family offices that use securities lending as a source of return, but many mutual funds and ETF issuers also use this as a common practice.

Not All Investors are Aware of It   However, still not all investors are aware of the functionalities. Indeed, some investors didn't even know about the existence of securities lending until a few years ago. At an ETF & Indexing Conference in London, the representative of a large British pension trust (who stated an hour before that they are increasingly active in using ETFs) outed himself after a presentation of a large ETF issuer covering this topic, that he had never thought about the implied counterparty risks involved and was not aware of the additional side revenue the ETF issuer might be generating through lending out securities which belong to the ETF's portfolio holdings. Meanwhile the gentleman reviewing the ETF issuer's collateral reports meticulously on a monthly basis.

In general, securities lending is not bad or particularly risky. It is all about having a transparent process in place, clearly disclosing to investors how much of the lending fee will finally be contributed to the ETF itself (and what share of the fee income the ETF issuer itself keeps) and accepting only collaterals which are quickly marketable in some way. Also, a collateral should remain valuable even in extreme market risk scenarios. This can be achieved by using only high-rated bonds and large-cap stocks as collateral. However, the ultimate decision maker in this process is the ETF issuer not the ETF investor.

Well-Established Process   The process of securities lending is well established and standardized (Figure 2.7): At first, a financial institution or hedge fund approaches the ETF issuer (or ETF portfolio manager if the portfolio management is outsourced) with the request to temporarily borrow a specific security from the ETF's portfolio. For instance, a sector ETF holds a thinly traded small cap automobile-supplier stock which a hedge fund trader wants to borrow as he intends to short the stock. Both parties agree for a securities lending fee (the hedge fund has to pay to the ETF issuer) and the hedge fund must provide a collateral – mostly cash or securities that must meet certain quality standards – to the ETF. All terms agreed, the ETF holds the collateral to secure repayment in case the hedge fund fails to return the loaned stocks at the end of the lending agreement. Also, the value of the collateral must exceed the value of the loaned security, to provide the ETF with a kind of "safety cushion" (2–5%) in order to prevent losses if the borrower isn't able to return the loaned security at maturity of the securities lending agreement. If the stock pays dividends while out on loan, the

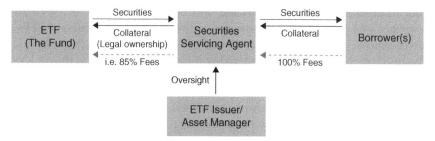

FIGURE 2.7   Securities Lending Revenue Streams
Source: Bloomberg, Markit, and BlackRock

borrower has to send the ETF the appropriate amount. Another fact that is not commonly known: The portfolio manager can sell securities regardless of whether the security is on loan or not. The lending agent (or the portfolio manager's middle office) has the responsibility of ensuring that sold securities are recalled from the securities borrower in time to effect a smooth settlement.

How Much Does the ETF Holder Get from the Lending Fee?   This is the most relevant question for investors and differs to some extent between some ETF issuers. For example, ETF issuer BlackRock disclosed that iShares ETFs receive 71.5–80%, depending on which kind of securities each ETF holds, of the additional income generated from securities lending. The remaining money is shared between BlackRock, affiliates and third parties serving the securities lending process.

Leveraged and Inverse ETFs

Unlike classic ETFs, which basically mirror the underlying index performance 1:1, leveraged ("geared") and inverse ("short") ETFs reflect a multiple of gains or losses in their underlying index. Also, these products often claim multiples or inverse participation in their names, such as "XYZ ETF 2×" or "ABC 3× Short ETF". They are constructed to achieve investment results that target the daily returns of their underlying benchmarks and are reset at the beginning of each new trading day. This mechanism is called "path dependency". Because of the path dependency, leveraged and inverse ETFs should be used predominantly for a short-term investment time horizon as they are not really suitable for long-term investors. In particular, inverse ETFs – which gain in value if the underlying declines – may be used to hedge parts of the portfolio against losses over a short time horizon.

Path Dependency Important to Understand To illustrate the price behavior of leveraged and short ETFs, let's assume an investor buys two different ETFs: a two-times leveraged ETF and a two-times inverse ETF on an equity index. Assumed on the first day, the underlying index increases by 3%, the 2× leveraged ETF gained 6% (2 × 3%), while the 2× inverse (short) ETF lost 6% (−2 × 3%), as shown in Table 2.5.

Both ETFs behaved as they should: The leveraged product performed twice of the positive value of the underlying index. The inverse product, which essentially bets on short price movements in the underlying index, lost 6% in value because the underlying gained 3%. If the underlying index had lost 3%, the leveraged ETF would have gained 6% – twice the negative performance in the underlying.

On day 2 (Table 2.6), things changed a bit. The massive decline in the equity index led to a meltdown of the positive performance of the leveraged ETF. Instead of $1,060, the ETF is worth $975.20. The inverse ETF, which suffered a loss on day 1, gained on day 2 impressively and jumped from $940 starting value to $1,015.20. However, the total returns show that the price movements are highly volatile.

Embedded Options Leveraged and inverse ETFs need to be rebalanced each day after market close. Thus, the ETF will tend to buy on up days and sell

TABLE 2.5   Market Close on Day 1

	Starting Value	Performance Return on Day 1	Value at End of Day 1	Total Performance Return
Index Value	100	+3%	103	+3%
2× Leveraged ETF	$1,000	+6%	$1,060	+6%
2× Inverse (Short) ETF	$1,000	−6%	$940	−6%

TABLE 2.6   Market Close on Day 2

	Beginning Value on Day 2	Performance Return on Day 2	Value at End of Day 2	Total Performance Return for Two Days
Index Value	103	−4%	98.88	−1.12%
2× Leveraged ETF	$1,060	−8%	$975.20	−2.48%
2× Inverse (Short) ETF	$940	+8%	$1,015.20	+1.52%

on down days, with the trade typically larger during volatile trading sessions. This means that on a day with declining prices in the underlying, the short ETF sells in order to add exposure while the long ETF sells positions in order to reduce its exposure. As the leveraged or inverse product buys high and sells low, this effectively reduces performance in a volatile market. However, in a steadily trending market (increasing or declining), it compounds gains day by day – exaggerating the momentum, and of course the exposure. Mathematically speaking, this effect is similar if the investor is short a put option (sold the right to purchase a security) and the market is falling; then the speed at which the put option loses value continues to accelerate because of negative Gamma. (Just a little option pricing digression: Gamma is the mathematical expression for the rate of change of an option's Delta. And Delta is nothing more than the number that tells the investor how much the option price will change if the option's underlying changes by a one-point move. As Delta is not fixed and fluctuates, it is helpful to have a specific measure – the Gamma.)

Essentially, adding leveraged or inverse ETFs to a portfolio makes sense if the portfolio manager has a short investment horizon and wants to actively play a market opportunity in a certain sector, market or commodity. The investor could overweight a specific market segment without using additional cash, but when trading these types of ETFs, you should have a serious understanding of what you are doing. In particular, because of the daily resets of the product's performance calculation and subsequently their path dependency, the individual performance of leveraged and inverse ETFs may differ substantially from their specific underlying over time. A careful and prudent risk assessment is highly recommended.

Tax Surprises? Last but not least, one surprising fact to some investors is the taxation of leveraged and inverse ETFs. Unlike traditional ETFs, which are generally tax-efficient because the in-kind creation and redemption mechanism limits the effective portfolio turnover (purchases and sales of securities), leveraged and inverse ETFs have usually a high portfolio turnover as they rebalance their ETF portfolio on a daily basis to reflect the market movements. Also, leveraged and inverse ETFs do not experience a significant level of in-kind creation or redemption transactions and use mostly swaps and other derivative instruments to replicate the desired payoff structure. As a direct consequence, leveraged and inverse ETFs are not tax-efficient. Investors are well advised to have a brief look to the short-term capital gains distributions stated on ETF issuers' websites. Almost all ETF issuers publish this figure more or less prominently.

ETFs vs. Futures

Today, some ETFs that trade on major indices have become an alternative to investing in futures. Thanks to the meanwhile remarkable deep liquidity in broad-based equity ETFs (like SPY, VOO, EEM or IWM), both instruments are almost identical. ETFs can simplify the internal trading process, while decreasing operational costs. Thus it is little wonder that an increasing number of active asset managers are now rethinking their product toolkits. Also, banks are reviewing the options: As most institutional investors are using futures for their long exposure, banks have to match the supply-demand situation and take the short exposures. Due to increasing costs of capital caused by regulatory frameworks such as Basel III, this has changed. Banks face higher costs which are passed on to future buyers in the form of increased prices. Especially the December roll becomes rich, as banks do not want the short exposure in futures contracts. Time will show if regulatory changes or other "short takers" enter the market. Meanwhile an increasing number of investors embrace ETFs over futures. Nevertheless, one should carefully look into the details of both instruments.

General Differences   Although ETFs and futures are similar in many ways, there are some major differences. ETFs do not expire. They are open-ended investments, whereas futures expire on a regular basis, quarterly for instance, and have to be rolled, which means that the invested contract must be sold prior to maturity and the following contract (maturing e.g. in three months) has to be bought. Another difference is the fee structure. Futures do not have explicit holding costs. As they expire regularly, transaction costs (execution, bid-ask spread, clearing) appear on a rolling date and can be substituted for holding costs. ETFs face a management fee and further costs depend on the replication method and the rebalancing framework. Last but not least, there is a big difference between futures and ETFs in their funding structure. Futures are unfunded, which means that not the whole exposure has to be invested, but only the initial margin. The difference between the notional and the paid margin can, for instance, be invested into "risk-free" assets. ETFs are fully funded and do not have any leverage when buying them (except leveraged ETFs).

Counterparty Risk   Since the occurrences of September 2008 (the "Lehman effect"), three issues have become increasingly important to most traders and asset managers. First of all, counterparty risk has become a major topic. Nowadays, as we all know, asset managers around the globe are significantly less comfortable with any sort of counterparty risk. This is why swaps, the classic over-the-counter product, are no longer the "ultra" instrument for portfolio management, even though there are not many alternatives when it comes to gaining exposure to things such as correlation. However, many institutions struggle with the involved counterparty risk and switch to the plain vanilla exposure of futures and ETFs. The amount of outstanding equity- and commodity-linked swaps has decreased dramatically since the financial crisis. Obviously, many traders and asset managers are keeping their hands off swaps – except with currency and foreign exchange deals. In the global swap trading environment, FX-linked swaps still dominate the marketplace. A first market study done in the year 2010 by EDHEC-Risk Institute found a further reason why swaps linked to some asset classes are no longer state of the art: many respondents believe that ETFs generally perform much better (and closer to the benchmark index) than total-return swaps. It should be mentioned that, ironically, this "better performance" or reduced tracking error in the specific ETF is because of the usage of total-return swaps between the ETF issuer and an investment bank.

Fees and Spreads – the Devil is in the Detail The second and third topics include liquidity and spreads. Today, many asset managers focus on the liquidity of a product and its bid and ask spreads during various market conditions. Few in the financial community are interested in a situation where portfolio positions are becoming rapidly illiquid and creating large bid and ask spreads. Here is a brief thought on the cost of ETFs: When buying and selling ETFs, each transaction will incur more than just a trading commission. As with other securities, there is a difference between what the market maker will charge an ETF buyer and what that same dealer will pay a seller ("bid-ask spread"). For asset managers, the smaller the spread, the lower the cost. This is a very important issue when the ETF position is used for cash equitization or tactical asset allocation reasons. When there is little trading activity in the ETF, bid-ask spreads can get quite wide; but the devil is in the details. Some funds have larger expense ratios (i.e. 0.30%) but a smaller average bid-ask ratio (i.e. 0.05%). The higher the trading frequency, the more an asset manager has to research which fund is finally the better choice. As a rule of thumb, the more exotic and unconventional the indices are (as stated in this book many times), the higher their expense ratios, both bid-ask spreads and overall liquidity.

Soaring Inflows Boost Liquidity Levels ETFs mastered all three issues – counterparty risk, liquidity and spread size – superbly during the financial meltdown. For instance, during the last 12 months, equity, fixed-income and commodity-based ETFs enjoyed heavy inflows from institutional investors. In addition, the soaring numbers of retail investors which switched from traditional mutual funds or structured retail derivatives into ETFs, particularly in Europe and Asia-Pacific, have boosted the liquidity levels of many exchange-traded funds dramatically. The average intraday volume in most ETFs remained stable on high levels. For example, the afore-mentioned SPDR S&P 500 Index Fund (SPY) currently has an average daily volume (ADV) of approximately US$20 billion[15] and is the most liquid ETF worldwide. On the other side of the Atlantic, the ETF market in Europe has to set its sights much lower when compared to the eleven-digit figure of the SPDR S&P 500 or the ten-digit ADV of the iShares Russell 2000 Index Fund. The ADV of the top-ranked Lyxor Euro STOXX 50, the ETF brand of Société Générale group, is just about EUR 100 million. The turnover of ETFs in the Asia-Pacific region is still lower. The Nikkei 225 ETF's average daily volume is US$55 million. However, investors should notice that the so-called "on-screen" liquidity – what the ADV effectively is – in most cases is only half of the truth.

Let's imagine a portfolio manager wants to buy $100 million of a less-often traded ETF linked to a European mid-cap index. The asset manager notices that the specific ETF's 20-day ADV is only about $10 million (consolidated across listings). This is the moment when the asset manager should contact an ETF broker (better known as an authorized participant or AP) to ensure that liquidity exists for the desired trade. The AP internally considers the best way to source liquidity for that larger-than-usual-ADV order. In this particular example, it's determined that new units of the ETF should be created. Even though the portfolio manager's order is more than ten times the hypotheticical ETF's ADV, an AP can source liquidity for the trade using the ETF creation process.

Leverage, Margins and "Speed Controls"   More than ever, leverage is still a double-edged sword and the wrong tool for traders and asset managers whose skills are not refined or for highly skilled portfolio professionals going through a slump. Yet, with the ability to trade ETFs with an intraday leverage, the futures advantage has diminished a bit. But if an asset manager prefers real leverage without surprising "reset effects" over a longer time horizon, the futures still get the edge there. Here it's important to distinguish between the money management issue when using ETFs vs. futures and the leverage effect itself ("daily reset"). In this paragraph we focus on the money management, better known as the margining process. A key point when writing about leverage and margins is the amended policy ("regulatory notice 09-53") on leveraged ETFs of the U.S. market regulator FINRA, which came into effect in September 2009. Since then, the required intraday margins doubled for bull leveraged ETFs and tripled for bear leveraged ETFs, meaning that the required margins on leveraged ETFs will range from 50% to 90% of the ETF price. All U.S.-based brokers amended their margin policy accordingly. Some require a 100% cash or securities backing when keeping 3× leveraged ETFs overnight. Hence any account which reports a margin deficit under the amended rule is subject to immediate liquidation by the broker. Another important guideline was set in December 2015 by the Securities and Exchange Commission. The new derivatives rules for Registered Funds limit the amount of notional exposure to derivatives a fund can have to 150% of a fund's net assets for most funds, or to 300% if the fund actually offers lower market risk because of that notional exposure. In this way, the ETF lost some of its advantage regarding the minimum cash amount an asset manager needs to keep in its account in order to trade. This all depends on the future position; i.e. in the e-mini S&P 500 (Ticker ES), a market position could be established with a minimum amount of US$5,625 (initial overnight margin) and US$4,500 (maintenance margin)[16]. This is the amount needed to carry one contract through the closing of the day session. In other words, an asset manager who trades the e-mini S&P 500 futures contract trades at around US$106,000 (US$50 times the value of the S&P 500 stock index) for a margin requirement over US$5,625. The corresponding ETF on the S&P 500 (SPY) is trading currently at just over US$193 – but you have to maintain at least usually 25% of the amount into your brokerage account. This equates a leverage of 4 to 1 at the ETF, while the future offers a higher leverage ratio of 1:18.

ETFs – A New Rival for e-Mini Futures? Some market participants believe that heavily traded ETFs, including the SPDR S&P500, iShares Russell 2000 and PowerShares QQQ, could be a substitute for some future contracts, most especially the CME Group's e-Mini futures. For example, one future contract for the e-Mini S&P 500 equals 500 ETF shares. It was introduced by the Chicago Mercantile Exchange on September 9, 1997, after the value of the existing S&P 500 contract became too large for traders managing smaller portfolios who were looking for a hedge with more precise exposure to the S&P500 index. Nowadays an asset manager could easily use the ETF instead of the future in order to gain short-term beta exposure to the U.S. equity market. Other market participants argue, however, that e-Minis are traded nearly around the clock during the weekdays on the CME Globex system, whereas ETFs are only traded with sufficient liquidity during normal and extended U.S. exchange trading hours, which means 6 AM to 8 PM Eastern Standard Time. The truth is probably somewhere in the middle of both arguments.

But this won't lead to an end of the downsized future contracts or a serious disruption in trading volume. Quite the contrary; the EUREX

Exchange launched a new mini-future: the DAX Mini. Unlike most other international indices, the DAX index family are performance total return indices, which means that the payment of dividends is not reducing the index level, but is fully reinvested. This contributes to the growing index levels, which result in growing notional of the DAX future. Therefore, in spring 2015, DAX futures had a notional value of approximately EUR 300,000 – much more than all comparable equity index futures worldwide. This size presents a significant challenge when hedging certain types of products, e.g. retail derivatives or similar financial products. It has also excluded semi-professional investors from getting engaged via futures in the main index they are tracking. As a result, Eurex Exchange introduced Mini-DAX futures as a supplement to the ordinary DAX futures in October 2015. The Mini's contract size is one-fifth of the original DAX futures. Meanwhile, the new Mini contract gained a lot of open interest, making this debut a great success story – fully complementary to ETFs linked to the DAX index.

Another point one should consider in the context of ETFs vs. futures are the spreads on futures. No doubt, when using futures rather than ETFs, liquidity and spreads are in most cases very competitive. The minimum price movement between the bid and ask of a future is known as a tick. For example, the e-Mini S&P 500 future trades in 25 US cent increments (1 tick equals 25 cents; 4 ticks equal 1 point). Broad-based equity ETFs in the U.S. have similar tight secondary market spreads (for example, SPY, EEM or QQQ) and therefore are equally competitive. However, all more esoteric equity ETFs or ETFs linked to small- and mid-cap indices will probably never become a substitute for futures.

Simplifying the Trading Processes Nevertheless, in the U.S. and Europe, more and more asset managers jump on the bandwagon in favor of ETFs, though they have motivations caused by different reasons. They prefer ETFs not only for their lower costs and the more advantageous tax and regulatory issues, but also because they have fewer operational constraints. By using ETFs, asset managers can reduce some of the hassle that their back offices usually have with the daily margin management and reconciliation process, as well unburdening the trading operations from calculating exact allocations for smaller portfolios and tracking the future contracts' collaterals. Today, confirmation that the trade cleared and is on the futures commission merchants (FCM) books is not enough. Clients now want more detailed reports and the FCMs want to know exactly where they and their customers stand. Furthermore, everybody who already witnessed a margin call from an exchange or future broker now knows about the latent risk of having future positions in the market; particularly when the market moves into the opposite direction. To say it clearly: A future is no riskier than an ETF, but using futures produces more complexity and sometimes needs more operational resources and IT infrastructure. This is especially true for smaller asset management companies and investment advisors, so this definitely gives ETFs an advantage over futures.

Expanding the Universe Compared to Futures Futures are available on the most liquid markets, but if investors seek exposure to a more exotic country/theme, futures are limited. ETFs, however, offer access to a variety of exposures such as sectors or even emerging markets single countries. Also, the growth in different bond markets doesn't stop. Furthermore, alternative asset classes such as REITs, private equity or hedge funds are addressed. As futures are almost only available on market capitalization-weighted indices, different weighting schemes in ETFs, known as "smart beta", are becoming more and more popular.

Portfolio Manager's Quick Read: Things to Consider When Using ETFs

Anatomy of ETFs

Exchange-traded funds (ETFs) are structured much like mutual funds, in that they hold an underlying basket of investments in which investors have proportional ownership stakes. Like a stock, ETFs can be bought and sold on an exchange throughout the trading day. Basically each ETF is linked to a specific (predefined) index. Most famous are broad equity indices like the S&P 500®, Euro STOXX 50®, FTSE100® or Hang Seng®.

The ETF will track the performance (up and down) of the underlying index. For example, if the S&P500® gains 2% on a trading day, an ETF linked to the S&P 500® will increase its value proportionally. Basically, the closer the price movements between the index and the ETF itself are, the better the specific ETF represents a specific market. This behavior is called "tracking difference". The tracking error is the volatility of this difference in total return between an ETF's value and its underlying index. Usually the ETF will follow its underlying index like a shadow.

Trading ETFs

An ETF can be traded through various channels: direct market access to the exchange or via the over-the-counter market, which means contacting the authorized participant or market maker for buy or sell orders.

APs are brokers with the ability to create and redeem ETF units, thanks to the AP's direct relationship with the specific ETF issuer. ETFs can be traded during the regular trading hours of the exchange (i.e. NYSE, LSE, Xetra or SGX) – usually from 9 AM until close of business. When entering a buy or sell order, always use price limits – in this way you avoid bad execution surprises. Trading is possible intraday, there are no minimum or maximum holding periods. Retail investors can trade ETFs for low commissions or even commission-free meanwhile.

Creation and Redemption

While ETF trading occurs on an exchange like stocks, the process by which their shares are created is significantly different. Unless a company decides to issue more shares, the supply of shares of an individual stock trading in the marketplace is finite. When demand increases for shares of an ETF, however, authorized participants have the ability to create additional shares on demand. Through the so-called "in-kind" transfer mechanism, the AP creates ETF units by delivering a basket of securities to the ETF issuer equal to the current holdings of the ETF. In return, they receive a large block of ETF shares (typically 50,000), which are then available for trading in the secondary market. This process also works in reverse. If an investor wants to sell a large block of shares of an ETF, even if there seems to be limited liquidity in the secondary market, APs can readily redeem a block of ETF shares by gathering enough shares of the ETF to form a creation unit and then exchanging the creation unit for the underlying securities. This ETF creation and redemption process helps to keep ETF supply and demand in continual balance. The creations/redemptions provide a hidden layer of liquidity.

Spreads

One important thing which investors should look closely at is the spread of an ETF. The spread is the difference between the bid and the ask price of a security. There are three main factors which influence the spread: volatility of the underlying, depth of liquidity of the underlying and finally the market maker sentiment. In brief: Extreme price movements in the underlying index will cause larger spreads.

Also, you will see wider spreads if you trade ETFs linked to a market or index which is in a different time zone. If you trade an ETF tied to U.S. stocks when Wall Street is closed, the ETF's market maker will charge a larger spread compared to the time when the U.S. markets are open for trading. Also, ETFs linked to less-liquid indexes (i.e. exotic markets or sophisticated strategies) will have larger spreads than ETFs linked to broad, highly liquid bases like the S&P500, EuroStoxx50 or Hang Seng.

The Different NAV-types

A NAV is calculated as the total value of a fund (assets plus cash and accruals minus fees/liabilities) divided by the number of shares in issue. ETFs usually trade close to their NAVs, which provide investors with the knowledge that the market price closely reflects the value of the underlying assets. The activity of market makers and other traders normally ensures that the price of an ETF does not substantially deviate from the NAV.

Additionally, the stock exchange or, alternatively, a service provider contracted by the issuer calculates an approximation of the ETF value every 15 seconds. This price is called iNAV. Other expressions are IIV (intraday indicative value) or IOPV (indicative optimized portfolio value). For investors, this means additional transparency and comparability. Professional investors can optimize their risk management by means of the iNAV.

Replication Methods

ETFs can use different methods to track/replicate their specific underlying index. Full replication means replicating an index by buying all of the constituents in exactly the same weightings as they are present in a benchmark. This is a derivatives-free approach. For example, an ETF tracking the DAX 30®, Germany's largest equity index, would have to buy all 30 shares equal to the DAX 30® index. Full replication would also involve rebalancing the ETF whenever the index is rebalanced.

Optimization – or partial replication – seeks to track a benchmark by investing in a subset of the index constituents whose returns are judged based on a statistical optimization technique likely to match those of the index as a whole.

Synthetic replication means buying assets that may or may not be index constituents and entering into a swap transaction with the ETF's sponsoring investment bank to swap/exchange the return on these investments for the return of the index. There are "unfunded" and "funded" swap methods. Using "unfunded" swaps means that investors own a basket of securities (which are not necessarily the same, like the ETF tracks) as collateral in case the swap counterpart gets bankrupt. In an unfunded swap, the cash – which investors have paid to purchase the ETF – is not directly transferred to the swap counterparty. Instead, a proportion of the money is used to pay the swap fee. The rest of the money is managed by the ETF provider itself. In a funded swap, the cash investors have paid to buy the ETP is transferred to the swap counter-party ("fully funded"). In exchange, the counterparty will provide that amount of exposure to the underlying asset and deposit collateral equal to, or greater than, that amount with the independent ETF custodian.

Leveraged and Inverse ETPs

Leveraged and inverse ETPs have become very popular. Leveraged ETPs aim to deliver a magnified performance of a particular index. Most lev-eraged ETPs attempt to multiply daily index returns by two or three times. Short leveraged ETPs aim to deliver a multiple of the daily index performance but in the opposite direction to the underlying benchmark. Investors should be aware of the daily resets of leveraged and inverse ETPs. As a result, over a longer time period, the performance between the base index or base commodity and the ETP could differ significantly. Hence leveraged and inverse ETPs are a perfect instrument for partici-pation in intraday price movements or a short-term investment horizon. Also, investors should be aware of the tax consequences while holding leveraged and inverse ETPs. They may have large short-term capital gains, which will cause hefty tax consequences.

EXCHANGE-TRADED COMMODITIES – HEAVY METAL EVEN FOR LIGHTWEIGHT INVESTORS

Globally, commodities are an integral part of advanced investment portfolios. Thanks to ETCs, investors could conveniently get access to an increasing range of commodities and commodity indexes, including metals, energy and agriculture. But differences between ETFs and the mechanisms in the com-modity markets need to be understood before investing.

Precious metals, namely gold and silver, have fascinated humans for thousands of years. Whether it was the gold treasure of the Andean Incas which lured the Spanish conquistadores or the pirate tales – like the adven-tures of Captain Blackbeard – about shiploads full of silver coins hidden on tiny, uninhabited Caribbean islands, the possession of such commodities has been always seen as a perfect means for wealth diversification – and alternative investment compared to cash, bonds and stocks. However, nearly impossible, or at least terribly costly, for investors was and is the physical possession of other commodities like oil and natural gas, copper or bushels of wheat. Also, the operational risks (storage and custody) for commodities such as energy, industrial metals and soft commodities are inherently complex.

Commodities – An Asset with a Long History

An alternative way to possess and invest in these commodities can be achieved through standardized derivative financial instruments, or so-called futures. They trade on dedicated commodities exchanges. A financial future is a contract in which two parties (the buyer and the seller) agree to exchange, at a future date, a certain amount of a particular commodity for a predetermined price ("strike price"). One of the world's oldest commodities exchanges is the London Metal Exchange (LME), which was officially established by a group of metals traders at the peak of the Industrial Revolution in Europe in the year 1877. They started first with trading copper contracts. Their aim was to manage the permanent price risk from the time they bought a certain metal from remote parts of the world till the shipload arrived in an English port and could be traded to a steel mill. By negotiating standardized contracts at the then new exchange, the traders could hedge their risk of a decline in prices while the ordered goods were on their way to the port of destination. Asia plays also an important role when it comes to commodities markets. For example, Japan is home of the world's first organized commodities futures market, the Osaka Rice Exchange. It was established in 1730.

The Midwest of the United States is home to the world's oldest commodities exchange and to most dominant commodities exchanges worldwide: the Chicago Board of Trade (CBOT). The CBOT was founded in 1848 by Chicago merchants keen to establish a central marketplace for grain and give farmers the possibility of securing a predetermined price before they transported their trainloads of grain to the "windy city". Formal futures contracts, as we know them today, were introduced on the CBOT in 1865. In 2007, CBOT and its rival Chicago Mercantile Exchange (CME) agreed to merge into the CME Group. Today, CBOT and its associated exchanges, New York Mercantile Exchange (NYMEX) and New York Commodities Exchange (COMEX), now operate as designated contract markets of the CME Group. Several of the youngest commodities exchanges in the world are the Dalian Commodity Exchange (DCE), based on the Liaodong peninsula in China's Northeast, and rapidly growing with regards to traded contracts, the Zhengzhou Commodity Exchange (ZCE) and the Shanghai Futures Exchange (SHFE). The DCE and the ZCE are the leading agricultural commodity exchanges among non-OECD countries.

Historically, commodities trading through futures, forwards and even options has been the exclusive home turf of institutional investors, commercial hedgers and professional traders. Also, in terms of portfolio allocation, commodities played more of a niche role, mostly because of the requirement for high minimum investments, daily maintenance of margins, and repositioning of consecutive futures contracts in order to maintain exposure to relevant commodity (so-called "rolling"). Retail investors have been almost unable to participate in the commodities market, except for buying some gold bars or silver coins, due to these burdens.

ETCs Democratize Investing in Commodities

Things changed with the introduction of ETCs. Operating in a similar way to stocks, they allow investors to participate in the performance of a certain commodity or commodity index without dealing with future contracts and margin requirements. In other words, an ETC is an exchange-traded turn-key solution for investors to get instant access to a desired commodity or commodity index. The first listing of an ETC took place in March 2003, when the Australian Stock Exchange began trading Gold Bullion Securities (a predecessor to the London-headquartered investment product provider ETF Securities). Although ETCs are simple and flexible to use, investors should be aware of the sometimes complex mechanisms of the commodities markets.

Commodity ETF vs. ETC: Same Goal, Different Features

Investors may read or hear in the financial media about "commodity ETFs", tracking a commodity index, a basket of commodity stocks or a commodity future. Basically, a commodity exchange-traded fund has the same purpose as an exchange-traded commodity but has a different structure. Investors should be aware of regional differences. In Europe, according to UCITS rules, an ETF must be diversified and cannot be invested in just one single underlying. All products exposed to a single commodity (gold, silver, oil) are structured as an ETC – not as an ETF. This means ETCs are not UCITS products, a fact that portfolio managers should be aware of and should match with the fund's individual compliance rules. Some portfolios may allow non-UCITS products, others may not.

Does this mean there are no single commodities ETFs available in Europe? No, there is one rare exception. On German exchanges, i.e. Börse Frankfurt and Börse Stuttgart, the cross-listed SPDR Gold Shares ETF (symbol GLD) is available for trading. These listings have been initiated by German securities brokers which act as independent market makers and are not associated or endorsed by the issuer or GLD's promotor, State Street Global Advisors (SSgA). SSgA does not offer this single commodity ETF in Europe because of the UCITS regulations. The details about single commodity ETCs, as they are offered and distributed in Europe, are explained below.

In the United States, there are some structures, wrapped into an ETF, that allow the issuer to offer exposure to just one single commodity. The SPDR

Gold Shares ETF is a good example of this. This is the world's largest single commodity ETF on physical gold and uses a grantor trust as its legal structure. Investors interested in securities law should note that this trust is not an investment company registered under the Investment Company Act of 1940 or a commodity pool for the purposes of the Commodity Exchange Act. Shares of grantor trusts are not subject to the same regulatory requirements as mutual funds but effectively behave from a trading and clearing perspective like common ETFs.

Another prominent example of a commodity ETF is the VanEck Vectors Gold Miners ETF. This ETF is structured as an open-ended fund, not as a trust. It tracks the performance of a basket containing the largest gold mining companies in the world. This product does not include a single ounce of gold – instead, this ETF is delivering a kind of indirect exposure to the gold price because the stock prices of gold miners are highly dependent (correlated) on movements in spot gold prices. This commodity ETF is traded and cleared like any other ETF. The creation and redemption process of commodities ETFs, exposed to commodity stocks but not to the underlying commodity itself, is absolutely equal to equity ETFs.

In addition to "classic" commodity ETFs, there are an increasing number of leveraged commodities ETFs available in the market. They offer two or three times the positive performance, or loss if things go south, of the underlying index. In most cases leveraged and inverse ETFs use commodities futures as their underlying. ETF providers like Velocity Shares and Direxion are among the few specialized in these leveraged and inverse commodities ETFs.

How are ETCs Constructed?

From a legal point of view, ETCs on single commodities are debt securities issued by a special purpose vehicle (set up or initiated by the ETC product provider, such as ETF Securities, Deutsche Bank, Source or the United States Commodities Funds, to name just a few), like a trust or a dedicated issuance company that pay no interest ("Zero Bond"), and are linked to a predefined commodity, commodity basket or commodity index. ETCs issued by an SPV have the advantage that the product's assets are segregated from the ETC's promotor or product provider and would not be affected by a bankruptcy or a credit event of the product provider itself. ETCs do not involve any active or discretionary management, and there is no investment policy. Each ETC is a passive product that directly tracks the price of the specific commodity. The performance in the specific commodity, which is quoted as the pro-rata product price on the exchange, is generated by holding either the physical asset (i.e. gold bars) or a derivative that gives exposure to that asset. Technically this derivative is mostly a collateralized commodity swap.

The collateral, often top-rated corporate or Government bonds and liquid stocks, ensures that in case of bankruptcy of the counterparty, the money invested into the ETC is still secured.

Different Product Designs

There are three possible forms in which ETCs gain exposure to commodities. Probably the most transparent method is to physically back them.

Physically-backed ETCs   Physically-backed ETCs are guaranteed by raw materials deposited in the vaults of a third-party (for example, a Swiss bank vault in Zurich or the Federal Reserve's vault in Manhattan) hired by the ETC issuer. The ETC's value, and effectively what the investors paid in to the ETC when purchasing ETC units, is directly invested into the specific commodity and therefore linked to the spot price of this commodity. As an illustration, take a gold ETC holding gold bars worth US$10 million today, which has issued 1 million ETC units. The value of one ETC unit is US$10. Assuming that the gold price appreciates, the total holdings might be worth US$10.2 million the next day. What is the ETC's unit price now? Correct, US$10.20.

Swap-based, Collateralized ETCs   In contrast to holding physical commodities in an ETC, there are many products that use the synthetic approach and thus hold futures or swaps rather than the physical asset. One of the reasons for using a futures-based or swap-based approach are the costs associated with the physical custody in high-security vaults or the perishable nature of physical investments like wheat, orange juice or coffee. However, the use of commodities futures or swaps is more convenient for the product's issuer but could lead to a tracking error in the ETP's performance because of certain rollover risks ("contango" vs. "backwardation"). Both phenomena in the futures market are explained later in detail.

Sources of Return

An investor's main motivation to trade and use ETCs is to track the performance of a certain (single) commodity or a commodity index. For ETCs that are futures-based, their performance is generated and influenced by three sources:

- *Commodity future price fluctuation*, which is largely affected by changes in the spot commodity price.

- *Commodity future roll*, which means the process of rolling the front month future into the near (next) month. Usually, there is a price difference between the two, which is after the roll directly reflected in the price of the ETC.
- Finally, the *interest rate on the collateral* plays a role, as all financial futures, including commodity futures, are margined instruments. The collateral (cash or high-grade securities) bears interest and this is also reflected in the ETC.

Fees of ETCs

Similar to exchange-traded funds and other financial products, ETCs charge their investors fees. As in the world of ETFs, ETCs have total expense ratios (TER). The TERs are found on almost all product documentation (term sheet, website, prospectus etc.) and state the annual fee. Most ETCs linked to the same underlying, for example physical silver, have similar TERs, though certainly not identical. Based on a current market snapshot, the three largest ETC issuers in Europe charge for their physically-backed silver ETCs TERs between 0.40% and 0.49% – even if the difference is tiny on paper, an investor could save instantly $900 with a $1 million trade. Hence fee comparisons are recommended.

Portfolio Manager's Quick Read: Things to Consider When Using ETCs

Anatomy of ETCs

Basically, ETCs are similar to ETFs, as both strive to reflect the performance of an underlying asset. However, ETCs are able to track the price of just one specific underlying – which a fund cannot do, for regulatory reasons. Also, ETCs are mostly debt securities issued by a special purpose vehicle associated with the issuer and are *not* a mutual fund structure like ETFs. With ETCs, the performance in the specific commodity is either generated by holding the physical asset (i.e. gold bars) or a derivative (swap or futures contract) that gives exposure to that asset. As swap-based ETCs do not hold the physical asset, they are secured by collateral, often top-rated corporate or Government bonds and highly liquid stocks. This is the place where the ETC investor's money is put. The performance is "mirrored" by the swap into the ETC's portfolio.

Contango vs. Backwardation

Some commodity ETPs are linked to commodity futures. Futures contracts have by their nature a fixed term and expire at specific dates. Hence there are many different "contract months" for each specific commodity futures market. When investors buy a long-ETP which invests into (commodity) futures, the issuer has to "roll" the underlying exposure from contract month to contract month. This roll creates a positive impact ("backwardation") or a negative impact ("contango") to the future's new value. Why? Because a backwardation is caused if the new contract is cheaper than the existing (old) one, which means that the investor gets more future contracts for the same investment amount. The opposite happens in contango situations: The roll will cause in these situations a (slight) loss to the ETF's NAV as the new contract is more expensive than the existing one. Contango and backwardation situations may be different depending on the underlying commodity and also varies over time. Oil may be in contango, while copper could be in backwardation.

Trading ETCs and Spreads

As the name implies, ETCs can be traded on an exchange. The New York Stock Exchange, NYSE Arca in particular, is home of a few pure exchange-traded commodities (organized as grantor trusts) like the SPDR Gold Trust (Ticker GLD) or the ETFS Physical Swiss Gold ETF (SGOL). In the U.S. pure ETCs are rare, though there are more than 140 commodity ETFs which track a commodity index. In Europe, Xetra/Börse Frankfurt and London Stock Exchange are the most dominant trading venues for pure ETCs. Like ETFs, ETCs can also be traded via over-the-counter (OTC). As ETCs mirror commodity futures markets, their liquidity and tradability is highly determined by the related commodity futures exchanges like CBOT, NYMEX or LME. Most commodities are traded on U.S. exchanges. Hence the spread between bid and ask prices of ETCs is tightest when the U.S. exchanges are open.

Creation and Redemption

ETCs which are physically-backed by a specific commodity (i.e. gold) can use the same primary market mechanism as ETFs. The "creation and redemption in-kind" process at ETCs works similarly to the process in ETFs: An authorized participant can request the creation or redemption of the physically-backed ETCs by exchanging with the ETC's custodian the exact quantity of raw material (i.e. gold bars). Some minimum lot sizes for in-kind transactions may apply.

Replication Methods

Similar to ETFs, ETCs also have different replication methods. Physical replication at exchange-traded commodities means that an ETC buys the underlying asset (i.e. gold) it is designed to track and keeps it physically in a vault or other appropriate storage facility.

Leveraged and Inverse ETCs

Like their peers on the ETF side, there are some leveraged ("geared") and inverse exchange-traded commodities available in the market. Leveraged ETCs aim to deliver a magnified performance of a particular commodity or commodity index. Most leveraged ETCs attempt to multiply daily index returns by two or three times. Inverse ("short") ETCs aim to deliver a multiple of the daily performance but in the opposite direction to the underlying benchmark. Here it is important to know that these ETCs will be reset on a daily basis. Thus over a longer time period, the performance between the base and the ETC could differ significantly. Leveraged and short ETCs are more interesting due to participation in intraday price movements or a short-term investment horizon. Also, investors should be aware of the tax consequences while holding leveraged and inverse ETCs. They may have large short-term capital gains, which will cause hefty tax consequences.

EXCHANGE-TRADED NOTES – THE UNDERDOG

Unlike ETFs, in which assets are segregated in a fund structure, ETNs are a type of a flexible debt security. They behave like ETFs and track almost every asset class – from broad equities to exotic commodities. Also, ETNs are offered as leveraged or inverse versions. The biggest challenge ETN investors face is the implied issuer risk.

ETNs are a kind of underdog in the world of exchange-traded products and don't hold much glamour compared to ETFs. As the name states, ETNs are listed notes and can be bought and sold throughout the exchange for the whole trading day. More specifically, ETNs are unsecured notes (not bank-guaranteed), issued by various financial institutions. Their promise is to deliver the performance of the underlying market index, basket or other benchmark. Compared to thousands of ETFs listed in the U.S. there are currently around 200 ETNs listed on NYSE Arca and a few on Nasdaq. In Europe, most ETNs are available for trading on Xetra/Börse Frankfurt (approximately 130). Nearly all of the ETNs listed in Europe are leveraged or inverse.

How are ETNs Constructed?

The issue process of an ETN is pretty straightforward, as they can bypass the tight restrictions associated with launching an exchange-traded fund. Speaking in U.S. regulatory terms, an ETN is not a mutual fund or any other type of "investment company" within the meaning of the Investment Company Act of 1940 and, subsequently, is not subject to regulation thereunder. Also, ETNs offered on European exchanges are not covered by fund rules or UCITS regulations. This gives the issuer total flexibility to create ETNs linked to almost any tradable underlying. Hence there are various types of ETNs available linked to indices or baskets, such as commodity futures (e.g. oil, grains, industrial metals etc.), foreign currencies (e.g. Euro/US dollar, Japanese yen/US dollar), and equities (sector, regions etc.). The ETN issuer creates the performance stream by entering into a swap agreement with another financial counterparty or purchasing futures. Depending on how the ETN is designed, a trustee, a custodian, a clearing broker and authorized participants are involved in the day-to-day operations of the ETN.

Trading and Early Redemptions

ETNs typically have long maturities, from 10 years up to 30 years. A special feature, it is possible to redeem existing units at their intrinsic value directly with the issuer before maturity in a so-called "early redemption", which is effectively an ETN embedded call feature. A well-functioning redemption process is absolutely critical for pricing the ETN fairly. If no proper redemption process is installed, the ETN would immediately start trading more like a closed-end fund, where prices are driven mainly by supply and demand and not necessarily by the underlying assets. In some cases, ETNs may trade at a premium over their underlying value or at a discount.

- Issuer call right: The ETN issuer may call the notes for redemption, depending on the individual prospectus, during the term. The investor will receive on the applicable redemption date a cash payment per ETN equal to the closing indicative value of the note on the issuer redemption valuation period end date. Some fees and distributions may be subtracted/added accordingly.

- **Investor call right:** Provided the investor redeems at least a certain amount of notes, it is possible to deal directly with the ETN's issuer. The investor will receive a cash payment per note equal to the closing indicative value of the ETN on the valuation date following the business day on which the ETN issuer receives a notice of redemption by the investor within a predefined time (4 PM). But this feature doesn't come for free: Investors should be aware of additional redemption charges – somewhere between 0.05% and 0.10% – as one-off fee, additional to the management fee.

The Issuer is Gone, Your ETN is Gone

As mentioned above, ETNs are unsecured, unrated debt securities and fully tied to the creditworthiness of the issuing bank or financial institution. Hence the issuer's credit rating is an important consideration for ETN investors. Prominent examples of how things could go south are Bear Stearns ("BearLinx ETNs") and Lehman Brothers ("Opta ETNs"). Both fallen banks offered ETNs. While J.P. Morgan, back in 2008 additionally funded by the Federal Reserve, adopted the Bear Stearns products, the Lehman notes vanished in the same moment the company declared bankruptcy on September 15, 2008. A lesson learned, investors have to realize and monitor any actual or anticipated changes to the issuer's credit ratings or credit spreads that may adversely affect the value of the ETN. If the issuer defaults, the whole investment will be at risk and, ultimately, the ETN may result in a total loss of the money invested – a scenario that hopefully will not happen again in the near future.

NOTES

1. Pensions & Investments, October 19, 1998
2. Assets under Management as of October 31, 2016
3. Bienkowski, 2013
4. China Asset Management SME ETF Launch Report, May 2006
5. Joint-Staff Report of the U.S. Commodity Futures Trading Commission and the U.S. Securities and Exchange Commission published on September 30, 2010.
6. SIX Swiss Exchange data, as of October 31, 2016
7. ICI Research Report, "Profile of Mutual Fund Shareholders 2015", published March 2016

8. Dillon Eustace, 2009
9. The Vanguard Group, ETF Structures at a Glance, August 2015
10. SPDR ETFs, The Basis of Product Structures, July 2014
11. The Vanguard Group, ETF Structures at a glance, August 2015
12. The Vanguard Group, ETF Structures at a glance, August 2015
13. Data by ETF.com as of October 30, 2016
14. Blocher and Whaley, 2015
15. Market data of ETF.com as of October 31, 2016
16. CME Future margins as of October 31, 2016

CHAPTER 3

Index Evolution

When Charles Dow and his two colleagues began picturing the collective performance of North American railroad and industrial stocks, eventually the world's first benchmark equity index was created. A publicly visible benchmark that pictures a defined market, updated after each trading day. Today, most indices are calculated every three seconds but the basic idea of Charles Dow – picturing the price developments of selected securities over time – is still the same. The mission of a benchmark index is to reflect a specific sector (i.e. railroad stocks or mobile device producers), a single country or region or, as another example, a type of commodity. Within the last five years, the number of indices exploded, fueled by a mushrooming number of index-linked products, particularly ETFs. Depending on which statistic one relies on, there are currently more than a million indices calculated globally. Of course, just a handful of these are globally important for investors and deserve the name "benchmark". The most relevant benchmarks are described and compared on the following pages.

Nevertheless, there are still plenty of indices which are kind of benchmarks but not investable or not (yet) easily investable. Examples are found in the real estate sector and the macroeconomic space (trade imbalances etc.). However, we expect that the trend of indexation will continue and that indices or markets which are today not yet fully investable or have low public visibility may draw more attraction the moment the segment or market becomes investable. Due to the nature of certain markets, i.e. real estate prices or inflation, the investment product on such indices can only be created in a synthetic way, for example via a swap agreement, as it is impossible to hold a "basket of inflation units" in one's portfolio.

BENCHMARK INDICES

Index investing, as we mentioned above already, was pioneered in the 1970s and has been increasingly embraced by investors since the late 1990s. An index itself, then and today, should be a perfect yardstick to measure, visualize and compare the performance of a predefined investment universe and make it comparable with other investment choices. It is crucial that the beta, which means the systematic market return, can be reliably measured – this is the only way to judge the out- or underperformance of any active asset management.

In the early years of indexing, classic benchmark indices of the first generation, which represent what is broadly known as "the market", have been established. Prominent examples are the Dow Jones Industrial Average Index (Ticker INDU) or the Standard & Poor's 500 Index (Ticker SPX). They have been – and are still – calculated pretty straightforwardly. For example, the Dow Jones Industrial Average's index value has been computed by adding the share prices of each stock divided by the number of its 30 components. Today, the divisor is adjusted to smooth out the effects of potential stock splits and other composition changes. Additionally, most of the established and well-known benchmark indices are market capitalization weighted. We will explain the details and relevant facts below.

However, choosing the "right" benchmark is in practice not as simple as one might think and also choosing the "right" index to invest. Furthermore, the methods of how the index is composed and the selection criteria should be understood well by the investor and portfolio manager. For example, the MSCI World Index, which sounds like an investment exposure across the globe, is heavily exposed to just one single stock market: the United States (ca. 60%). The remaining 40% of the index is allocated to other developed markets including 8% to Japan and 7% to British stocks. Hence investors shouldn't simply rely on the label name of an index but dig into the details. An investor with home exposure to the S&P 500 Index would, by adding the MSCI World Index to its portfolio, drastically increase the concentration risk towards U.S. stocks – and not really diversify its portfolio. A smarter solution would be to choose a different version of the MSCI World Index or research about regional indices and add a number of country indices to the base portfolio in order to diversify the overall market exposure.

Before investing into indices, an investor should make itself aware of the methodology and the weightings of the index itself.

Market Cap Weighted Indices – "The Bigger, the Better"

This calculation method is based on the principle that the biggest companies (with the largest share price multiplied by the number of outstanding shares) should have the biggest impact on the index and its performance. Market cap weighted indices are usually adjusted by their free-float, meaning that share portions held by the Government or the company itself are excluded from the weighting. When using market cap weighted indices in a portfolio, the investor effectively puts the most money into stocks which have already increased in price, as their higher stock price increases automatically (and by the index's rules) the weighting within the index. In bull markets, market cap weighted indices will be driven by a few hyped stocks. As soon as these sky-high valued "poster boy companies" get in trouble and their share price tumbles, the index and the associated product (i.e. ETF) will feel the heat of the downturn. On the flip side, investing into market cap weighted indices means that an investor indirectly sticks to well-established, very large companies – with hopefully sustainable and solid revenues.

Equal-Weighted Indices – "One Stock, One Vote"

As the name says, this method of indexing is focused on an equal impact of all index members and continuously keeps all shares with a fixed (equal) percentage weighting. This method is probably the easiest to understand. For example, if an index consists of 20 stocks then this means that each stock accounts for 5% of the index, and the movement of each stock has the same effect – no matter how large or small the company's market capitalization. As a result, equal-weighted indices give more emphasis to smaller companies and do not only consider the largest companies (with the highest share price) in the index. To some extent, this could lead to more volatility in the index as mid- and small-sized companies tend to be more volatile than large-cap stocks.

Fundamentally Weighted Indices – "New Age Parameters Count"

This approach is one of the newer ways to construct indices. Particularly in the bond market, this kind of calculation method sometimes makes much more sense than sticking to the largest debtors in the market. Fundamental weight factors could be earnings, debt-to-equity ratio, book value etc.

Factor Indices – "The Growing Zoo"

This weighting method comprises a pretty wide range – some pundits have already described it as "factor zoo" because of the massive increase of factor indices. The whole factor world is also known as "smart beta" or "alternative beta".

All these methods of indexing are not exclusive; a blending of various approaches would not be uncommon. Hence it is possible that an institutional investor demands to limit the single stock exposure in a market-capitalized index. Also, all of the mentioned weighting methods are not exclusively reserved for a certain asset class.

Benchmark Questions for Investors

Investors have to consider how they wish to implement and manage their benchmarks. This includes the question of which benchmark is right for the specific portfolio. Also, how much active management does the investor want versus a benchmark? The more active bets are allowed in the portfolio, the greater the tracking error against the benchmark. An increasingly important factor, despite melting nominal interest rates, is the currency of the portfolio benchmark(s). Are there turnkey solutions like currency-hedged versions available – or is it smarter to stay in local currency? Also, with equity sector indices a careful due diligence check could save an investor many basis points of performance as sector indices that sound the same could exhibit different returns. A helpful indicator is the industry classification. This is something we will focus on in the next sections.

The following pages contain a comprehensive overview of some of the world's most relevant benchmarks. These indices are well-known and highly regarded within the global investment community. However, from a portfolio management perspective it is important to understand the limitations and objectives of each benchmark. Also, we have added some comments from a portfolio manager's perspective to each of these indices. Therefore, we state the websites of the index sponsors where investors will find the current index details.

Please note: All data are as of June 2016 and some weighting figures may change over time.

Equity Benchmarks

Tables 3.1 to 3.13 give an overview to different equity benchmarks used heavily within the fund industry. Here benchmark-specific aspects and advantages and disadvantages are highlighted.

TABLE 3.1 Dow Jones Industrial Average Index

Dow Jones Industrial Average Index	
Ticker:	INDU
Year established:	1896
Index Universe/Objective:	The index universe is defined as all U.S.-listed stocks of companies that produce non-transportation and non-utility goods and services. The definition of 'industrial' is kept intentionally broad to provide an indicator that reflects the performance of the entire U.S. economy.
Benchmark focus:	Large-Cap Stocks
Region:	United States
Currency:	USD
Constituents:	30
Constituent Cap:	n/a
Weight largest constituent:	10.7%
Weight Top 10 constituents:	58.1%
Weightings:	Price-Weighted Index
Dividends:	No inclusion; price return index
Review/Rebalancing:	At sole discretion of index sponsor; no annual or semi-annual reconstitution.
Index sponsor:	S&P Dow Jones Indices (www.spdji.com)
Investment products (U.S. and/ or European exchanges – selection only):	DIA, DOG, SDOG, DXD, DDM, CBINDU
Portfolio Manager's view:	As mentioned already, the stock selection process in the Dow Jones Industrial Average Index is not governed by quantitative rules. Furthermore, a stock typically is added to the index at the sole discretion of the index provider. The most obvious disadvantage of the INDU is the limited universe of just 30 companies and the fact that the index is price-weighted. This means that a company with a share price of USD 50 makes up five times more of the index than a company with a share price of just USD 10, even if the lower-priced stock produces twice the profits or has more shares trading in the market. Nevertheless, "the Dow" fits as benchmark for concentrated U.S. portfolios or actively managed large-cap stocks.
✓	Well-recognized proxy for U.S. equities
➖	No quantitative rules for index inclusion. Only 30 companies, which are price-weighted

Source: Authors, S&P Dow Jones Indices

TABLE 3.2   Standard & Poor's 500® Index

Standard & Poor's 500® Index	
Ticker:	SPX
Year established:	1957
Index Universe/Objective:	The S&P 500® is widely regarded as the best single gauge of large-cap U.S. equities. There is over USD 7.8 trillion benchmarked to the index, with index assets comprising approximately USD 2.2 trillion of this total. The index includes, as the name implies, the 500 leading companies domiciled in the U.S. (ADRs are not eligible) and captures approximately 80% coverage of available market capitalization. The final determination of domicile eligibility is made by the U.S. Index Committee.
Benchmark focus:	Large-Cap Stocks
Region:	United States
Currency:	USD
Constituents:	505
Constituent Cap:	n/a
Weight largest constituent:	3.0%
Weight Top 10 constituents:	17.7%
Weightings:	Market capitalization weighted
Dividends:	No inclusion; price return index
Review/Rebalancing:	Quarterly, at sole discretion of index sponsor.
Index sponsor:	S&P Dow Jones Indices (www.spdji.com)
Investment products (U.S. and/or European exchanges – selection only):	SPY, VOO, IVV, XSPX, IUSA, LSPU, SPXS
Portfolio Manager's view:	The S&P 500 Index is one of the most suitable index solutions to track the U.S. equity market, and probably also the cheapest. The index is highly correlated to the Dow Jones Industrial Average Index (ca. 0.97) and also highly correlated to the Nasdaq 100 Index (0.94). The index is probably the world's most-used benchmark for equity portfolios – whether actively or passively managed.
✅	Representative U.S. equity benchmark; very attractive pricings (low fees) for index tracking
➖	Strong sector concentration (ca. 36%) towards information technology and financials

Source: Authors, S&P Dow Jones Indices

TABLE 3.3 Nasdaq 100® Index

Nasdaq 100® Index	
Ticker:	NDX
Year established:	1985
Index Universe/Objective:	As the name implies, the Nasdaq 100 consists of the hundred largest stocks (by market capitalization) out of the Nasdaq Composite Index, which effectively contains all Nasdaq-listed stocks. The companies have to be listed on Nasdaq for at least two years. The index aims to reflect America's most important companies across all sectors.
Benchmark focus:	Large-Cap Stocks
Region:	United States
Currency:	USD
Constituents:	100
Constituent Cap:	n/a
Weight largest constituent:	10.6%
Weight Top 10 constituents:	49.8%
Weightings:	Market capitalization weighted
Dividends:	No inclusion; price return index
Review/Rebalancing:	Annually, in December at sole discretion of index sponsor. Ad-hoc changes of the composition occur in the case of a stock delisting.
Index sponsor:	Nasdaq OMX (http://business.nasdaq.com)
Investment products (U.S. and/ or European exchanges – selection only):	QQQ
Portfolio Manager's view:	The Nasdaq 100 Index has an implied sector exclusion as the index does not contain financial stocks by design. Also, there are no utilities, oil and gas, and basic materials stocks in the Nasdaq 100. Despite these characteristics, the correlation to the S&P 500 Index is surprisingly high: 0.94. The ETP fees of the NDX are higher than those of the S&P 500 Index. However, over a longer period of time the non-financial sector component could exhibit a performance advantage (as happened in the 2012–2016 period).
✓	Representative U.S. equity benchmark with rules-based sector exclusion for financials and oil and gas; implied outperformance opportunity
⊖	Relatively high fees for ETPs compared to other U.S. equity benchmarks

Source: Authors, Nasdaq OMX Group

TABLE 3.4   Russell 3000® Index

Russell 3000® Index	
Ticker:	THY
Year established:	1984
Index Universe/Objective:	The index is one of the broadest equity benchmarks in the U.S. market. It contains, as the name implies, 3,000 US-headquartered stocks listed on NYSE, Nasdaq or NYSE AMEX and represents 98% of the total market capitalization of the U.S. equity market. The Russell 3000 Index combines the components of the Russell 1000 Index and Russell 2000 Index.
Benchmark focus:	Entire U.S. stock market Small-Cap Stocks
Region:	United States
Currency:	USD
Constituents:	3,018
Constituent Cap:	n/a
Weight largest constituent:	2.5%
Weight Top 10 constituents:	14.5%
Weightings:	Market capitalization weighted
Dividends:	No inclusion; price return index
Review/Rebalancing:	Annually, at sole discretion of the index sponsor.
Index sponsor:	FTSE Russell (www.ftserussell.com)
Investment products (U.S. and/or European exchanges – selection only):	IWV
Portfolio Manager's view:	Despite its very large universe, the Russell 3000 has a surprisingly high correlation to the S&P 500 Index (0.99) and even to the blue chip benchmark Dow Jones Industrial Average (0.97). The total market capitalization of all constituents equals ca. $25 trillion. The fees of the index-linked ETF (IWV) is fair-priced but not competitive against the other, highly correlated U.S. equity benchmarks.
✓	Broadest U.S. equity benchmark available
➖	In context to other U.S. equity benchmarks the Russell 3000 ETF is relatively expensive

Source: Authors, FTSE Russell

TABLE 3.5 Bovespa® Index

Bovespa® Index	
Ticker:	IBOV
Year established:	1968
Index Universe/Objective:	The Bovespa Index is the globally recognized indicator of the Brazilian stock market's average performance, representing more than 80% of Brazil's stock market.
Benchmark focus:	Large-Cap Stocks
Region:	Brazil
Currency:	BRL
Constituents:	59
Constituent Cap:	n/a
Weight largest constituent:	10.0%
Weight Top 10 constituents:	52.0%
Weightings:	Market capitalization weighted
Dividends:	Inclusion; gross total return index
Review/Rebalancing:	Quarterly, at the sole discretion of the index sponsor.
Index sponsor:	BM&F Bovespa (www.bmfbovespa.com.br)
Investment products (U.S. and/or European exchanges – selection only):	RIO FP
Portfolio Manager's view:	The Bovespa Index, also called Ibovespa, is still an important benchmark for emerging markets equity investors. In the aftermath of the BRIC slowdown (Brazil/Russia/India/China) in the last two years, the Bovespa suffered on its relevance. Due to the high weighting of its Top 10 components, investors will get a concentrated exposure to the largest Brazilian listed companies by adding this benchmark to their portfolio.
✓	Important emerging markets benchmark
⊖	Just one ETF available; listed derivatives in Brazil only

Source: Authors, BM&F Bovespa

TABLE 3.6   EURO STOXX 50® Index

EURO STOXX 50® Index	
Ticker:	SX5E
Year established:	1998
Index Universe/Objective:	The index strives to reflect the performance of Eurozone large-cap stocks ("supersector leaders") and is derived from the EURO STOXX index and represents the largest free-float market-capitalized listed companies.
Benchmark focus:	Large-Cap Stocks
Region:	European Monetary Union ("Eurozone")
Currency:	EUR
Constituents:	50
Constituent Cap:	10%
Weight largest constituent:	5.2%
Weight Top 10 constituents:	37.4%
Weightings:	Market capitalization weighted
Dividends:	No inclusion; price return index
Review/Rebalancing:	Annually, in September at sole discretion of the index sponsor.
Index sponsor:	STOXX (www.stoxx.com)
Investment products (U.S. and/ or European exchanges – selection only):	FEZ, EXW1, DBX1EU
Portfolio Manager's view:	This benchmark is widely used for Eurozone equity portfolios. However, the EURO STOXX 50's sector mix is biased towards banks (14%) and industrial goods and services (10%). Also, this index does not – like other price indices – reflect dividend payments in its performance. Hence by investing into ETPs linked to this benchmark, the investor does not participate on the sometimes decent dividend yields that Eurozone blue chip stocks pay out.
✓	Representative Eurozone benchmark; various low fee ETPs available for index tracking
➖	No dividends included; sector exposure of banks and industrial goods and services

Source: Authors, STOXX Ltd.

TABLE 3.7   FTSE 100® Index

FTSE 100® Index	
Ticker:	UKX
Year established:	1984
Index Universe/Objective:	The FTSE 100 aims to represent the performance of the United Kingdom's 100 largest blue chip companies. The index measures stocks that are traded on the London Stock Exchange and passed screening criteria for size and liquidity.
Benchmark focus:	Large Cap Stocks
Region:	United Kingdom
Currency:	GBP (EUR version available too)
Constituents:	100
Constituent Cap:	10%
Weight largest constituent:	5.4%
Weight Top 10 constituents:	39.8%
Weightings:	Market capitalization weighted
Dividends:	No inclusion; price return index
Review/Rebalancing:	Quarterly in March, June, September and December at the sole discretion of the index sponsor.
Index sponsor:	FTSE (www.ftserussell.com)
Investment products (U.S. and/or European exchanges – selection only):	CSUKX, HUKX
Portfolio Manager's view:	The FTSE 100, called the "Footsie" among traders, is a good proxy for the UK's hundred largest companies listed on the London Stock Exchange. Due to the relatively high dividend yields that British stocks pay out to their shareholders, simple index tracking of the price return version (which is the benchmark) doesn't pay off over the long term. Hence a full replication of the Footsie or switching to the Total Return version (i.e. comstage FTSE100 TR ETF) may make more sense.
✔	Highly liquid proxy for Britain's large-cap equities
➖	No dividends included; biased towards mining stocks and the financial sector

Source: Authors, FTSE

TABLE 3.8   DAX 30® Index

DAX 30® Index	
Ticker:	DAX
Year established:	1988
Index Universe/Objective:	The DAX index is the globally recognized benchmark for Germany's 30 largest publicly listed companies trading on the Frankfurt Stock Exchange.
Benchmark focus:	Large-Cap Stocks
Region:	Germany
Currency:	EUR
Constituents:	30
Constituent Cap:	10%
Weight largest constituent:	9.3%
Weight Top 10 constituents:	64.5%
Weightings:	Market capitalization weighted
Dividends:	Inclusion; total return index
Rebalancing:	Annually, in September at the sole discretion of the index sponsor. Additionally, irregular adjustments (through fast-exit- and fast-entry-rule) in March, June and December possible.
Index sponsor:	Deutsche Börse (www.dax-indices.com)
Investment products (U.S. and/ or European exchanges – selection only):	DAX, EXS1, XDDX, C001, EL4A
Portfolio Manager's view:	For years the DAX has been the best proxy for Germany's export-oriented large-cap companies. Investors should consider the large influence of the Top 10 constituents (around 65% weighting) on the total index performance. Also, the DAX is one of the few total return indices. This means that all dividend payments go directly into the index's performance. This is an important fact as most German large-cap stocks have decent dividend yields. Also, there are many low-priced ETPs available in the market.
✓	Total return benchmark for German large cap stocks; various low-cost ETPs available
➖	Large influence of Top 10 weightings onto total index performance

Source: Authors, Deutsche Börse Group

TABLE 3.9   MDAX® Index

MDAX® Index	
Ticker:	MDAX
Year established:	1996
Index Universe/Objective:	The MDAX index reflects Germany's mid-cap sized listed companies. Like the big brother, the DAX index, the MDAX components are selected according to market capitalization and stock exchange turnover
Benchmark focus:	Mid-Cap Stocks
Region:	Germany
Currency:	EUR
Constituents:	50
Constituent Cap:	10%
Weight largest constituent:	9.8%
Weight Top 10 constituents:	45.7%
Weightings:	Market capitalization weighted
Dividends:	Inclusion; total return index
Rebalancing:	Quarterly at the sole discretion of the index sponsor
Index sponsor:	Deutsche Börse (www.dax-indices.com)
Investment products (U.S. and/or European exchanges – selection only):	ETF007, MDAXEX
Portfolio view:	The often-cited "German Mittelstand" is perfectly pictured through the MDAX index. The bias towards its Top 10 is less concentrated than in its "big brother", the DAX. Nevertheless, as it is a mid-cap index, volatility is slightly higher. The index exposure can be accessed through index products. However, MDAX ETFs are currently listed in Germany only.
✔	Total return benchmark for German large cap stocks; various low-cost ETPs available
⊖	Large influence of Top 10 weightings onto total index performance

Source: Authors, Deutsche Börse Group

TABLE 3.10   Hang Seng® Index

Hang Seng® Index	
Ticker:	HSI
Year established:	1969
Index Universe/Objective:	The index aims to reflect the performance of the largest companies of the Hong Kong stock market. Its 50 constituents represent roughly 60% of the capitalization of the Hong Kong Stock Exchange. Also, Mainland China enterprises that have H-share listing in Hong Kong will be eligible for inclusion in the HSI if they meet certain criteria.
Benchmark focus:	Large-Cap Stocks
Region:	Hong Kong (and HK-listed China Mainland stocks)
Currency:	HKD
Constituents:	50
Constituent Cap:	15%
Weight largest constituent:	11.3%
Weight Top 10 constituents:	61.0%
Weightings:	Market capitalization weighted
Dividends:	No inclusion; price return index
Rebalancing:	Quarterly at the sole discretion of the index sponsor
Index sponsor:	Hang Seng Indexes Co. Ltd. (www.hsi.com.hk)
Investment products (U.S. and/or European exchanges – selection only):	Tracker Fund of Hong Kong, Voya Hang Seng Index Portfolio, ETF022, LYXHSI GY, HSI SP.
Portfolio Manager's view:	Investors seeking liquid exposure to China mostly use the Hang Seng Index as appropriate proxy. The well-known benchmark includes the largest and most liquid stocks listed on the Main Board of the Hong Kong Stock Exchange. Largest drawback is the record high dominance of financial stocks in the index (44%). From an asset manager's perspective, the sector bias should have considered carefully.
✔	Liquid benchmark which reflects multi-national, Hong Kong and Mainland China headquartered companies
➖	One of the world's largest concentration risks towards the financial sector (44%)

Source: Authors, Hang Seng Indexes Co. Ltd.

TABLE 3.11 Nikkei 225® Index

Nikkei 225® Index	
Ticker:	NKY
Year established:	1950
Index Universe/Objective:	The index reflects the 225 largest companies from 36 sectors listed on the Tokyo Stock Exchange and has become the premier benchmark for Japanese equities. The formal name of the index is the "Nikkei Stock Average".
Benchmark focus:	Large-Cap Stocks
Region:	Japan
Currency:	JPY
Constituents:	225
Constituent Cap:	15%
Weight largest constituent:	6.9%
Weight Top 10 constituents:	32.0%
Weightings:	Price weighted
Dividends:	No inclusion; price return index
Rebalancing:	Annually, in October at the sole discretion of the index sponsor
Index sponsor:	Nihon Keizai Shimbun (http://indexes.nikkei.co.jp/en)
Investment products (U.S. and/or European exchanges – selection only):	JPXN, ETF020, SXRZ
Portfolio Manager's view:	Unlike the Chinese equity benchmarks, the Nikkei 225 Index is biased towards the industrial sector, Consumer Discretionary and Information Technology (Top 3 Sectors account for 54% of the whole index). For some years, the correlation with other Western equity benchmarks has been low due to the special nature of the Japanese economy and certain domestic stimulus programs. A few ETFs are available to track this index, with very fair fee levels.
✔	Good reflection of Corporate Nippon's leading stocks, which are mostly export-oriented
➖	Dominant influence of three sectors to the total index performance

Source: Authors, Nikkei Inc.

TABLE 3.12 MSCI World® Index

MSCI World® Index	
Ticker:	MXWO
Year established:	1968
Index Universe/Objective:	The MSCI World Index strives to capture large- and mid-cap listed companies across 23 developed markets. With more than 1,600 constituents, the index covers approximately 85% of the free float-adjusted market capitalization in each country.
Benchmark focus:	Large-Cap Stocks
Region:	Industrial nations
Currency:	USD
Constituents:	1,639
Constituent Cap:	n/a
Weight largest constituent:	1.7%
Weight Top 10 constituents:	9.9%
Weightings:	Market capitalization weighted
Dividends:	No inclusion; price return index
Rebalancing:	Quarterly (February, May, August and November) with the objective of reflecting change in the underlying equity markets in a timely manner, while limiting undue index turnover. Also, semi-annual index reviews (May and November) including rebalancing; the large- and mid-capitalization cutoff points are recalculated.
Index sponsor:	MSCI (www.msci.com)
Investment products (U.S. and/or European exchanges – selection only):	URTH, IQQW
Portfolio Manager's view:	The MSCI World Index, the widely used and recognized proxy for developed market stocks, is not as global as it may sound. It is quite heavily exposed to one single stock market: the United States (ca. 60%). The remaining 40% of the index are allocated to other developed markets, including 8% to Japan and 7% to British stocks. Hence investors should review the correlation before and after adding MSCI World exposure to their portfolio simply to avoid inherent concentration risks or a large overlapping with their U.S. equities exposure. The correlation against the S&P 500 Index is around 0.95.

Liquid exposure to the world's most relevant developed economies; various low-cost ETPs available

Largely biased towards the U.S. equity market

Source: Authors, MSCI

TABLE 3.13   MSCI Emerging Markets® Index

MSCI Emerging Markets® Index	
Ticker:	MXEF
Year established:	2001
Index Universe/Objective:	A well-regarded benchmark, the MSCI Emerging Markets Index tracks large and mid-cap companies across 23 Emerging Markets (EM) countries. With 837 constituents, the index covers approximately 85% of the free float-adjusted market capitalization in each country.
Benchmark focus:	Mid- and Large-Cap Stocks
Region:	Emerging markets
Currency:	USD
Constituents:	837
Weight largest constituent:	3.4%
Weight Top 10 constituents:	19.5%
Weightings:	Market capitalization weighted
Dividends:	No inclusion; price return index
Rebalancing:	Quarterly (February, May, August and November) with the objective of reflecting change in the underlying equity markets in a timely manner, while limiting undue index turnover. Also, semi-annual index reviews (May and November) including rebalancing; the large and mid-capitalization cutoff points are recalculated.
Index sponsor:	MSCI (www.msci.com)
Investment products (U.S. and/ or European exchanges – selection only):	EEM, HEEM, EGUSAS SW, DBX1/XMMD
Portfolio Manager's view:	For investors seeking exposure to the world's emerging markets, the MSCI EM Index is inevitably the ultimate benchmark. However, the index contains a very broad variety of countries (from Hungary to Thailand), has inherent currency risk (HEEM strives to reduce FX risks) and its strongly biased towards Asia (China 24%, South Korea 15%, Taiwan 12%, India 8%). Also, the local markets replicated in this index are open for trading in different time zones. Accordingly, a physical replication of this index in a portfolio seems to be very exhaustive. Finally, due to the local restrictions in certain markets (buying local stocks in India still is a nightmare), the brokerage execution is a costly venture. Hence ETFs on the MSCI EM are the most convenient way to add emerging markets exposure to the portfolio. Investors should be aware that the benchmark and the ETF may have a significant tracking error due to the reasons mentioned above.
	Highly regarded benchmark which is accessible through ETFs; total expense ratios are mostly fair-priced in the light of managing a still exotic collection of emerging markets
	Very complex composition with inherent FX risk; Strong bias towards Asian equity markets (60%/top 4 markets)

Source: Authors, MSCI

Sector Indices

Beside the equity benchmarks listed on the previous pages, there are various sector indices which represent selected industries. When it comes to sector investing, there is always the question of how companies are classified and categorized. As mentioned earlier, investors should not trust a sector name alone. For example, only a few expert investors are probably aware that a financial sector ETF like the Financial Select Sector SPDR® Fund would bring your portfolio a 20% exposure to the U.S. real estate market, including a hotel and resort management company. Another example is a sector index focused on oil and gas. This sector does not only include fossil energy companies, as the sector name suggests. In fact, the index (and effectively your portfolio exposure) would include solar, wind and other renewable energy companies. This fact came as a surprise to some investors when their performance was very positively impacted in the 2006/07 period. However, when the stock prices of wind energy and solar manufacturing companies temporarily went south in 2013, the sector performance was stressed additionally. We provide an overview of the most-used classification models and the relevant sector indices below.

Sector classification models:

- **Industry Classification Benchmark (ICB):** As seen in figure 3.1, the Industry Classification Benchmark (ICB), maintained by index provider FTSE International, is a definitive system categorizing over 70,000 companies and 75,000 securities globally. The categorization is done through the primary source of revenue of each company. The ICB consists of 114 subsectors, 41 sectors, 19 supersectors and 10 industries.
- **The Global Industry Classification Standard (GICS®):** This classification standard, as seen in Figure 3.2, jointly developed by Standard & Poor's

FIGURE 3.1 Industry Classification Benchmark
Source: Authors, FTSE

FIGURE 3.2 Global Industry Classification Standard
Source: Authors, MSCI

Financial Services and MSCI in 1999, consists of 10 sectors, 24 industry groups, 67 industries and 156 sub-industries. The categorization of a company towards a specific sector/industry etc. is also done through the business activities that generate the majority of the company's revenues.

Selected Sector Indices Overview

As there are different country-based benchmarks, specific sector indices are also quite popular and accepted within the fund industry (Tables 3.14 to 3.16).

TABLE 3.14 Dow Jones Sector Titans™ Indices

Dow Jones Sector Titans™ Indices	
Year established:	2001
Benchmark focus:	Large-Cap Stocks
Region:	Global
Currency:	USD (EUR)
Categorization:	Proprietary classification system (supersectors-oriented)
Constituents:	30
Weightings:	Market capitalization weighted
Dividends:	No inclusion; price return index
Index sponsor:	S&P Dow Jones Indices (www.spdji.com)
Comments:	Mostly strong U.S.-biased components, 10% capping per constituent

Source: Authors, SPDJI

TABLE 3.15   S&P Select Sector Indices

S&P Select Sector Indices	
Year established:	1998
Benchmark focus:	Large-Cap Stocks
Region:	U.S.
Currency:	USD
Constituents:	Different holdings number per sector index out of S&P 500 Index
Weightings:	Modified market capitalization weighted
Dividends:	No inclusion; price return index
Index sponsor:	S&P Dow Jones Indices (www.spdji.com)
Comments:	Attractive sector benchmarks for U.S. equities; low-cost ETFs linked to these indices available from State Street Global Advisors SPDR

Source: Authors, SPDJI

TABLE 3.16   STOXX Europe 600 Sector Indices

STOXX Europe 600 Sector Indices	
Year established:	2000
Benchmark focus:	Mid- and Large-Cap Stocks
Region:	Pan-Europe (not only Eurozone)
Currency:	EUR
Categorization:	ICB
Constituents:	Different holdings number per sector index out of STOXX 600 universe
Weightings:	Market capitalization weighted
Dividends:	No inclusion; price return index
Index sponsor:	STOXX (www.stoxx.com)
Comments:	Europe's leading sector benchmarks with relatively low-priced ETFs from BlackRock/iShares available. Largest company is capped at 30% and the second largest at 15%. Hence in some cases strongly biased to a single stock.

Source: Authors, STOXX

Fixed-Income Benchmarks

In the fixed-income universe the focus is on the following benchmarks:

TABLE 3.17   Bloomberg Barclays Global Aggregate Index

Bloomberg Barclays Global Aggregate Index	
Ticker:	LBUSTRUU
Year established:	1973
Index Universe/Objective:	The Bloomberg Barclays Global Aggregate Index, formerly the Lehman Brothers Global Aggregate Bond Index, is a flagship measure of global investment-grade debt from 24 local currency markets. This multi-currency benchmark includes Treasury, government-related, corporate and securitized fixed-rate bonds from both developed and emerging markets issuers. Various coupon types are allowed; bonds of at least one year until final maturity are eligible.
Benchmark focus:	Cross sector fixed-income
Region:	Global
Currency:	USD
Constituents:	16,315
Weight largest constituent:	0.78
Weightings:	Market capitalization
Minimum Rating Quality:	Investment-grade (Baa3/BBB or higher)
Rebalancing:	Bonds are moved monthly and added on the last day of the month, with the rebalancing taking effect from the first day of the following month.
Index sponsor:	Bloomberg (www.bloombergindices.com)
Investment products (U.S. and/or European exchanges – selection only):	IAGG, XBAE
Portfolio Manager's view:	Incredibly broad bond spectrum with more than 16,000 securities in the benchmark. Hence this is more a hypothetical benchmark. There are unhedged and hedged versions available, depending on the risk appetite. A slightly different index version can be tracked conveniently through the iShares Core International Aggregate Bond ETF linked to the Barclays Global Aggregate ex USD 10% Issuer Capped (Hedged) Index.
	Extraordinarily broad fixed-income benchmark; almost untapped spectrum.
	No exact tracking through an ETF possible. However, slightly different index versions available. Broadness is sometimes questioned.

Source: Authors, Bloomberg

TABLE 3.18   World Government Bond Index

World Government Bond Index	
Ticker:	SBWGU
Year established:	1984
Index Universe/Objective:	The World Government Bond Index (WGBI) measures the performance of fixed-rate, local currency, investment-grade sovereign bonds. The WGBI is a widely used benchmark that currently comprises sovereign debt from over 20 countries, denominated in a variety of currencies. The WGBI has also sub-indices in any combination of currency, maturity or rating. The index is calculated daily.
Benchmark focus:	Sovereign bonds
Region:	Global
Currency:	USD (EUR, GBP, JPY available too)
Constituents:	1,003
Weight largest constituent:	32.7%
Weightings:	Market capitalization
Minimum Rating Quality:	Entry: A- by S&P and A3 by Moody's. Exit: Below BBB- by S&P and below Baa3 by Moody's
Rebalancing:	Once a month at month end
Index sponsor:	Citigroup
Investment products (U.S. and/or European exchanges – selection only):	No ETPs available; IGLO (proxy to SBWGU) linked to Citigroup Group-of-Seven (G7) Index.
Portfolio Manager's view:	The WGBI is a well-known Government bond benchmark. However, the relevance of sovereign fixed-income bonds has decreased somewhat in the light of ultra-low interest rates. Also, investors should be aware that the WGBI is largely exposed to U.S. treasuries (32%) and the Eurozone (31%).
✓	Versatile developed markets Government benchmark
⊖	Developed markets in favor, strongly biased towards U.S. and Eurozone (63%).

Source: Authors, Citigroup

TABLE 3.19   J.P. Morgan Emerging Market Bond Index

J.P. Morgan Emerging Market Bond Index	
Ticker:	EMBI
Year established:	1999
Index Universe/Objective:	The EMBI was formed after the issuance of the first Brady bond and has become the most widely published and referenced index of its kind. This benchmark measures the total return performance of international government bonds issued by emerging market countries (issued in other than local currency). Minimum remaining time to maturity of 1 year for existing index bonds, and 2.5 years for new bonds entering the index. There are three different EMBI indices variances: EMBI+, EMBI Global and EMBI Global Diversified.
Benchmark focus:	Sovereign bonds
Region:	Emerging markets
Currency:	USD
Constituents:	457
Weight largest constituent:	n/a
Weightings:	Market capitalization
Minimum Rating Quality:	No rating criteria
Rebalancing:	Monthly
Index sponsor:	J.P. Morgan (www.jpmorgan.com/country/US/EN/ jpmorgan/investbk/solutions/research/indices/ product)
Investment products (U.S. and/or European exchanges – selection only):	IEMB
Portfolio Manager's view:	Well-known, broad hard currency emerging markets sovereign bond benchmark, which is conveniently tradable through IEMB, an iShares ETF. Since 2005, two additional benchmarks have been launched: Government Bond Index-Emerging Markets series and the Corporate Emerging Markets Bond Index series, both of which have become the new standard for local market and corporate EM benchmarks, respectively.
✅	Broad hard currency EM bond benchmark; tradable via ETF
➖	Slightly outdated because of market developments ("yield meltdown").

Source: Authors, Bloomberg

Additional Fixed-Income Benchmark Families

Besides accepted single benchmark indices, the index families in Tables 3.20 and 3.21 are well recognized.

TABLE 3.20   markit iBoxx Indices

markit iBoxx Indices	
Year established:	2002
Benchmark focus:	iBoxx™ bond indices offer broad benchmarking and liquid tradable index solutions that track bond markets globally. Fueled by multi-source pricing, iBoxx provides transparency to bond market performance. iBoxx rules-based methodologies are publicly disclosed and designed to be replicable.
Regions:	Global, U.S., Europe, Asia
Currency:	USD, EUR
Index sponsor:	markit (www.markit.com/Product/IBoxx)
Investment products (U.S. and/or European exchanges – selection only):	LQD, HYG, XYPD, TDTT
Comments:	iBoxx has become a well-known set of benchmarks. The ETFs we mentioned above represent one of the products with the largest AuM and are probably the best benchmark-tracking products: Markit iBoxx USD Liquid High Yield Index, Markit IBOXX € Sovereigns Eurozone Yield Plus Index and FlexShares iBoxx 3-Year Target Duration TIPS Index Fund.

Source: Authors, markit

TABLE 3.21 BofA Merrill Lynch Indices

BofA Merrill Lynch Indices	
Year established:	1976
Benchmark focus:	The suite of BofA Merrill Lynch Fixed-Income Indices tracks the performance of the global investment-grade, high-yield and emerging debt markets.
Regions:	U.S., Europe
Currency:	USD, EUR, GBP
Index sponsor:	Bank of America Merrill Lynch (www.mlindex.ml.com)
Investment products (U.S. and/or European exchanges – selection only):	CJNK
Comments:	Merrill Lynch, before its takeover by Bank of America in September 2008, had a long history of publishing bond benchmarks and continued doing so after the corporate rebranding to BofA ML. Today, the BofA ML indices are a well-regarded benchmark for fixed-income investors, particularly in the investment-grade as well as the high-yield segment. An often-discussed fact is the huge amount of corporate bonds included in BofA ML's flagship indices (ML Glbl. Large Cap IG Index contains 6,718 bonds issued by 1,201 firms; ML Glbl. HY Index contains 3,552 bonds issued by 1,687 firms). Opinions are divided, as with the Barclays indices, as to whether such a broad universe is good or bad.

Source: Authors, Bank of America Merrill Lynch

Commodities and Alternative Benchmarks

More exotic but still very important for multi-asset portfolios are commodities and alternative benchmarks. The most important ones are named in Tables 3.22 to 3.24.

TABLE 3.22   S&P Goldman Sachs Commodity Index

S&P Goldman Sachs Commodity Index	
Ticker:	SPGCCITR
Year established:	2007, predecessor GSCI Index was launched 1991
Index Universe/Objective:	The S&P GSCI™ is one of the most widely recognized benchmarks that is broad-based and production-weighted to represent the global commodity market beta. The index comprises the principal physical commodities that are traded in active, liquid futures markets. Also, the index is published in three versions: excess return, total return and spot.
Benchmark focus:	Broad commodities
Currency:	USD, EUR, CHF, SGD, AUD, GBP
Constituents:	24 (energy, agriculture, industrial metals, livestock, precious metals)
Weight largest constituent:	Energy (59.3%)
Weightings:	Market capitalization
Rebalancing/Rolling:	Monthly
Index sponsor:	S&P Dow Jones Indexes
Investment products (U.S. and/or European exchanges – selection only):	GSG
Portfolio Manager's view:	The S&P GSCI™ is an often-cited benchmark and well-known in the asset management industry. However, investors should be aware that the index is heavily biased towards energy commodities, namely both sorts of crude oil.
✔	Easily accessible commodity benchmark; various index versions available
➖	Heavily biased towards energy commodities

Source: Authors, SPDJI

TABLE 3.23   Thomson Reuters Core Commodities CRB Index

Thomson Reuters Core Commodities CRB Index	
Ticker:	CRY
Year established:	1957
Index Universe/Objective:	The Thomson Reuters Core Commodities CRB Index consists of 19 commodities, with 39% allocated to energy contracts, 41% to agriculture, 7% to precious metals and 13% to industrial metals. The index acts as a representative indicator of today's global commodity markets. There are also various index versions, which exclude certain energy subsectors like energy.
Benchmark focus:	Broad commodities
Currency:	USD
Constituents:	19 (energy, agriculture, industrial metals, livestock, precious metals)
Weight largest constituent:	Crude oil (23%)
Weightings:	Market capitalization
Rebalancing/Rolling:	Monthly
Index sponsor:	Thomson Reuters
Investment products (U.S. and/or European exchanges – selection only):	GCC, LYY6
Portfolio Manager's view:	As one of the oldest commodities benchmarks, the CRB Index is relatively well-balanced (compared for example to the GSCI) and therefore a good indicator for the broad commodities market. In the U.S. ETF market, the GCC provides similar exposure to the original Reuters/Jefferies CRB Index but in an equal-weighted way (5.88%) – which is nothing bad.
✔	Broad commodity benchmark with one of the longest real market histories available
➖	Still dominant exposure to energy sector; no directly linked ETF in the U.S. available

Source: Authors, ThomsonReuters

TABLE 3.24 UBS Bloomberg CMCI® Total Return Index

UBS Bloomberg CMCI® Total Return Index	
Ticker:	CMCITR
Year established:	2007
Index Universe/Objective:	The CMCI Composite Index is the most diversified index available to investors in the CMCI family. It comprises 27 commodity futures contracts representing the energy, precious metals, industrial metals, agricultural and livestock sectors. On top of this comes a balanced weighting of all available maturities (from 3 months up to 3 years) for each commodity. This means that the index is also diversified across the time dimension, which the traditional index approach neglects.
Benchmark focus:	Various commodity sectors/single commodities
Currency:	USD, EUR, CHF
Constituents:	28 (energy, agriculture, industrial metals, precious metals)
Weight largest constituent:	Brent Crude Oil (10.3%)
Weightings:	Market capitalization
Rebalancing/Rolling:	Monthly
Index sponsor:	UBS (www.ubs.com/cmci)
Investment products (U.S. and/or European exchanges – selection only):	CCUSAS SW, UIQK GY
Portfolio Manager's view:	The CMCI family is a well-regarded, diversified offering across a range of commodities and is pretty international in its scope. The CMCI methodology extends beyond short-dated futures contracts and diversifies investment opportunities across the maturity curve. By providing investors with access to "constant maturities", it not only gives a more continuous exposure to the asset class and avoids the speculative activity that usually may occur on the monthly "rolls" of traditional indices, but can also minimize exposure to negative roll yield, making the index more representative of the underlying market price movements. Also, the CMCI family includes indices with different tenor.

(Continued)

TABLE 3.24   *(Continued)*

UBS Bloomberg CMCI® Total Return Index	
✅	Well-balanced commodity benchmark with smart implied roll mechanism. Unlike other commodities benchmarks, the weight on energy is comparatively low (37%).
➖	To fully benefit from the CMCI mechanism, an investment horizon of at least four to five years is recommended. On a shorter time horizon, the correlation with the other two commodity benchmarks mentioned is relatively high.

Source: Authors, UBS

SMART BETA INDICES (SECOND GENERATION OF INDEXING)

It's probably the most overused expression in the financial world: smart beta. The expression suggests that there are dumb and smart betas – which is clearly not the case. However, there are more innovative index concepts and more classic index concepts. In general, smart beta indices are nothing new. It all began in 1964 with the One-Factor Model, also known as the Capital Asset Pricing Model. That factor was called beta. Beta was (and still is) the measure of how much each stock moved in relation to the stock market as a whole. A high beta stock is one that moves more compared to the general market, and a high beta stock is usually associated with higher risks (higher volatility) but also higher expected returns. On the other side, stocks that move less than the general market are called low beta. Subsequently, these are expected to have lower risks (lower volatility) and also in some cases lower returns compared to the general market.

In 1992, Eugene F. Fama and Kenneth R. French spiced up the one-dimensional perspective by combining beta with two new factors. Their Three-Factor Model became the most widely-cited paper in the financial industry. The duo of Fama and French found that small-capitalized stocks (Factor Two) got higher returns than large-capitalized stocks, and that stocks with reasonable valuation compared to the general market and dividend strength (Factor Three) got higher returns than sometimes overvalued growth stocks. The reason for higher returns is the higher risk exposure and the need of investors to compensate for this extra risk.

If you find an open-ended fund that outperformed its benchmark for the last three years, the question is: has this been due to luck or skill? Fama and French regressed the selected stocks on their three factors and found evidence that many "outperforming" portfolios are tilted towards value and small-capitalization stocks.

With the rise of passive investments, these factor exposures were made available for investors in transparent and rules-based smart beta indices. It was a win-win situation for product providers and investors. New products were available for sale with an edge – passive, yet different – and investors got cheap access to risk premiums.

Defining Smart Beta – A Tough Challenge

There are thousands of definitions and understandings of what smart beta is and how it is defined. So it is not possible to find the one fits all definition. But to keep it simple, let us concentrate on the aims of smart beta. It seeks to improve returns, reduce risks or provide a systematic factor exposure. It combines characteristics of both passive and active investing. Russell defines it as "transparent, rules-based indexes designed to provide exposure to specific factors, market segments or systematic strategies". We like this definition as well as the separation of the smart beta world into two segments: "alternatively weighting strategies and factors".[1]

Factor Investing

Factors are the heart of every single smart beta strategy. Understanding that different factor exposures are the key driver of risk and return is essential. Every security and so every portfolio is chased by different factors. For example, energy stocks tend to move together as they are highly dependent on the development of commodity prices. Typical factors are:

- Value
- Size
- Momentum
- Low volatility
- Quality
- Dividend yield

We want to highlight the relevant facts associated with each of the factors listed above on the next pages. Also, we highlight advantages and potential disadvantages or shortcomings of each of these factors.

Value A typical value strategy is defined by undervalued securities, which means that you select stocks, bonds or commodities which are cheaper than their actual fair value. Value is one of the oldest factors. Fama and French defined value with the book-to-market-ratio, favoring securities with the highest ratio. There are a lot of different definitions out there, taking into account for example the P/E-ratio or the P/CF-ratio.

Historically value outperformed a broad market index, but the factor outperformance is not steady (Figure 3.3 and Table 3.25). In particular, the

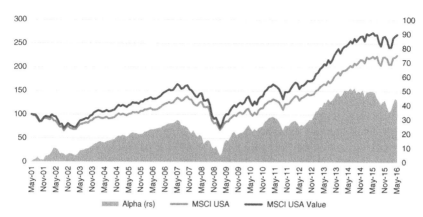

FIGURE 3.3 MSCI USA Index vs. MSCI USA Value Index
Data Source: FactSet

TABLE 3.25 MSCI USA Index vs. MSCI USA Value Index

05/01–05/16	MSCI USA	MSCI USA Value
Performance	125.45%	169.02%
CAGR	5.57%	6.82%
Volatility	14.76%	16.40%
Sharpe Ratio	0.38	0.42
Max. Drawdown	−50.65%	−55.86%

Data Source: FactSet

period around the financial crisis in 2007/2008 was marked by a cyclical underperformance and caused the high maximum drawdown of −55.86%. All in all, value outperformed the market-cap weighted MSCI USA Index by 43.57% in total or 1.25% on an annual basis since May 2001. This good performance attribute is partly compensated by a higher volatility of the value index which leads to a slightly better Sharpe ratio.

One of the most important questions one should ask is: Why are the selected securities cheaper than their competitors? Is there a reason such as a profit warning? The typical "value trap" appears when securities which are cheap become even cheaper and cheaper and the discount compared to competitors turns out to have been justified.

Advantages

- Selection of "cheap" securities compared to the market
- Historically outperformed a broad market index
- Highly accepted premium in the market

Disadvantages

- "Value trap" – cheap securities can become even cheaper
- Possible cluster risks in specific sectors

Size   Size is relative, also when it comes to indexing. The size premium, just like the value factor, is a highly accepted premium as described by Fama and French. They showed that there is a return premium in selecting stocks with a low market capitalization (small caps) in favor of stocks with a high market capitalization (large caps). The reason why these securities outperform is highly discussed. In the efficient market view, Fama and French originally hypothesized that small caps have higher systematic risk (beta) which allows them a higher return premium. Other researchers suggested that the outperformance comes from a higher default risk or a higher information uncertainty in smaller stocks.

The historical outperformance of the size factor is, as with the value premium, not steady. Due to the usually higher beta of a small cap portfolio, the factor delivers outperformance in a rising market environment and underperformance in down markets. The alpha chart in Figure 3.4 demonstrates this behavior and shows the accompanying periods. The really good return properties made the factor achieve an outperformance of 119.85% in total or 3.04% on an annual basis, as shown in Table 3.26. This overcompensated for the higher volatility compared to the MSCI USA Index. The risk-return ratio (Sharpe ratio) has been increased from 0.38 to 0.45. Due to the high beta the maximum drawdown of the MSCI USA Small Cap Index is slightly higher than the broad market index.

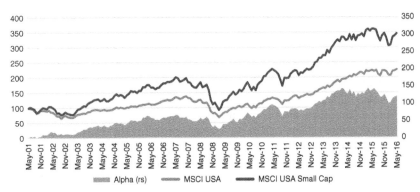

FIGURE 3.4   MSCI USA Index vs. MSCI USA Small Cap Index
Data Source: FactSet

TABLE 3.26   MSCI USA Index vs. MSCI USA Small Cap Index

05/01–05/16	MSCI USA	MSCI USA Small Cap
Performance	125.45%	245.30%
CAGR	5.57%	8.61%
Volatility	14.76%	19.03%
Sharpe Ratio	0.38	0.45
Max. Drawdown	−50.65%	−54.03%

Data Source: FactSet

Advantages

- Selection of smaller companies with a trend for higher growth potential
- Historically outperformed a broad market index
- Highly accepted premium in the market

Disadvantages

- Usually underperformance in falling markets
- Higher distress risk
- Low turnover can cause higher bid-ask-spreads

Momentum   An often-cited jargon term in the asset management world is "the trend is your friend". In academic words, investment professionals refer to "momentum". As Fama and French were focused on the Three-Factor Model, Carhart (1997) explained momentum as a persistent investment driver of returns and added it as an explanatory variable to the model. The momentum factor reflects future excess returns to securities with stronger past performance. So winners continue to win and losers remain losers. To add value, stock prices have to show trends over certain horizons. Jegadeesh and Titman (1993) proved in one of the first seminal studies on momentum in the U.S. stock market that buying past winners and selling past losers produced significant "abnormal" returns in 1965–1989.[2] Other studies showed that the momentum effect is strongest within 3–12 months and disappears after this time frame. Due to the short horizon it requires a very high turnover, which is at the same time a disadvantage of the strategy.

While value and size are explained by the Efficient Market Hypothesis, momentum can only be explained with behavioral biases. The most common reason why stocks tend to trend and show momentum is that investors over-react to information and love to buy what others are buying (herding).

As with all the other factors, the momentum factor has times of out- and underperformance as well. In sum, the MSCI USA Momentum Index outperformed the MSCI USA Index by 104.32% in total or 2.71% on an annual basis, as shown in Figure 3.5 and Table 3.27. Compared to the small cap factor, this outperformance has been achieved with similar volatility to the MSCI USA Index, which increases the Sharpe ratio to 0.56. The weaknesses of the momentum factor can be seen in the chart below.

In the financial crisis there has been a severe momentum crash, as past winners started to heavily underperform – mainly the financial sector. Investors suddenly favored defensive, non-cyclical stocks such as in the health care sector. This caused a large break in alpha generation and a slightly higher maximum drawdown as the momentum strategy needs some time to adopt its weightings.

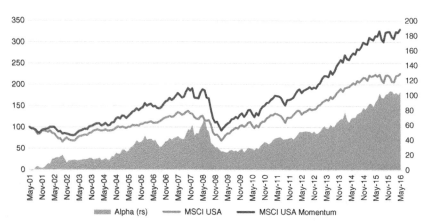

FIGURE 3.5   MSCI USA Index vs. MSCI USA Momentum Index
Data Source: FactSet

TABLE 3.27   MSCI USA Index vs. MSCI USA Momentum Index

05/01–05/16	MSCI USA	MSCI USA Momentum
Performance	125.45%	229.77%
CAGR	5.57%	8.28%
Volatility	14.76%	14.79%
Sharpe Ratio	0.38	0.56
Max. Drawdown	−50.65%	−51.72%

Data Source: FactSet

Advantages

- Selection of momentum securities improves performance in trending markets
- Historically outperformed a broad market index
- Highly accepted premium in the market

Disadvantages

- Usually high turnover
- Underperforming in trendless markets
- High concentration risk when a specific theme shows momentum

Low Volatility Usually one of the first things you learn in portfolio management is the Capital Asset Pricing Model (CAPM), which says that riskier stocks (higher volatility/beta) should be compensated with a higher return than less risky ones. The low volatility factor shows that the opposite is true and less risky stocks outperform the broad market and riskier competitors.

The low volatility factor strategy invests in securities with the lowest risk (lowest volatility) and is one of the most favoured and successful factors. The explanations for its historical outperformance are mostly behavioral. The most common explanation is the "lottery effect", which means that investors tend to take bets with a small expected loss but a large expected win, even though the probability of a loss is much higher than the win, and the weighted average of the outcome may be negative. That's why investors tend to buy low volatility stocks at a premium to the market.

Low volatility stocks characterize as outperforming in falling equity markets and lagging in up-markets. Due to the base effect, which shows the asymmetry of returns, low volatility stocks usually outperform over a market cycle. "Earning more by losing less" is the mystery here. When the market portfolio loses 50% in a crisis it needs 100% gain to recover, but if your low volatility portfolio only loses 40%, you just need 67% to recover.

The low volatility factor in Figure 3.6 and Table 3.28 expressed by the MSCI USA Minimum Volatility Index is a real success story. In the last 15 years it performed with an annual growth rate of 8.63% compared to the MSCI USA Index with 5.57%. But this isn't the whole story. It also achieved this superior performance with a volatility of just 10.89% and so was able to double the Sharpe ratio to 0.79. As mentioned, one part of the mysterious performance comes with the approximately 10% lower drawdown.

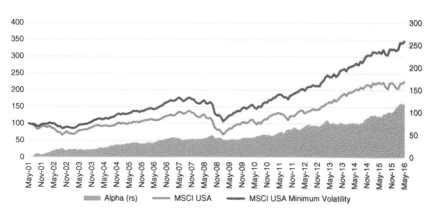

FIGURE 3.6   MSCI USA Index vs. MSCI USA Minimum Volatility Index
Data Source: FactSet

TABLE 3.28   MSCI USA Index vs. MSCI USA Minimum Volatility Index

05/01–05/16	MSCI USA	MSCI USA Minimum Volatility
Performance	125.45%	246.24%
CAGR	5.57%	8.63%
Volatility	14.76%	10.89%
Sharpe Ratio	0.38	0.79
Max. Drawdown	−50.65%	−39.83%

Data Source: FactSet

Advantages

- Selection of low volatility stocks generates a very good risk-return profile
- Historically outperformed a broad market index
- Highly accepted and favored premium in the market

Disadvantages

- Low beta strategy – usually lags in rising markets
- Concentration risk in defensive sectors such as utilities or consumer staples

Quality   The quality factor tries to earn the excess return of "high-quality" companies. There are many ways to define a quality company. The most common method is to rank the investment universe using fundamental figures from the balance sheet or income statement such as a company's efficiency, growth, leverage, profit sustainability or return-on-equity (ROE).

The reason for its superiority is much discussed, but becomes clear when you think in terms of a business owner. You don't want a highly leveraged company that has a high variability in its earnings and growth rate. Investors seek companies that manage their capital carefully and reduce the risk of over-leveraging. A steady growth in earnings will further reduce its need for capital market financing, which will support its stock price. This will trigger a positive feedback loop making the company more competitive in the eyes of its customers and investors.

Figure 3.7 and Table 3.29 show that the quality factor also historically outperformed a broad market index within the last 15 years. Here the excess return is 48.9% and the volatility has been reduced by 1.53%, which results in a Sharpe ratio of 0.53. The quality factor started to really outperform

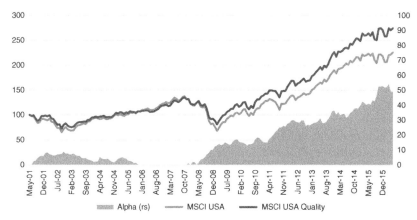

FIGURE 3.7   MSCI USA Index vs. MSCI USA Quality Index
Data Source: FactSet

TABLE 3.29   MSCI USA Index vs. MSCI USA Quality Index

05/01–05/16	MSCI USA	MSCI USA Quality
Performance	125.45%	174.35%
CAGR	5.57%	6.96%
Volatility	14.76%	13.23%
Sharpe Ratio	0.38	0.53
Max. Drawdown	−50.65%	−40.49%

Data Source: FactSet

after the financial crisis as investors were more aware of a company's fundamentals. As with the low volatility factor, the success comes with the reduced maximum drawdown.

Advantages
- Selection of quality stocks reduces volatility and beta
- Historically outperformed a broad market index
- Highly accepted premium in the market

Disadvantages
- Many possible figures to implement the factor
- Low beta strategy – usually lags in rising markets

Dividend Yield　Dividend yield is also a very important, persistent and "old" factor to invest in. It aims to capture the outperformance of high dividend yield stocks compared to a broad market index. The key driver of the superior returns is the compounding of dividend reinvestments. Dividends account for the majority of stock returns, depending on the index and country. Those companies that pay a consistent dividend with a steady growth have particularly attracted investors within the last years. There are many factor strategies covering dividends to invest in. Index strategies that focus only on the dividend yield run the risk of the above-mentioned "value trap" as a high dividend yield can also be the outcome of a sharp stock price decline. Another risk is the sudden cut of future dividends. As dividend stocks in particular are valued with dividend discount models, a dividend cut could disrupt the whole valuation model and cause severe stock price volatility.

As a conclusion for investors, high dividend factor strategies such as the MSCI USA High Dividend Yield Index outperformed a broad market index showing lower volatility and superior returns (Figure 3.8 and Table 3.30).

Advantages
- Selection of high dividend yield stocks delivers a steady return distribution
- Historically outperformed a broad market index
- Highly accepted premium in the market

Disadvantages
- "Value trap"
- Risk of a dividend shortfall results in severe losses

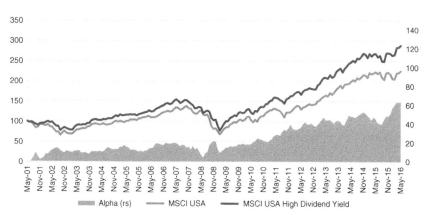

FIGURE 3.8 MSCI USA Index vs. MSCI USA High Dividend Yield Index
Data Source: FactSet

TABLE 3.30 MSCI USA Index vs. MSCI USA High Dividend Yield Index

05/01–05/16	MSCI USA	MSCI USA High Dividend Yield
Performance	125.45%	189.26%
CAGR	5.57%	7.34%
Volatility	14.76%	13.22%
Sharpe Ratio	0.38	0.56
Max. Drawdown	−50.65%	−50.05%

Data Source: FactSet

Factor Investing Summary These factors (Table 3.31) are the most accepted ones within the so-called "factor zoo", where issuers develop more and more factors to promote new index strategies or derive them from classic index strategies.

Alternative Weighting Strategies

The previously mentioned factors are just one side of the smart beta coin. To concentrate on specific risk premiums is a good strategy to diversify a portfolio or to get a specific risk exposure. Another method to get factor exposure and a diversified investment is to implement alternative weighting strategies.

TABLE 3.31   Overview of Factor Exposures

Factor Exposures	Thesis	Usually measured via
Value	Companies cheaper than their fair value deliver excess returns	Price/book ratio
Size	Smaller companies deliver excess returns to larger ones	Market capitalization
Momentum	Strong past performers deliver future excess returns	Historical relative performance
Low Volatility	Stable companies with low price fluctuation deliver excess returns to the market	Standard deviation
Quality	Good companies with low debt, high returns and stable earnings deliver excess returns	Degree of debt, high return on equity
Dividend Yield	Companies that pay higher dividends deliver excess returns	Dividend yield

Source: Authors, FactSet

For a long time, capitalization-weighted indices were the one and only weighting method to invest in. They have a lot of advantages, such as low turnover, high liquidity and the focus on large companies. In a market capitalization weighted index the weight of a company is calculated as the share price times the (free float-adjusted) outstanding shares divided by the market-cap of all stocks. This leads to the bias to large caps discussed previously.

However, there are some disadvantages which led to the success of smart beta strategies. Market-cap weighted indices are highly pro-cyclical as the weight of a company rises when its share price increases, so these indices can face a high concentration risk in specific securities and sectors during market bubbles such as the financial crisis.

On the other hand, alternatively weighted indexes became more popular as they addressed the disadvantages of their market-cap weighted competitors. There are many ways to calculate the weighting of securities within these rules-based frameworks. The simplest method is a naïve equal weighting with a steady rebalancing frequency. Another method is a fundamental weighting scheme, which weights stocks by economic factors, resulting in a weighting scheme that is independent of price-based market measures of size. Furthermore, there are risk-based mathematical weighting methods, which are most often based on a Markowitz optimization. The minimum-variance approach can be mentioned here, which tries to reduce the volatility of a portfolio to the minimum or an equal risk contribution or maximum diversification method, which is discussed in detail later. All alternative weighting schemes have different payout profiles and try to achieve certain objectives but they indirectly address different factor exposures. It is very important to know and understand the associated risk exposures.

Equal Weighting   As mentioned, the simplest way to weight a portfolio of stocks is to give each security the same amount of capital. This makes sense when you don't know which one will perform best and simultaneously reduces the concentration risk in your portfolio. A good example where equal weighting would reduce the risk towards a handful of stocks is the Nasdaq 100 Index. Here the Top 10 stocks make up 50% of the index, as shown in Table 3.32. So the remaining 90 stocks share the other half. Certainly, the high weighting of Apple can be an opportunity when enough smartphones are sold and the company grows enough, but what happens if there is another competitor like Samsung taking Apple's market share or a new technology arises, which Apple didn't recognize early enough? In an equally weighted index the stock-specific risk is reduced to a minimum, as in the Nasdaq 100, for example, Apple's weight would have been reduced to 1%, along with Microsoft and Cisco. As a result, stocks with a smaller market capitalization such as Mattel increase their weighting from 0.2% to 1%.

This larger allocation towards small-capitalization stocks in comparison to a capitalization-weighted index shows that from a factor perspective an equally weighted index displays a bias towards the size factor. But this isn't the only factor addressed by an equal weighting. Due to a regular rebalancing framework towards the same capital amount, an equally weighted

TABLE 3.32   Top Holdings Nasdaq 100

Apple	10.6%
Microsoft	8.0%
Amazon	6.5%
Facebook	5.2%
Alphabet C	4.9%
Alphabet A	4.2%
Comcast	3.0%
Intel	2.9%
Cisco Systems	2.8%
Gilead Sciences	2.3%

Source: Authors, FactSet, Data as of June 30 2016

index profits from the mean-reverting behavior of the stock market, as on a rebalancing date profits in winning stocks are realized and losing stocks are rebought cheaper. This counter-cyclical behavior lifts a small portion of the value premium.

As small caps tend to outperform in rising markets, an equally weighted index usually performs better than a classic cap-weighted benchmark in an upward trend and underperforms in a fearful environment.

Advantages
- Historically outperformed a market-cap weighted index
- Implementation of a more balanced industry structure
- A pro-cyclical index calculation and thus a distortion of the markets is avoided
- Counter-cyclical acting by regular rebalancing of index components

Disadvantages
- Tilt towards small cap stocks increases systematic risk (beta)
- Higher bid-ask spreads in smaller companies and rebalancing increase trading costs

Fundamental Another example of weighting securities within an index is fundamental weighting. Here a company's weight is not given because of its market capitalization. Rather, the economic scale is the important factor for defining a weighting. The most famous example within the industry is Research Affiliates (RAFI), which uses mainly four fundamental measures such as sales, cash flow, book value and dividends. Unlike an equal weighting approach, a company's fundamental size is highly correlated with its market cap, so fundamental indices tend to have similar size and liquidity characteristics as a cap-weighted strategy and therefore do not earn the size premium. Caused by its weighting scheme and focus on good fundamental ratios and figures, such strategies face a severe tilt towards the value factor. A regular rebalancing also boosts the value premium.

Advantages
- Historically outperformed a market-cap weighted index
- Small tracking error to a cap-weighted index compared to other weighting schemes
- "Cheap" valuation ratios
- Counter-cyclical acting by regular rebalancing of index components

Disadvantages

- Risk of "value trap" due to tilt towards "cheap" stocks
- Possible cluster risks in specific sectors

Minimum Variance Now it becomes exciting for nerds who love mathematics. Minimum-variance indices are based on a risk-return optimization which is based on Markowitz's theory and invests in the portfolio with the lowest volatility on the efficient frontier (all portfolios with the highest return for a given risk). All that is needed is a volatility and correlation forecast (index calculators often use historical data) for each single security. In theory this portfolio would be quite risk-averse and achieve just a small return, but what does the reality say?

Can I achieve a higher return with lower risk? The standard portfolio theory would clearly say "no" to that – the cornerstone of the portfolio theory by Markowitz and the Capital Asset Pricing Model (CAPM) of Sharpe is based on the assumption that higher risks on the capital market should lead to systematically higher risk premiums.

The reality is, however, the opposite – stock investments and diversified equity portfolios with lower risk structure show a more attractive risk-return profile over longer periods than the standard theory would suggest – and these results are consistent and robust across different time periods or even regions. The empirically well-tested minimum-variance anomaly is mainly due to the fact that the capital market does not reflect the highest level of information efficiency and different factors require a negative capital market line.

In an unconstrained implementation the minimum variance portfolio would show a high concentration in a few defensive companies and sectors. To avoid this, almost every index provider employs constraints such as maximum stock or sector weights. This reduces the concentration risk and increases the diversification.

Focusing on the factor exposure, a minimum variance index is tilted towards the size premium, which means that there is an overweight in small-cap stocks relative to the cap-weighted index, although to a lesser extent than the equally weighted index. The second marked factor exposure is low volatility, which is a natural outcome of the stock selection process as the main focus is on defensive stocks.

Caused by the excellent risk-return characteristics, more and more institutional equity portfolios and index-based ETFs or mutual funds have devoted themselves to the minimum-variance strategy in recent years.

Ever since the financial crisis and low interest rates, the need and demand for equity strategies has increased, which can reduce the drawdown risk but also use the yield potential of stock premiums.

As with the low volatility premium, the message for minimum variance is "earning more by losing less".

Advantages
- Historically outperformed a market-cap weighted index
- "Earning more by losing less"
- Superior risk-return figures
- Lower drawdown in crises

Disadvantages
- Low beta – underperforms in rising markets
- Possible cluster risks in specific sectors depending on constraints

Equal Risk Contribution   Another mathematical alternative weighting method is Risk Parity or Equal Risk Contribution. As the name suggests, the strategy is characterized by the fact that contrary to the classical monetary equally weighted asset allocation, a distribution is implemented based on the risk contributions per security. This has the advantage that "risky" assets (mostly categorized by volatility) do not dominate the performance respectively risk result and thus leads to a much more balanced portfolio structure.

Another important advantage is that the investment process of the risk parity strategy is not dependent on fragile market and return forecasts. The management of risk parity between securities can be implemented on the basis of risk prediction, so that the inherent weaknesses of market forecasts are ruled out in this strategy. Risk predictions are, for most issuers, historical volatility parameters. The aim is that each security has the same volatility contribution to the whole portfolio. This results in an overweighting of low volatility stocks and disfavors stocks with a higher volatility. So the factor tilt is similar to the low-volatility premium. However, it is essential to detect the driving factors of the strategy and to take these into account.

Advantages
- Historically outperformed a market-cap weighted index
- Tilt towards low volatility stocks
- Superior risk-return figures
- Lower drawdown in crises

Disadvantages

- Low beta – underperforms in rising markets
- Possible cluster risks in specific sectors depending on constraints

Maximum Diversification   In recent years, new techniques especially geared towards risk diversification were developed in the area of portfolio construction which have become particularly popular. This success was able due to the growing recognition that a traditional capitalization-weighted index shows weaknesses and can be developed through adjustments to a better risk-return ratio.

The basic idea behind the maximum diversification approach is to implement a portfolio that converts the highest degree of diversification – thus maximizing the "diversification ratio". For this purpose, the strategic asset allocation is dynamic, therefore regularly adjusted to market conditions. The weight of an asset class or security is reduced when its volatility or its correlation rises to another asset class.

The portfolio management of the maximum diversification approach is only based on risk prediction, so that there are no market and price forecasts adopted in the investment process. As a basic strategy for risk-averse investors, the maximum diversification approach can occupy a valuable space in a portfolio.

Advantages

- Historically outperformed a market-cap weighted index
- Highly diversified portfolio
- Superior risk-return figures

Disadvantages

- Pro-cyclical strategy
- Based on volatility and correlation forecasts

Getting Smart about Beta

As shown in this chapter, a wide variety of indexing methodologies exists adding complexity to understand the risks and benefits of the different smart beta strategies. It is very important for investors to focus on transparent, simple and scientifically well documented weighting methodologies, as these have the necessary economic significance where the investors can justifiably

	Quality	Value	Small tilt	Momentum	Low volatility
Quality	1.00				
Value	0.54	1.00			
Small tilt	0.36	0.85	1.00		
Momentum	−0.09	−0.18	−0.21	1.00	
Low volatility	0.79	0.24	0.09	0.02	1.00

FIGURE 3.9   Smart Beta Correlations
Source: PowerShares by Invesco

expect to earn a risk premium over a complete capital market cycle. Obviously, different factor weighting strategies are showing different levels of outperformance at different times. Another key observation is that different smart beta strategies are showing low correlation to each other[3] (Figure 3.9).

The important implication for portfolio construction is that the meaningful combination of different factor smart beta ETFs can additionally reduce the risk structure of a diversified portfolio. In a recent study Invesco PowerShares analyzed the performance and risk properties of various smart beta strategies and alternative weightings in different market cycles and different market environments[4]. Their results showed that smart beta strategies showed a clear pattern of outperformance relative to market-cap weighted indices within a time frame of over two decades – a period that included five different market cycles and other forms of market uncertainty. Figure 3.10

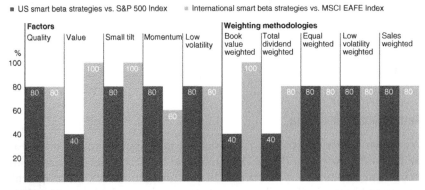

FIGURE 3.10   Performance of Smart Beta Strategies
Source: PowerShares by Invesco

shows that most smart beta strategies outperformed during a majority of market cycles studied.

Despite these very favorable results supporting smart beta strategies, it is important for investors to understand that these performance and risk results are dependent on the time frame of the holding or observation period. As each factor shows a different performance path, longer time frames of underperformance must be accepted to reap the long-term risk premium benefit.

In the same study – shown in Figure 3.11 – Invesco PowerShares also calculated the longest periods of underperformance of the various smart beta strategies compared to the S&P 500, which varied from 4 to 10 years.

This is a very important implication, as it shows that with the deviation from the market cap weighting scheme there is no automatic outperformance achieved, which can usually be reaped only with a sufficient holding period. As longer periods of underperformance can be observed, investors do need the patience to hold on to their smart beta investments as time is needed so that an alternative weighting scheme can show its superior risk-adjusted performance compared to the naïve market cap weighted indices.

Additionally, several smart beta factors are showing different performance properties in different capital market cycles. An important example is the recent outperformance and run towards so-called low volatility strategies, which profit from the low interest rate environment which is a critical factor for this weighting strategy. Unsurprisingly, Invesco PowerShares confirms in their study as shown in Figure 3.12 that in rising rate environments, low volatility strategies tend to massively underperform.

Investors should be aware of this fact as most investors are altering their asset allocation from bonds towards equities because of the secular low-yield environment in bonds. But going out of bonds and into for example

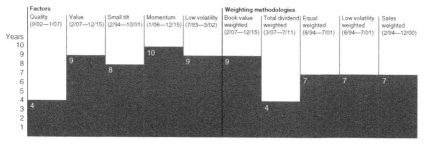

FIGURE 3.11   Longest Periods of Underperformance
Source: PowerShares by Invesco

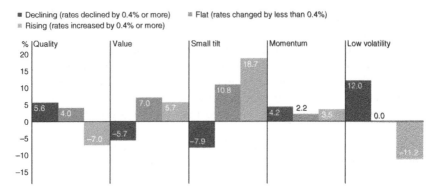

FIGURE 3.12   Performance Dependent on Interest Rate Moves
Source: PowerShares by Invesco

low-volatility stocks (as a low-beta equity alternative) might not be optimal as interest rate sensitivity is still the most in Low Volatility stocks.

NEXT GENERATION INDICES (THIRD GENERATION OF INDEXING)

As the previous chapters have showed, the evolution and development of indexing and the triumphal march of passive investing in the last years led to increasing research and new strategy and index developments of ETF powerhouses but also specialists and focused niche players. By the time of writing this book, we are on the verge from moving from the second generation of indexing – led by the ever-increasing attention to factor investing and so-called "smart beta" strategies – to the third generation of indexing, in which the various advantages of optimized indexing are combined with different rules-based investment processes and transparent strategies.

Figure 3.13 shows the time line and evolution of indexing and ETF investing, which in the previous chapters the first generation and second generation were treated in depth.

The first generation of indexing started with plain vanilla market-cap weighted indices. The huge success of ETFs and continuing asset flows confirm the high value-added of these efficient, low-cost and transparent investment vehicles. With the growing success of ETFs on the well-known flagship indices, investors realized that there were some severe weaknesses with market-cap weighted indices such as pro-cyclicality or sectoral concentration risks.

Unsurprisingly, new weighting methodologies and invented index strategies emerged based on alternative index weighting methodologies such as

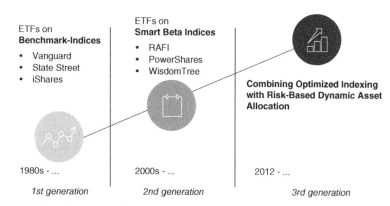

FIGURE 3.13 Evolution of Indexing
Source: Kula, Stahn 2015

low volatility or equal weighting – and thus the second generation of indexing was born. As a result, so-called "smart beta" indices and ETFs were launched, which enjoyed huge investor attention and inflows accordingly. These indices offer a potentially "smarter" approach to equity beta by addressing specific risk factors and risk premiums.

To put it differently, the main aim of the further evolution to the third generation of indexing is to provide investors with different payoff profiles and risk-return structures, which cannot be achieved by classical beta-1 indexing strategies, independent of which generation they belong. While the classical advantages of ETF investing and indexing are preserved, the third generation of indexing adds rules-based investment processes, which leads to a specific risk-return profile that would not be available with the traditional first and second generation of ETFs.

The main aim of this latest development in indexing is to provide investors with access to institutional investment strategies in a rules-based transparent index framework, which is packaged in efficient passive investment vehicles that offer an adjunct to classical indexing strategies and products. As an introduction, we now discuss several examples and aspects of the third generation of indexing, going into further detail about this important and exciting development in the following chapters.

Reducing Behavioral Gap

The triumphal march of ETFs and indexing was founded first and foremost on the notion that the majority of active investment managers do not add value for investors after costs and that – particularly in a continued low interest rate environment – significant cost reductions in investment products are increasing the return potential, particularly from a long-term investment perspective.

Nevertheless, as both arguments favoring the use of first-generation indexing products are still valid, another important aspect comes increasingly into consideration, driven by extensive research from the area of behavioral finance. This research field seeks to combine behavioral and cognitive psychological theory with conventional finance theory to provide explanations for why investors make systematically irrational financial decisions, leading to substantial underperformance compared to buy-and-hold investing. This underperformance of investors caused by bad market timing and other behavioral biases was addressed and quantified by different scientific studies, which showed that investors are suffering a massive "behavioral return gap"[5,6] (see Figure 3.14).

So one main objective of the third generation of indexing is becoming more obvious – to offer an investment strategy or framework based on efficient indexing which is additionally supporting investors in reducing the long-term disadvantages of emotional bad investment decisions and thus leading to a significantly reduced behavioral gap return profile. The important point is that by using rule-based investment strategies to control for and to mitigate costly behavioral biases, far more value-added can be achieved

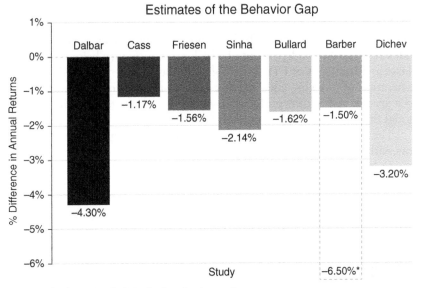

*given for the most actively trading investors in sample.

FIGURE 3.14   Behavioral Return Gap
Source: Betterment

compared to solely optimizing the average cost structure of investment port-folios, which was the main aim of first-generation indexing and ETFs.

By combining efficient indexing with rule-based investment strategies, the massive behavioral return gap can partly be closed and the average underperformance to fair benchmark indices can be substantially reduced – by earning behavioral alpha.

Adding the Risk Perspective to Indexing

Another advantage of third-generation indexing comes from analyzing the risk structure of the first and second generation of indexing strategies and products. Irrational, volatile and noisy capital markets require flexibility and an immediate capacity to act, particularly to control for severe down-side risks in equity markets. The technology bubble (2000–2002) or the great financial crisis (2008) are examples of substantial downside risks for equity market investors, which led to huge losses in investment portfolios and the missing of important risk-return targets for most investors. Institutional investors in particular, like pension trusts, endowments and similar capital-preservation and liability-driven investment plans, have been hit hard by these two extreme events, occurring within just six to eight years. This is actually fewer than might be expected looking at the historical pattern and is a good example of the unpredictability of market events.

With classical first or second generation indexing strategies or ETFs, investors face a static beta and thus suffer severe losses in bear markets as their holdings are always fully invested in the chosen ETF. Figure 3.15 shows an analysis which compares the maximum drawdown properties of individual weighting methods applied to the U.S. capital market[7].

In this analysis the capitalization-weighted index (S&P 500 Net Total Return, first-generation index) is compared to an equal-weighted index (S&P 500 Equal Weight Index NTR), a minimum volatility index (MSCI USA Minimum Volatility Index) and a fundamental index (FTSE RAFI US 1000 Index) – all indices classified under second-generation indices. The chart shows impressively that independent of which weighting-scheme is applied, substantial market-beta risk still remains for investors.

Therefore, an additional potential application of third-generation index solutions becomes apparent. By combining efficient indexing with some sort of rules-based risk overlay strategies – which are often applied by institutional investors, as they have some sort of limited risk budgets by regulators or beneficiaries – costly drawdowns, which can substantially impair wealth and long-term returns for investors, can be cushioned.

After delivering some introductory thoughts regarding the latest step of the evolution of indexing and passive investing, the following chapters will

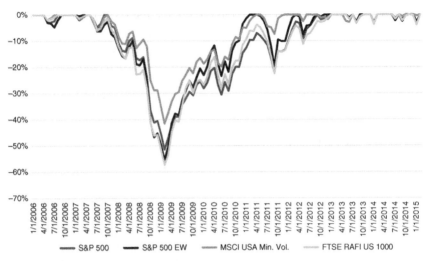

FIGURE 3.15 Maximum Drawdown Comparison
Source: Aykan Kula, 2015

present further in-depth information about third-generation strategies and potential product solutions, analyzing the advantages and disadvantages of these latest developments in indexing.

Factor Rotation Strategies

Factor investing has become widely recognized with the rise of smart beta indexing solutions, as risk factors help to explain systematic sources of returns. As previously shown, second-generation indexing strategies are targeting to systematically earn risk premiums, which have been assiduously researched and confirmed scientifically. Obviously, using a conscious risk factor allocation approach in portfolio construction does add significant value compared to the classical asset allocation approach, as we will show later in detail.

The main advantage of risk factor investing is that investors can seek exposure to systematically rewarded risk premiums, such as, for example, the value premium or the small cap premium, first confirmed in the seminal work of Fama/French[8]. It may well come as a surprise to most readers that the foundations of the massive "smart beta" trend were laid at the beginning of the 1990s, so some could say that the idea of smart beta is nothing new – but that's another story. What is important with the surge of efficient and transparent investment products targeting specific risk factors is that nowadays investors have a huge investment opportunity set to actively manage their portfolio based on risk factor allocations. With the recent surge of optimized indexing strategies, investors are nowadays in the position to exactly harvest risk premiums which exist alongside the "traditional" CAPM equity market risk premium.

The impression may be given that putting together a smart factor ETF portfolio alone would solve most investor problems in today's complex capital markets. Certainly, compared to classical asset allocation and active investment strategy solutions, focusing on efficient factor investing products definitely improves long-term performance of investor portfolios. But it is very important to understand that risk premiums are not stationary but cyclical in nature. As Figure 3.16 shows, each of the analyzed factor indices have shown different relative return paths compared to the market-cap weighting index, confirming the cyclical nature of the different targeted risk premiums.

Unsurprisingly, the analyzed factors showed significant difference in their risk-return characteristics, as Figure 3.17 shows.

One important aspect is that although all analyzed factors exhibit significant alpha, higher Sharpe ratios and outperformance compared to the market-cap weighted index, this outperformance is only reaped in the long term if investors hold onto their position, even though longer periods of underperformance may occur.

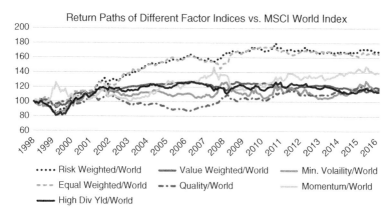

FIGURE 3.16 Return Paths of Different Factor Indices
Data Source: Bloomberg

Risk / Return Characteristics of Different Factor Indices
(Performance Data from 12/98 to 02/17)

○ Risk Weighted   ⊘ Value Weighted   ◎ Min. Volaility   ⊖ Equal Weighted
◉ Quality   ● Momentum   ● High Div Yld

FIGURE 3.17   Risk-Return Characteristics of Different Factor Indices
Data Source: Bloomberg

For example, the value factor is very solid and has been observed over many decades. But value investors have suffered significant periods of underperformance. Similarly, the momentum factor is well researched within different periods and internationally confirmed, but occasionally stormy momentum crashes occur, leading to large relative underperformance for investors.

As behavioral traits often result in pro-cyclical investor behavior, rules-based third-generation factor strategies can be one possible solution to cope with factor cyclicality.

Multi-Factor Index Solutions and Investment Products   The aim of multi-factor index solutions is to provide intelligent risk factor portfolios that match the specific needs of investors. By setting up a diversified portfolio of different risk factors, the cyclical nature of single factors can be alleviated, as the different risk factors show low correlation among themselves. With a rules-based rebalance schedule, the price movements of the specific factors can be addressed in a counter-cyclical way, as better-performing risk factors are systematically reduced to policy weights, whereas underperforming factors are increased.

It is important to recognize that this next generation of index solutions is by no means a "panacea". Nevertheless, multi-factor strategies show a distinct advantage to the investor, as they can achieve a cost-effective and transparent diversification of chosen factors. As forecasting the current or future market phase is very difficult to achieve (bull market, bear market), bundled multi-factor strategies can minimize the risk of investors over-weighting the wrong factors and seizing the opportunity to be invested in the correct factor. In the long run, a multi-factor approach is less volatile than the underlying single factors individually considered.

Unsurprisingly, different efficient multi-factor ETFs have been launched, aiming to provide investors with bundled factor portfolios with some sort of rebalancing schedule. One of the first providers of a multi-factor ETF was Indexing Research Powerhouse Scientific Beta, which partnered with Global X to start different multi-factor ETFs in the U.S.[9]. The multi-factor ETF combines four factors – value, small cap, low volatility and momentum. For example, the value factor includes only those stocks that show up as cheapest. Scientific betas methodology then allocates weightings to each of these factors, combined with periodic rebalancing. Another new product offering was started by global ETF leader BlackRock iShares, which partnered with MSCI to start different factor-select ETFs, offering investors a diversified packaged factor exposure portfolio, also for European investors[10].

Before continuing with another solution for factor investors, some caveats and difficulties of multi-factor strategy solutions should be highlighted. Most importantly, the risk-return payoff of the bundled multi-factor portfolios are dependent on the correct selection of risk factors which have low intra-correlation behavior. A static selection of risk factors which might be optimal at the time of the product launch may not necessarily be optimal after some time has passed.

Additionally, the main advantage of passive investing becomes more and more diluted as multi-factor strategies increase complexity and reduce transparency for investors, ultimately leading to increasing total expense ratios, which can be already observed in second-generation smart beta ETFs. Time will tell whether these new developments will offer significant value after costs compared with low-cost cap-weighted first-generation Total Market ETFs.

Flexible Factor Rotation Strategies   Another solution that tries to take advantage of the varying and cyclical factor premiums is trying to time specific favorable factors dependent of the prevailing market cycle. As risk factors are showing different risk and performance characteristics within a capital market cycle, a factor rotation strategy targets to dynamically allocate into an available pool of risk factors.

The key difference to the multi-factor index solutions previously shown is that, while static weighting between risk factors already delivers a significant level of diversification and hence value-added, a dynamic tactical allocation can add even more value in terms of portfolio risk and performance. As single risk factors also exhibit persistence and momentum in the short term, investors can exploit these short-term return patterns by dynamically rotating between risk factors.

Certainly, the task of forecasting future factor returns and risk premiums is as challenging as classical market return predictions – if not impossible. The disappointing real track record of classical active forecast-based strategies and investment products is showing that strategies based on market predictions are not robust and reliable. Unsurprisingly, most active flexible factor allocation strategies show disappointing real-time results compared to the promised backtesting-based return potential.

Therefore, the focus now is based on flexible factor allocation strategies which are not dependent on forecasts. One possible way to set up a robust investment process is to allocate to sets of risk factors dependent of current market cycle. As the various risk factors show different risk-return properties in different market cycles, straightforward but compelling allocation strategies can be implemented. To choose an appropriate factor or factor combination for the flexible factor allocation strategy, the important criteria are risk structure, correlations with other factors and the performance of the specific factors in different business and market cycles. To begin with, a classification of the various single factor strategies to different market conditions matrix is necessary, as Table 3.33 demonstrates:

The main idea of the dynamic factor allocation strategy is to allocate factors based on the prevailing market cycle or regime. For example, in an upward trending bull market cycle, pro-cyclical factors like Momentum or

TABLE 3.33 Overview of Factor Indices

Factor	Historical Risk	Historical Correlation	Historical Business Cycle
Value	Comparable to market	Low with Momentum and Quality	Pro-cyclical
Momentum	Comparable to market	Low with Value, Yield and Quality	Pro-cyclical
Low Size	Higher than market	Low with Min. Volatility, Yield and Quality	Pro-cyclical
Quality	Lower than market	Low with Value, Size, Yield and Momentum	Defensive
Low Volatility	Lower than market	Low with Value and Momentum	Defensive
Yield	Lower than market	Low with Size, Quality and Momentum	Defensive

Data Source: MSCI.Inc

Small Cap are invested, whereas in difficult bear market cycles the portfolio is shifted into defensive factors like Low Volatility or Yield to reduce drawdown risks by focusing on defensive factors. Of course, the determination of the prevailing market cycle is of utmost importance, and, as stated earlier, we do not believe that it is systematically possible to forecast market cycles. However, fortunately, transparent and simple technical indicators can help us to set up a stringent dynamic factor allocation strategy that is also implementable for do-it-yourself investors.

One possible simplistic methodology would be to use moving average rules to define prevailing market cycles. If the current market price is higher than a certain moving average (for example 10-month moving average), a bull cycle is determined, so the portfolio is allocated into factors like Momentum. As long as this condition holds, pro-cyclical factors are allocated to earn the systematic risk premium of the invested factors. On the other hand, if market prices fall below the chosen moving average, the portfolio is adopted into defensive factors like Low Volatility so as to set up an active factor rotation strategy. Even though this example may be very simple, with huge potential for further development, the main idea of active factor allocation strategies as the third generation of indexing can be shown.

In conclusion, the following active factor rotation strategy (Index: BIST 100, Turkish Large Cap Equities) can be introduced, which is based on a market cycle regime engine rotating between the Momentum factor and the Low Volatility/Dividend factor. Depending on the determined market cycle based on a quarterly rebalancing, the factors are implemented directly using concentrated stock positions (30 stocks equal-weighted). Figure 3.18 shows

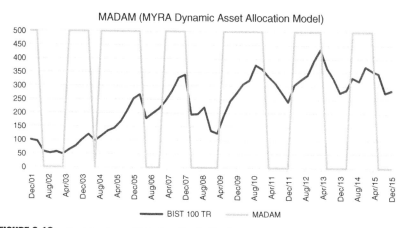

FIGURE 3.18 Positioning of Market Cycle Engine
Data Source: MYRA Capital AG

the results of the market cycle engine, which is solely based on a systematic, rules-based and quantitative process without explicit forecasts[11].

The market phases are determined on a quarterly basis, making the determination robust and reducing the rate of false signals. Macroeconomic and geopolitical factors play no role in the market phase determination. The goal of the strategy is to use two proven models of factor stock selection (Momentum, Quality Dividend) and to combine them with a rotation strategy to access an additional alpha source. As the historical analysis of the Dynamic Factor strategy (figure 3.19) shows, value-added can be achieved with this process.

Dynamic Risk and Asset Allocation Strategies

This section will take the notion of next-generation indexing to another level, as the main difference between classical indices (first generation of indexing) but also smart beta indices (second generation of indexing) is that risk-based asset allocation strategies dynamically and tactically alter the portfolio betas. Whereas the introduced factor rotation strategies were fully invested with a static beta-1 exposure into equities, the flexible factor allocation strategies aiming for a somewhat limited management of beta exposure by selecting different risk factors with different market betas.

But before we dig deeper into this latest development in the indexing business, the rationale for risk-based indexing strategies should be made. By consequently adding the risk perspective into the analysis, the advantages of

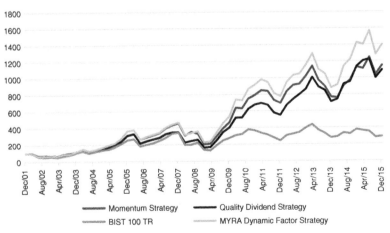

FIGURE 3.19 MYRA Dynamic Factor Strategy
Data Source: MYRA Capital AG

a modular enhancement of an efficient indexing strategy should be clear, depending on investor risk preferences. Often a simple buy-and-hold strategy would be the optimal positioning for investors in the long term, but only a small fraction of investors shows the behavioral strength to maintain the chosen strategy also in difficult capital market times.

Regardless of which index weighting method or smart beta strategy is implemented, systematic market risk remains as the indices and strategies are always fully invested. In downturn markets these various beta-1 indices will suffer large losses and drawdowns, hurting investor portfolios and threatening investor wealth objectives. A drawdown analysis of different weighting schemes and indices (S&P 500 Cap Weighted, S&P 500 Equal Weighted, MSCI USA Minimum Volatility Index, FTSI RAFI US 1000 Index) during the great financial crisis show the underlying rationale (Table 3.34). Independent of the applied weighting schemes, massive drawdown risks remain[12].

The analysis shows that even defensive weighting schemes or factor strategies like low volatility suffered a massive drawdown of more than −40% in the great financial crisis, putting investors at a significant risk. Low volatility does not translate into low risk.

From an institutional investor's perspective, the aftermath of the technology bubble and the global financial crisis in particular have led to risk budgets being significantly scaled down, leading to structurally low equity allocations in Europe, which is also partly driven by regulatory changes in the banking and insurance sector. Unsurprisingly, risk-based allocation and portfolio insurance strategies gained momentum since then.

TABLE 3.34 Risk-Return Analysis of Different Beta-1 Strategies

	S&P 500	S&P 500 Equal Weighted	MSCI USA Minimum Volatility	FTSE RAFI US 1000
Total Return	88.26%	117.19%	109.24%	82.72%
Total Return p.a.	7.22%	8.92%	8.48%	6.87%
Volatility p.a.	15.56%	18.44%	12.27%	18.01%
Maximum Drawdown	−51.44%	−55.35%	−41.59%	−57.31%
Low-Point Date	2/27/2009	2/27/2009	2/27/2009	2/27/2009
Time To Recover (Months)	58	44	41	67
Sharpe Ratio	0.35	0.39	0.55	0.29

Data Source: Aykan Kula, 2015

Nevertheless, also from the perspective of individual investors, a flexible, risk-centric approach is important to achieve long-term investment objectives. It is scientifically shown that behavioral biases like overconfidence and loss aversion lead to systematically inferior investment decisions, which result in a behavioral return gap in market returns. Pro-cyclicality in investment decisions can be better controlled if rule-based investment methods are implemented and combined with a consequent risk perspective.

Additionally, basic mathematics show the importance of avoiding large equity market drawdowns to protect and increase private wealth in the long term. As incurred investment losses have to be offset exponentially by future gains, the basic investor mantra could be "Earning more by losing less". Figure 3.20 shows this relationship in a very intuitive manner.

As the graph demonstrates, the gain necessary to offset the loss is not linear. The larger the loss, the larger the difference between the percentage loss and the percentage gain required to recover. As a result, it is particularly important to avoid large losses, as we observed in the aftermath of the technology bubble or the great financial crisis.

Rules-based investment strategies shifting dynamically between risky equity market exposure and a safe asset investment like treasuries or money market are also well known, termed "portfolio insurance investment strategies".

Volatile capital markets in the aftermath of the great financial crisis with large drawdowns increased popularity of portfolio insurance strategies

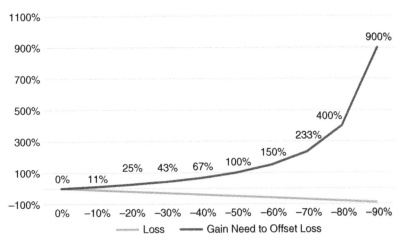

FIGURE 3.20   Upside-Downside Relationship of Returns
Data Source: MYRA Capital AG

as an important alternative for those investors who have only limited risk budgets to act. In particular, the institutional demand from continental Europe, particularly Germany, increased significantly in the last decade, which paved the way for the development of different risk overlay strategies aimed at systematic reduction of loss potentials and the de-risking of investment portfolios in times of capital markets distress.

Table 3.35 gives a short overview of various dynamic asset allocation (DAA) methods, with the corresponding strategy profiles and success factors[13].

In the following sections, two risk-based index and strategy solutions (third generation of indexing) will be introduced, which aim to deliver superior risk-adjusted returns with significant drawdown reduction properties.

TABLE 3.35   Dynamic Asset Allocation Strategies

Elementary Shifting Rules	Portfolio Insurance	Best-of-N Risky Assets	Protect Spending
Different Variants			
▪ Constant Mix ▪ Linear investment rule	▪ Dynamic Stop-Loss ▪ Synthetic Put ▪ CPPI ▪ TPPI	▪ Best-of-2 ▪ Best-of-2 with Risk-free ▪ Best-of-N with Risk-free	▪ Dybvig (1999)
Strategy Profile			
Constant Mix: ▪ "Buy Low/Sell High" ▪ Maintenance of target allocation Linear investment rule: ▪ Pro-cyclic behavior	▪ Absolute capital preservation ▪ Asymmetric payoff profile	▪ Relative or absolute capital preservation ▪ Asymmetric payoff profile	▪ Maintenance of financial solvency
Factors of Success			
Constant Mix: ▪ Oscillating markets Linear investment rule: ▪ Trend-prone markets	▪ Trend-prone markets	▪ Trend-prone markets ▪ Low cross-correlations	▪ Trend-prone markets

Source: Aykan Kula

Target Volatility and Risk Control Indices   One important strategy solution for risk-averse investors are so-called "target volatility indices" or "risk control indices", which dynamically adjust the equity exposure of the index to the money market in times of market distress and high volatility. These tactical asset allocation changes are aimed at significantly reducing drawdowns to protect the investor better for serious losses.

As volatility is one of the most popular risk metrics used in investment management, it is not surprising that indices were launched which target a predetermined specific volatility level target. As equity market drawdowns and turbulent markets are generally accompanied by higher volatility levels, a rules-based tactical shifting towards safe assets decorrelates the strategy from the equity markets to protect investors from serious losses when markets are falling. To put it another way, target volatility indices are aiming to hold the volatility of the strategy as close as possible to the aimed volatility level, whereas often several indices with different volatility target levels corresponding to different investor needs are offered by ETF issuers.

Basically, these indices decrease the allocation to the underlying equity index in times of equity market corrections, as the volatility of the underlying risky equity index increases. Simultaneously the exposure to a risk-free asset allocation component (generally cash or US Treasuries) is increased in this case and vice versa. Several index providers and ETF issuers launched target volatility strategies: the FTSE Volatility Target Index Series and the Dow Jones Volatility Risk Control Indexes, for example. In the next section the functioning of target volatility strategies is described based on the DJ Volatility Risk Control Index methodology[14].

Several predetermined volatility target levels are offered, typically 5%, 10%, 15% or 20% in the case of the Dow Jones index range. The targeted volatility level is achieved by tactically allocating between the equity index underlying and cash. The allocation between the equity underlying and cash index is a function of the realized volatility of the equity index. If realized volatility is higher than the target volatility, the allocation to the equity market is reduced. Otherwise, if the realized volatility is lower than the target volatility, the equity market allocation is increased.

Figure 3.21 shows a performance chart based on the comparison of the DJ Europe Titans 80 Index (equity market underlying) and the corresponding target volatility index with 10% target volatility level. Here the long-term characteristics of the volatility target strategy[15] can be seen very well.

Whereas in "normal" market cycles like the European bull market from 2003 to 2007 the underlying equity market index is outperforming the risk-based strategy, the main advantage of the target volatility strategy comes in times of great market drawdowns like those observed in the great financial

FIGURE 3.21 Target Volatility Strategy

Source: The S&P 500 Index is proprietary to and is calculated, distributed and marketed by S&P Opco, LLC (a subsidiary of S&P Dow Jones Indices LLC), its affiliates and/or its licensors and has been licensed for use. S&P® and S&P 500®, among other famous marks, are registered trademarks of Standard and Poor's Financial Services LLC, and Dow Jones® is a registered trademark of Dow Jones Trademark Holdings LLC. ©2016 S&P Dow Jones Indices LLC, its affiliates and/ or its licensors. All rights reserved.

crisis in 2008. Drawdowns are significantly reduced compared to the direct investment in beta-1 equities, as equity allocation is reduced to hold the target volatility of 10% constant.

Figure 3.22 shows the relationship between realized volatility and investment allocation to underlying equities.

The dynamic allocation nature of the target volatility strategy is best shown on the dynamic shifts during the financial crisis in 2008. As realized volatility reached record levels above 70% at the height of the financial crisis, the equity allocation was reduced to only 16% in the last quarter of 2008. As the volatility levels reverted back to normal levels, the strategy gradually increased the equity allocation to higher levels. In 2011 the equity allocation to the underlying index again reached 70%, corresponding to the lower volatility levels in 2011.

— Dow Jones Europe Titans 80 Index (EUR)
— Dow Jones Europe Titans 80 10% Volatility Risk Control Index (EUR)
— Percent Invested

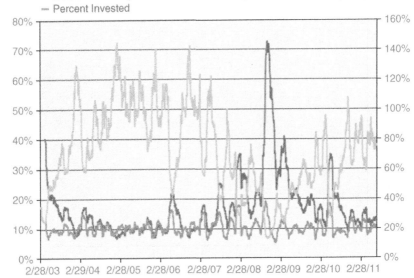

FIGURE 3.22 Target Volatility Strategy – Realized Volatility
Source: The S&P 500 Index is proprietary to and is calculated, distributed and
marketed by S&P Opco, LLC (a subsidiary of S&P Dow Jones Indices LLC), its
affiliates and/or its licensors and has been licensed for use. S&P® and S&P 500®,
among other famous marks, are registered trademarks of Standard and Poor's
Financial Services LLC, and Dow Jones® is a registered trademark of Dow Jones
Trademark Holdings LLC. ©2016 S&P Dow Jones Indices LLC, its affiliates and/
or its licensors. All rights reserved.

Comparing the long-term risk-return characteristics of target-volatility
strategies compared to the underlying equity market investments, the superior Sharpe ratio over the long-term over different market cycles becomes
evident. As the target-volatility strategy is changing the equity allocation
within the investment cycle depending on different volatility regimes, risks
are taken in favorable market conditions (low volatility) and risks are
avoided in unattractive equity markets cycles (high volatility). As volatility
clustering is a scientifically well-overserved property of volatility regimes,
times of high volatility tend to be followed by high volatilities and vice versa.

As Giese showed in his conclusion[16], investors in equity-based ETFs are
always better off in the long run investing in the corresponding target volatility ETF instead of the pure equity ETF. As drawdown markets are cushioned with the risk-based strategy indices, wealth is preserved in difficult
capital market conditions. Even if the participation rate in upward trending

markets is lower than direct equity investments, through the avoidance of permanent capital losses the investor is still better off in the long run.

In the next section another type of risk-based dynamic asset allocation indices is introduced as an alternative to target volatility index strategies.

Best-of-Assets – Dynamic Asset Allocation Strategy   Another rules-based dynamic asset allocation strategy is the best-of-assets strategy, which aims to significantly reduce the equity market drawdown by flexibly and tactically adjusting the equity allocation depending on the market cycle.

The best-of-assets strategy is a rules-based, systematic strategy which uses a dynamic asset allocation model to attribute the portfolio allocation to either equities (so-called "risky assets") or fixed-income (so-called "safe assets"). Depending on the specific market signals, the asset allocation can vary between 0% and 100% exposure to the equity market and the bond market. The strategy is fully invested in the market at any time, and both asset classes add up to a 100% allocation. Changes in the asset allocation can be executed on a monthly basis.

At the beginning of each calendar year the index is rebalanced and reset – according to the index methodology – towards 50% equities and 50% bonds. At each rebalancing date (monthly), the strategy determines the weightings of each of the two components by analyzing historical market returns and volatilities for each asset class and the historical correlations between each pair of components. In particular, the strategy methodology seeks to determine the asset portfolio that delivers the most attractive risk-return profile possible: reducing drawdown risks during a given calendar year combined with participation in upward markets. Within the calendar year the asset allocation will shift momentum-based to the better-performing asset class. This is combined with a rules-based rebalancing at each end of the calendar year (counter-cyclical).

As a result, an attractive asymmetric payoff profile is generated for the investor, which on the one hand significantly cushions losses due to unfavorable price developments, but at the same time is not giving up participation in positive market developments. Through a market cycle, a large part of the return potential of the "risky asset class" (for example U.S. equities) can be generated – which is achieved with a significantly reduced risk structure.

This described best-of-assets strategy is implemented in the NYSE Dynamic U.S. Allocation Index, which was launched by NYSE and MYRA Capital[17]. The underlyings of this index are the NYSE US Large Cap Equal Weight Index and the NYSE US 10 Year Treasury Future Index. As described earlier, the asset allocation shifts dynamically on a monthly basis between U.S. equities (NYLGCAPT) and U.S. treasuries (AXTEN). Hereby the whole range between 0% and 100% per asset class is exploited. On average the index was historically exposed 53% to U.S. equities and 47% to U.S.

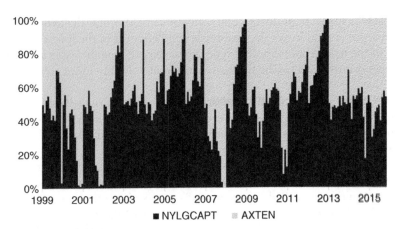

FIGURE 3.23   Asset Allocation Shifts Best-of-Assets
Source: Kula, Stahn, 2015.

treasuries, whereas the median equity allocation was 51%. By systematically allocating towards the better-performing asset class, large drawdowns are cushioned, without giving up performance in strong equity markets[18]. The asset allocation shifts are shown in Figure 3.23 and the drawdown behavior in Figure 3.24.

The large drawdown of the equity market in 2008 of more than −50% would have been cushioned to roughly –14% by reducing the equity allocation during the year. The effect of this is even stronger, as the equity market needs more than 100% gain to recover whereas the NYUSDA just needs 16%.

Besides the favorable risk figures of the NYUSDA, the performance metrics also show convincing results. With a return of 306% since 2000, the strategy outperformed the 50/50 allocation, as well as the bond and the equity index. The NYLGCAPT, which itself outperformed a plain vanilla market-cap weighted equity index such as the S&P 500, delivered a return of 209%. Nevertheless, it cannot compete with the NYUSDA, which shows even better performance statistics, with roughly half of the volatility of the equity market, delivering an impressive risk-adjusted return with a Sharpe ratio of 1.16, as shown in Figure 3.25 and Table 3.36.

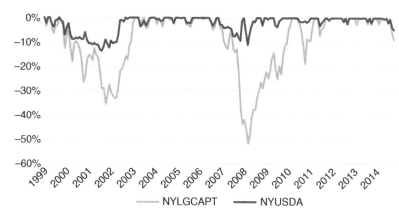

FIGURE 3.24 Maximum Drawdown Best-of-Assets
Source: Kula, Stahn, 2015.

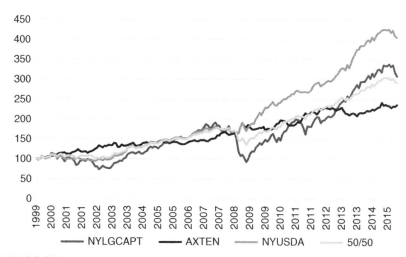

FIGURE 3.25 Performance Chart Best-of-Assets
Source: Kula, Stahn, 2015

TABLE 3.36 Risk-Return Figures Best-of-Assets

01/2000–09/2015	NYLGCAPT	AXTEN	NYUSDA	50/50
Total Return	209.32%	137.15%	305.95%	193.76%
CAGR	7.43%	5.64%	9.30%	7.08%
Volatility	16.70%	7.52%	8.04%	7.92%
Semi-Volatility	13.27%	4.76%	4.93%	6.47%
Sharpe Ratio	0.45	0.75	1.16	0.89
Sortino Ratio	0.56	1.18	1.89	1.10
Max. Drawdown (CY)	−39.61%	−9.89%	−6.75%	−13.42%
Year	2008	2009	2001	2008
Max. Performance (CY)	41.63%	20.25%	29.19%	20.33%
Year	2003	2008	2003	2003

Data Source: Kula, Stahn, 2015

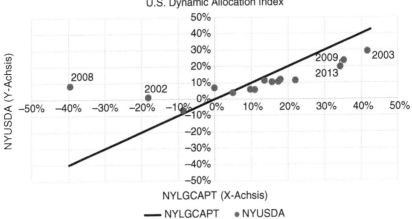

FIGURE 3.26 Yearly Returns Best-of-Assets
Source: Kula, Stahn, 2015

Figure 3.26 shows the yearly returns of the NYSE Dynamic U.S. Allocation Index compared to U.S. equities. As it is shown, the NYUSDA follows an asymmetric (right skewed) return distribution. It cushioned large losses of the equity market. In 2002, for example, the equally weighted equity index lost 18% whereas the dynamic asset allocation strategy ended the year with a positive return of 1%. In the financial crisis in 2008 the early shift into bonds preserved the investor's capital. In this year equities lost nearly 40%. In well-performing equity years such as 2003 or 2013, the strategy also performs well, though it cannot compete with a pure equity index.

All in all, the NYSE Dynamic U.S. Allocation Index offers an attractive asymmetric payoff profile, which on the one hand significantly cushions losses and on the other hand participates in rising equity markets. With this strategy, it is aimed at the medium term, to gain from the performance of the equity market with a significantly reduced risk structure.

NOTES

1. Russell Investments, 2014
2. Titman, 1993
3. Stoneberg and Smith, 2016: 9
4. Stoneberg and Smith, 2016
5. Term coined by Carl Richards, http://www.behaviorgap.com/
6. Patrick Burns, Betterment's Quest for Behavior Gap Zero, https://www .betterment.com/resources/investment-strategy/behavioral-finance-investing-strategy/betterments-quest-behavior-gap-zero/
7. Kula and Stahn, 2015: 8
8. Fama and French, 1993
9. Global X Scientific Beta U.S. ETF (Ticker: SCIU) http://www.globalxfunds. com/funds/sciu/
10. BlackRock iShares MSCI World Multifactor ETF, ISIN IE00BZ0PKT83, https://www.ishares.com/de/individual/de/produkte/277246/ishares-factorselect-msci-world-ucits-etf
11. MYRA Dynamic Factor Strategy, © MYRA Capital 2016
12. Aykan Kula, 2015: 27
13. Aykan Kula, 2015

14. Dow Jones Indexes, 2011
15. Introduction to the Dow Jones Volatility Risk Control Indexes, Page 1, https://www.djindexes.com/mdsidx/downloads/analytics_and_research/Dow_Jones_Volatility_Risk_Control_Indexes_White_Paper.pdf
16. Giese, 2012
17. http://ir.theice.com/press/press-releases/all-categories/2015/01-12-2015
18. Kula and Stahn, 2015

CHAPTER **4**

The Good, Bad and Ugly – A Critical Review of Today's Indexing Approaches

As illustrated in the previous chapters, indexing is becoming increasingly popular, achieving significantly higher allocations in investor portfolios, not only of institutional investors but also of private investors. In particular, the first generation of indexing solutions can be classified as a real invention in investment management, as these plain vanilla investment products optimally serve the need to gain low-cost beta-1 market exposure. With the ever-growing product space covering the first-generation classical indexing products, nowadays not only standard large-cap indices of developed markets are investable, but also satellite markets, such as single emerging markets countries, can be passively invested in with significantly lower costs than existing active products.

As the industry flows are still shifting from active managers to passive indexing solutions, a new active-passive equilibrium will only be achieved some years into the future, as there is still huge potential for passive strategies gaining global market share. The ongoing global low-yield environment is one important factor ensuring that low-cost investment solutions will gain further significant market share, whereas the bad track record of most active investment funds is another important catalyst for the secular trend towards passive investment strategies.

Nevertheless, despite the legitimate huge success of indexing strategies, a critical closer look at the latest developments is necessary, particularly with the ongoing marketing presence of "smart beta" strategies, the second generation of indexing strategies.

But before we dig deeper into the discussion of the advantages and weaknesses of smart beta strategies, some important points generally applicable to exchange-traded funds should be made which are of utmost importance for investors.

SYNTHETIC VS. PHYSICAL REPLICATION

As shown in the previous chapters, different replication strategies exist which are applied by ETF issuers, whereas the physical replication is the clear leader in terms of assets under management, as about 80% of indexed strategies, as of 2016, are physically replicated[1]. The aftermath of the great financial crisis has led to an increased investor awareness of the counterparty risk of products which are synthetically replicated and hence using derivatives to track the index underlying. Despite the fact that still more swap-based ETFs exist, investors showed a clear preference to the more transparent and understandable physical replication method where the ETF holds the index components depending on the optimization method. It seems that the conceptual simplicity of fully replicated ETFs has won the race.

As the demand structure of investors clearly favors physically replicated ETFs, more and more product developers are shifting from synthetic to physical replication. The latest most prominent changes came from the European ETF powerhouses, db x-tracker and Lyxor, which used to fully concentrate on synthetic derivative ETF replications and are now trying to switch their products to physical replication.

For those investors allocating to large and liquid standard indices like the S&P 500 or EuroStoxx 50, an investment to full replication ETFs is certainly the most advantageous as these liquid markets are easy and efficient to replicate so there is no need to use derivative replication products.

The situation changes if the investor wants to get an allocation to a difficult to track index such as, for example, the MSCI Emerging Markets Index or other not-so-liquid indices. In these instances, physical replication methods can be quite costly, even though some optimization is usually employed to control for costs. But in these instances, swap-based replication ETFs show their strength, as the index can be tracked far better than the classical replication methods, as the tracking error usually is significantly lower compared to fully replicated ETFs. So it does make sense for investors to use swap-based ETFs for those markets which are very difficult to track or even impossible to invest (e.g. volatility, commodity markets) with physical replication. The trade-off that investors are facing is that to reduce tracking error for a difficult-to-reach market, some swap counterparty risk and more complex product structures must be accepted. As always, the following important remark holds for investors: only invest in swap-based products if the functioning and risks are fully understood; otherwise, avoid these products.

Trading Costs of ETFs – Case Study "Flash Crash, August 24, 2015"

Before investing in an ETF, investors should think about the saleability of the product, as this will determine the final return for the investor. To highlight this hypothesis, let us have a quick look at August 24, 2015, which was a nightmare for many ETF investors in the United States. After a weak start in the markets, the prices of some passive index funds suddenly rushed sharply down. Even though the background of the "Flash Crash Monday" is still not entirely clear, one of the reasons for the sudden fall and deviation of ETF prices was the failed market making amid the high uncertainty, as sales orders of ETF investors could not be matched with buyers. The problem was ultimately largely attributed to specificities in the trading rules of the New York Stock Exchange, whereas in Europe, for example, the Deutsche Börse gave an assurance that such crashes are not possible under their trading systems. Despite these statements, investors are understandably concerned about pricing of products and exit costs in drawdown markets.

Obviously, there are large differences in the liquidity of individual ETFs, depending on the markets covered, the assets under management and the number of designated sponsors and market makers covering the ETF. These are the most important determinants of whether investors can sell their ETF shares at the desired time and at the desired price.

If investors want to ensure that their disposal of their ETF shares does not entail too many costs due to a lack of liquidity, they can pay attention to some easy key metrics. A good and easy-to-find indication of the tradability of ETFs is the volume of the respective ETF. In the large ETFs with highly liquid underlyings like the DAX or the S&P 500, anyone who wants to get rid of his shares should not have trouble with it at normal times. For smaller ETFs, which comprise often only a few hundred million euros, it might be more difficult to find a prospective buyer or seller just in time, so the implicit trading costs (also known as slippage) might be significantly higher to get into or sell the smaller ETF where the respective underlying is not as liquid compared to the popular and large indices.

If the investor arrives at a situation where from a risk management point of view a change in the ETF portfolio risk structure is immediately necessary in times of market turmoil, one important trading procedure could be to hold the ETF (for example the DAX ETF) and to hedge instead with the corresponding futures (Eurex DAX Futures), when available, for the ETF underlying. With this procedure the risk position of the portfolio can be adjusted as intended by the investor without incurring high ETF trading costs with high bid-ask spreads in market turmoil. If market volatility gets back again to "normal" levels, the ETFs can be disposed with far better conditions, so this could be one possibility for handling market disruptions like the flash crash observed on August 24, 2015.

SECOND GENERATION INDEXING CRITIQUE – THE BAD ONES

As already shown, cap-weighted indices do have certain weaknesses, so different weighting strategies can definitely add value to investors. Indexing strategies like naive equal weighting, fundamental weighting or other weighting schemes are based on different systematic risk factors which are scientifically well documented and viable.

In the last few years the passive investment industry massively pushed these strategies as more and more products were launched and correspondingly marketed by the respective sales departments. As the main scientific ideas behind smart beta investing dated from the 1990s following the seminal work of Fama/French, one could certainly wonder why, more than 20 years later, smart beta strategies are marketed as if they were an innovation. With the increasing availability of computational power, the value effect was quantified as early as the late 1970s, and the small-cap effect was documented in the 1980s. With the Three-Factor Model of Fama/French published in 1994, these two effects were combined with the market-beta as the third source of risk premiums to lay the foundations of risk factor investing. Unsurprisingly, these scientific findings found their way to the investment management industry in the early 1990s – Dimensional Fund Advisors (DFA) were the first investment company to focus on risk factor investing based on the Fama/French study. Properly stated, Dimensional Fund Advisors were the first "smart beta"-focused investment company, with huge success as the assets under management surged over USD 300 billion as of June 30, 2016.[2]

It is evident that the main ideas behind smart beta are not really new and are already applied by Dimensional Fund Advisors but also traditional active fund managers, who try to outperform cap-weighted indices by systematically applying a risk premiums-based strategy overweighting small-caps or other systematic risk factors. So what about all this hype around smart beta investment strategies and the launch of countless ETFs based on smart beta indices?

As is often the case, the main driver for product launches by ETF providers is the desire to increase the margins of their product range. As with cap-weighted standard ETFs, there is huge price competition on a global scale, so complex smart beta ETFs are an ideal way to increase margins for product providers. If standard plain vanilla ETFs are compared with smart beta ETFs, the pricing differential becomes obvious. Recent research calculated that smart beta ETFs are on average up to three times more expensive than their classical cap-weighted counterparts[3].

Besides the critical look to the higher cost basis of smart beta ETFs, only a small number of risk factors seem to be significant in economic terms which can be ultimately reaped by investors. As smart beta strategies are always based on or have a tilt towards one or more equity risk factors, the decisive question to select between those second-generation ETFs is to judge whether the strategy is targeting "real" equity risk factors. Harvey, Liu, and Zhu[4] examined 315 factors well researched in scientific studies and working papers. Adjusting for data snooping, they conclude that only a small number of equity risk factors are statistically significant. Unsurprisingly, the Fama/French factors like value, low volatility but also momentum were highly significant, whereas hundreds of others were not. Of course, product providers trying to capitalize on the whole smart beta hype have got the incentive to launch products with great back-tested equity portfolios and risk factor selection strategies with corresponding high Sharpe ratios for these strategies. But the reality tells another story. After launching these strategies, the real track record is not really showing up in superior paper back-testing results.

Vanguard[5] showed in an analysis that there is a significant change of generated alpha after the launch of a product. They used an event-study analysis to analyze the performance of several indices before and after the ETF product launch. They find that ETFs are likely to be launched when the corresponding smart beta indices showed an outperformance compared to classical cap-weighted US indices before the inception date. Unfortunately, after the product launch, on average the outperformance did not persist in reality, as shown in Figure 4.1.

So the lesson learned from these findings is that investors should beware of being too optimistic if a new exotic smart beta ETF is launched with high promises – the chances are high that the underlying risk factor combinations are only viable on paper and that in reality no value-added can be expected from these products.

Of course, risk factor investing is an important alternative to traditional asset allocation strategies, but investors need to understand the main drivers

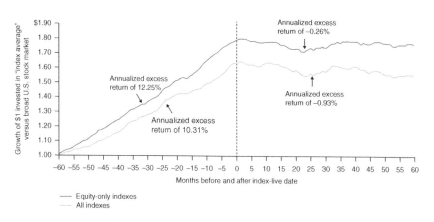

Notes: Analysis includes data from 370 indexes versus the total U.S. stock market (as measured by the Dow Jones Wilshire 5000 Index before April 22, 2005, and the MSCI US Broad Market Index thereafter). Dashed vertical line in figure separates "before" and "after" performance. See text for description of "index average return".

FIGURE 4.1   Performance Persistence of Smart Beta Indices
Source: © The Vanguard Group, Inc., used with permission

of risk premiums in order to focus on the real factors with economic significance. It is always important to ask what the main risk and return drivers
behind a certain indexing strategy and the observed historical paper back-
testing outperformance are. The naïve equal-weighting indexing strategy
can be one easy example for explanation of the key drivers. There is plenty
of international research documenting the long-term outperformance of
equal-weighting indices compared to classic capitalization-weighted indices.
If you have a closer look at the implications of equal-weighting, it becomes
clear that the small-cap risk premium and the value risk premium are the
key drivers of relative outperformance. As small- and mid-cap companies
are overweighted compared to large-cap indices and hence large caps are
underweighted, equal-weighting strategies have a tilt towards small- and
mid-capitalization companies. So it is not really surprising that equal
weighting can capture a part of the scientifically well-documented small-
cap premium.

Furthermore, as all indexing strategies deviating from capitalization
weighting have got some applied rebalancing scheme, underperforming
companies are regularly reinvested, whereas outperformer companies are
systematically cut back to target equal weightings. But if you have a look at
the risk metrics, unsurprisingly, the equal-weighting indexing shows in general higher volatility and drawdown figures compared to classical indices.
This is as expected, as in times of financial distress small- and mid-cap companies should be more hit by market turmoil due to lower liquidity and
higher risk compared to large-cap established companies.

To conclude, after looking behind the main drivers of the equal-weighting
indexing scheme, the observed outperformance but also the higher risk relative to capitalization-weighted indices becomes obvious and clear. As with
this example, investors should try to understand the main risk and performance drivers of indices or ETFs before investing into these strategies.

For now, we have covered the Good ones:

- Classical cheap ETFs on flagship indices
- "Smart beta" ETFs based on real risk factors like Momentum, Low
  Volatility, Value, Small Caps

and the Bad ones:

- "Smart beta" ETFs with some questionable indexing approach with no
  clear scientific founding.

But what about the Ugly ones?

Unfortunately, meaningful inventions and product developments are
often accompanied with product launches which are trying to improve upon
the great basic idea. This is also observed in the ETF/indexing space, as more

and more issuers are trying to participate in the phenomenal growth story of passive investments. As an early example, we already showed that product issuers are often motivated to increase the complexity in product structures so as to increase running costs for investors/margins for themselves ("expropriation coefficient"). Precisely this development is observable in the latest ETF issuance attributable to the second generation of indexing, the rise of smart beta products.

We want to give at this point some concrete examples of "ugly" product issues, which were certainly launched with good intentions, but demonstrated structural problems so that it was clear that investor expectations could not be met. As it is one of the most basic investing rules in play here, investors should definitively understand the strategy/product in full detail, including the advantages and disadvantages in different market cycles. If the investor is in doubt about an ETF or strategy, it is better not to invest in the structure. Obviously, this point is not only important in the indexing sphere but also generally for all investment products.

COMMODITY/ENERGY/OIL ETP PRODUCTS

To include commodity exposure to a broad diversified portfolio is definitely a very valid strategy to pursue in strategic asset allocation. Favorable correlation properties compared to equities and bonds and the liquidity of commodity futures are important facts favoring an allocation to this asset class. These instruments are particularly important to hedge the portfolio against potential unexpected inflationary pressures, as part of the consumer inflation rate is impacted by energy and other commodities.

Unsurprisingly, with the rise of indexing, the innovation also embraced the commodity asset class as more and more product issuers launched products with underlyings from a wide range of single commodities or commodity indices. Significant assets were acquired as institutional and private investors used these efficient passive instruments to add commodity exposure to their portfolios.

Nevertheless, the main idea to achieve beta-1 exposure to commodity indices or commodity prices like crude oil could not be achieved by the product offerings, as the ETPs replicated the exposure via commodity futures like the Brent Future, which exhibit different future curves relating to different maturities. If we look to the energy or soft commodity sector (e.g. grains), a so-called "contango" situation is structurally observed, meaning that within the necessary regular roll-over of futures the investor is achieving a loss, as the new commodity future is trading higher than the current one. Figure 4.2 shows a typical contango situation in the Crude Oil WTI Futures curve.

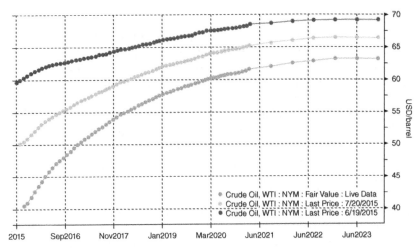

FIGURE 4.2   Futures Curve of WTI
Data Source: Bloomberg

If you compare the price of the commodity (WTI Oil Futures) over time and the associated ETPs (USO, OIL, USL), the difference becomes observable, as shown in Figure 4.3.

The underperformance of the ETPs compared to the commodity price increases permanently, so investors cannot achieve the intended 1:1 exposure to the relevant commodity.

But how should investors react to mitigate these problems which are inherent in commodity investing?

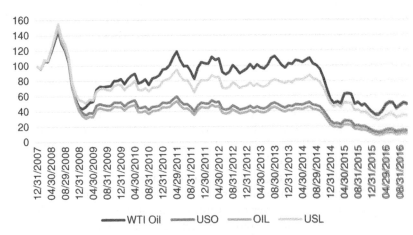

FIGURE 4.3   WTI Performance vs. Investment Products
Data Source: FactSet

One strategy could be to focus on commodities which don't have the structural contango problem as energy futures do. One possibility, for example, is to focus on a precious metal allocation (e.g. gold), as these futures do not exhibit the disadvantage of contango.

Another possibility is to select commodity strategies which are trying to optimize and adapt the positioning to the optimal commodity futures curve, some even going short on those commodities showing high contango. As these strategies are also rules-based concerning the roll-over strategies, they are often transparent as to their schedule and strategy.

A basic example is the United States 12 Month Oil Fund ETF (USL), which is also shown in the above performance comparison. It is conspicuous that the USL is significantly better-performing compared to the other two oil ETFs, as the USL invests in 12 different futures contracts at all times, whereas the other two ETFs are only investing in the futures contract of the nearest month. This has helped USL to avoid some of the dramatic costs of trading futures in periods of heavy speculation, when the near month contract is often the most expensive. Nevertheless, the USL has, despite the rules-based optimization, shown an underperformance compared to the spot-futures price of WTI Brent.

Only time will tell whether these and other roll optimizations are really delivering value-added to investors trying to implement an allocation in this asset class.

Of course, another possibility for investing in energy is to avoid futures contracts but to invest in energy companies to gain an indirect exposure to the oil price. Whereas this strategy is avoiding the negative contango forward curve as there is no exposure to futures, investing in oil stocks leads to another problem: that the diversification potential originally observed by the investor is completely disappearing, as energy stocks show high correlation to the equity markets.

VOLATILITY ETPS

Another example of a potentially "ugly" product relates to volatility index strategies and leveraged ETPs.

The Volatility measure is the primary gauge of market risk for most investors. As an important risk indicator, various volatility indices are calculated from global exchanges, trying to measure the "fear gauge" of the market. The most popular and observed are the Chicago Board Options Exchange (CBOE) Volatility Index (VIX) for the U.S. and the VSTOXX and VDAX calculated from Eurex for the European and German markets respectively. Looking to the long-term behavior of volatility, it typically increases in times of crisis, as observed in the technology bubble or the great financial crisis, as shown in Figure 4.4.

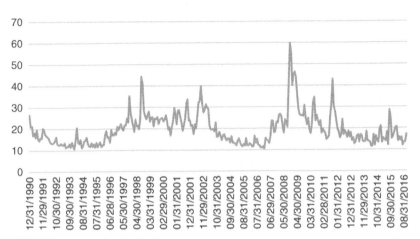

FIGURE 4.4   VIX Volatility Index
Data Source: FactSet

It is difficult to diversify portfolio exposure away by only focusing on conventional assets. With the secular low interest rate environment and global equity markets showing rich valuations, the pressure is increasing for investors to identify sources of return in alternative instruments not related to traditional asset classes. As observed in the last years, against this backdrop, more and more investors are turning to alternative, highly liquid risk premiums. In this process, volatility is increasingly attracting investor focus as an alternative asset class.

Buying volatility as an asset class is a fascinating topic for investors trying to use the favorable properties to insure their own portfolio. The main idea behind a long position in volatility is that in case of market turmoil and equity market drawdowns, the volatility product should increase significantly in value so as to insure part of the investor portfolio.

The most basic way to play volatility is to invest in options, but because of the complex functioning and the various influencing factors of the valuation of options, most investors do not have the possibility or the ability to invest directly in options like professional institutional investors.

Unsurprisingly, several ETPs were launched, trying to give investors access to investing into volatility with a single and liquid investment product. The main idea is that the Volatility ETPs are tracking the underlying volatility index, so the investor can participate 1:1 on the development of the volatility index. As good as the idea and the intention was at the start, looking at the performance of the various Volatility products compared to the underlying volatility index shows again the problem of futures contango leading to systematic underperformance.

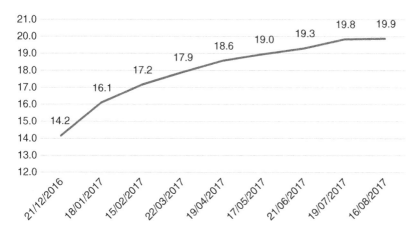

FIGURE 4.5   VIX Futures Term Structure
Data Source: FactSet

The VIX index is not directly investable for investors and ETPs, as the VIX index is synthetically and mathematically calculated by the index provider. Instead, the VIX ETFs are linked to the futures market where the volatility futures trade with different maturities. The volatility future is also showing the properties of contango, meaning that longer-dated maturities are more expensive. As the nearest and most liquid volatility future expires regularly, investors do need to rollover to the next contract to hold their exposure constant. Figure 4.5 shows the volatility future term structure, which is trading in contango.

As the volatility futures are showing this behavior, investors do not have the possibility of obtaining direct exposure to the volatility index. Unsurprisingly, the long-term performance of the most popular volatility index product, the iPath S&P 500 VIX ST Futures ETN (VXX), shows a massive loss since inception of this product in 2009 (see Figure 4.6).

Again, investors should not be allured by the investment case alone but should also understand the functioning of the underlying investment mechanics. As in the case of oil ETPs, volatility investing is an interesting case for diversifying the investment portfolio. But investors should always understand the products and potential drawbacks of strategies so as to avoid costly pitfalls which are difficult to make up even in the long term.

To sum up, the following main recommendations can be given to investors regarding the "ugly" part of the ETP universe:

- A simple trading or asset allocation idea can be extremely difficult to execute, so investors need to understand the working and the dynamics of the underlying.

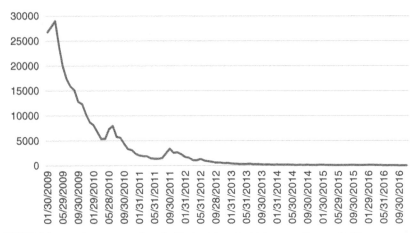

FIGURE 4.6 Performance of iPath S&P 500 VIX ST Futures ETN (VXX)
Data Source: FactSet

- The investor needs to understand how underlying futures markets work and understand that a systematic contango can lead to long-term underperformance and deviation of the ETP compared to the underlying.
- As for most complex investments or alternative investments, the investor should regularly observe futures prices and futures curves, as a buy-and-hold strategy in plain vanilla passive products can be really costly to investors.
- To avoid future disappointment, investors should be restrictive concerning which investment products are used in their portfolios. If in doubt, avoid complex products where the time factor is working against the investor because of the market underlying.

NOTES

1. Garcia-Zarate, 2016
2. https://eu.dimensional.com/de/unternehmen/ueberblick.aspx
3. Johnson, Bioy and Boyadzhiev, 2016
4. Harvey, Liu and Zhu, 2014
5. Vanguard, 2012

Advantages Unlimited – Portfolio Application Strategies for Superior Index Investing

After treating in depth in the previous chapters the important pillars of index investing and the latest developments and achievements in indexing and product design, the time has come to dig deeper into recommendations for investors to improve their portfolio construction to increase risk-adjusted returns over time. All parts of the investing game need to be addressed in this analysis, like a puzzle to solve for the often seemingly complex capital markets and products environment investors are faced with. As a general rule, which is also suitable in finance, simple dominates complex, so the investors should only use those financial products they fully understand. As a human behavior, high return promises which are presented by the product issuers in general may be exciting, but there is no alchemy in finance, so each potential gain could also result in an equivalent loss in the future. In this chapter, easy-to-grasp recommendations for action are presented to the reader, to help them avoid the biggest pitfalls in investing in general and indexing in particular.

NEVER UNDERESTIMATE THE IMPORTANCE OF INVESTMENT COSTS

It is important to focus on those variables which are under the control of the investor. Noisy capital markets may be constantly moving, but investors can control aspects like the asset allocation or costs of investment products and charges. As a matter of fact, ongoing charges, taxes and other investment costs are significantly eroding the value of the portfolio on a permanent basis. By minimizing these costs, investors can significantly improve the future returns of their portfolio.

Obviously, understanding and knowing all potential cost factors in the investment value chain is of utmost importance in order to get a transparent overview of all incurred costs.

To begin with, the following costs and cost components need to be considered to calculate the total costs of a product or portfolio. As the product providers typically don't show full transparency with regard to total costs, there is still a measure missing, which puts all product investment expenses in one number. Although regulatory changes are moving this topic in the right direction, investors still need to be aware of hidden charges depressing future returns.

Annual Management Fee

This cost factor is the single largest one, and covers the cost of managing the fund/product over the year. As this fee is stated in the issued prospectus, investors can easily compare this cost factor. Obviously, passive investment products charging only a fraction of active manager's annual fee have a significant advantage on this point.

Additional Operational Fees

For most investment products, there will typically be additional running costs which are charged directly to the product. These running fees include custodian fees, auditing fees, publishing fees, regulatory fees etc. The total expense ratio, which is often published by the product providers, typically includes the annual management fee and the running additional operational fees.

Transaction Costs

As an investor, one might think that there should be no further costs incurred in the fund or ETP. But as the asset manager is executing his strategy or the passive investment product does some sort of rebalancing trades, this may have explicit (trading fees) and implicit (for example bid-ask spread, slippage) cost implications for investors. Unfortunately, to date the product providers do not have to state the total incurred transaction costs, so investors cannot take this important cost factor easily and transparently into consideration. Of course, depending on the executed strategy, investors should avoid strategies with high portfolio turnover ratios as the transaction costs could severely impact long-term returns.

Performance Fee

Some products have a performance fee provision which gives the manager an additional financial bonus if pre-stated benchmarks are exceeded. Typically, the performance fee is only designed one way in favor of the asset manager, as in underperforming years no credit is given back to the investors. This asymmetric optionality in favor of the asset manager, highlights moral hazard problems (too much risk-taking) and other agency problems. As the performance fee is not considered in the total expense ratio or ongoing charges figure, investors should check before investing in a product whether a performance fee is charged. As the investor is already paying for the asset management service covered by the annual management fee, the investor should avoid products or strategies with performance fee provisions.

Other Fees, Like Initial Charges and Redemption Fees

Although the trend for efficient passive investing has already significantly depressed sales charges like initial charges, some product categories still burden the investor with such additional charges. Often the investor has the choice inbetween different share classes of the investment product. Here investors should choose those classes without ongoing distribution costs or initial charges (often called institutional share classes). Compared to the "standard" retail share classes, these institutional share classes often have a significant reduction in the annual total running costs, directly enhancing investor returns.

Comparison of Active Fund Management Fees vs. Passive ETFs

With the triumphal march of passive investing in the last decade, the cost structure of investment products has come under severe pressure, which has been reinforced by the secular low-yield environment in the aftermath of the financial crisis. Retail and institutional investors have never enjoyed such historically low fee structures in portfolios, leaving a higher ratio of the investment results in their own pockets. The good news is that this evolution does not seem to have come to an end, as the asset management business is under severe pressure not only from cost-efficient ETFs, but also from rising fintech and robo-advising companies, which are at the moment disrupting the investment management industry.

Looking at the evolution of investment fees over the last years in Figure 5.1, the massive reduction becomes very clear[1].

Low-cost innovator Vanguard, with a crystal clear positioning as the cost-efficient ETF provider, is aggressively implementing its strategy and vision to provide the most cost-efficient ETFs in the market. This decisive strategy is not only further forcing active management companies to rethink their pricing strategies, but also forcing peer ETF providers to further cut costs in favor of investors.

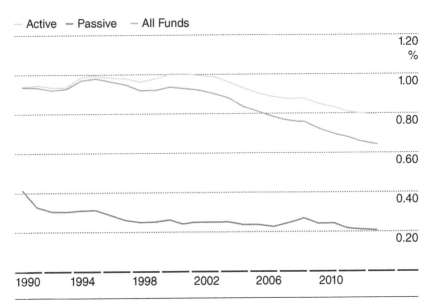

FIGURE 5.1   Expense Ratios of Active vs. Passive Investments
Source: © The Vanguard Group, Inc., used with permission

Depending on the invested asset classes and the different markets, an investor can easily reduce portfolio costs by switching from active investment products to efficient passive investments in the range of 0.5–1.0% p.a., which translates to an identical increase in expected future returns for the investor.

The power of compounding returns makes it clear that minor differences in product costs can also have a massive impact on an investor's wealth. A simple calculation in Figure 5.2 shows the different wealth levels dependent on the annual management charge for the investment[2].

The term "expropriation coefficient" is the right term that investors should have in mind as each basis point of extra costs is reducing their return level. As investors should focus on things they can control – and costs are definitely under the control of the investor – the critical regular review of investment costs is one of the most important factors for future investing success.

The readers of this book already took a very important step in the investment process, as you know already the great importance of structurally reducing the running costs to improve long-term investment results. Obviously, the main reason for the victory run of passive investing in the last decades is the discontent with the performance of active managers and the high costs incurred by traditional active investment management.

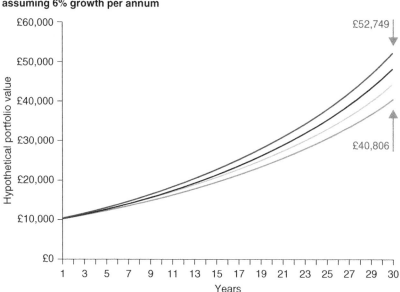

Growth of a £10,000 initial investment over a 30 year period, assuming 6% growth per annum

FIGURE 5.2   The Power of Compounding
Source: © The Vanguard Group, Inc., used with permission

The global low-yield environment as a policy response of global central banks to counter the great financial crisis in 2008 has further accelerated this trend as future expected investment returns seem to be significantly reduced because of the elevated valuations of most asset classes.

Unsurprisingly, several scientific studies validate the hypothesis that the average cost structure of investment portfolios is highly negatively correlated with future success of these investment portfolios, calculated on a risk-adjusted basis.

Morningstar showed that the total expense ratio of an investment product is the most important determinant of future outperformance. Morningstar's study[3], which focused on US-domiciled active funds, found that funds with lower expense ratios consistently outperform their more expensive peers across all asset classes.

As an example, the results of the analysis for the peer group "US equity" are shown in Figure 5.3, where the relationship between costs and performance was found to be strongest.

5-Year Average—Oldest Share Class (1/1/2011 to 12/31/2015)	US Equity				
Expense Ratio Quintile as of 12/31/2010					
Average Expense Ratio as of 12/31/2010	0.61	1.01	1.27	1.54	2.69
# Funds 5-Year Return Statistics	500	447	512	311	91
Total Return (Annualized)	11.05	10.29	9.62	9.18	7.71
Percent Rank in Category	34	46	54	60	72
Batting Average	77.00	59.96	47.46	36.66	21.98
Success Ratio	63.95	49.72	37.33	28.43	16.13

FIGURE 5.3   Returns Based on Expense Ratios
Source: © 2016 Morningstar, Inc. All Rights Reserved. Reproduced with permission.

The funds in the lowest-cost quintile had an annualized return of 11.05% over five years, compared to just 7.71% for the highest-cost quintile, a remarkable performance difference of over 3% p.a.

As a final remark, passive investment products are certainly championing the topic of efficient investment costs. Nevertheless, with the rise of smart beta or next-generation indexing products, these ETF fees are significantly higher than classical market cap-weighted ETFs. Product issuers facing the massive pressure to reduce margins of their product offerings are happy to use and market "smart" products to investors to increase average margins to offset for margin reductions in traditional products. So investors shouldn't blindly assume that with the term "ETF" in the product name it is automatically cost-efficient. As stated earlier, the analysis of the total cost of the investment product may be the most important due diligence task, as fund costs are the most reliable predictor of future success.

SMART BETA DECONSTRUCTION[4]

After the in-depth look at the cost economics of investments, it is time to move on to the next financial industry characteristic causing a lot of investor pain and disappointment: the sell-side, marketing and storytelling side of the business. Obviously, investor knowledge and awareness concerning weighting schemes and deficiencies regarding classical market weighting schemes are an important part of structurally improving long-term risk-adjusted performance in investor portfolios. Although the basic idea and the advantages of the shifting away from market cap-weighted indices based on known weaknesses are already treated and analyzed in great detail[5] in financial academia, the financial selling industry is doing its best to transform the smart beta hype into a disappointment to investors as expectations are raised which are not realistic. It is intriguing how the product management and marketing units of the passive and active investment management industry promoted the idea of "smart investing" as something completely new and as a holy grail to all investment problems. Even large and educated institutional investors are considering investments in these smart beta products, as the asset under management statistics show significant inflows to this product new segment.

Here we will analyze in detail the pitfalls and misunderstandings of smart beta so as to enable the knowledgeable investor to differentiate between real economic risk premiums and other factors showing up in the famous "factor zoo"[6] without economic significance. We will show in this section that there is not really anything new or smart with smart beta, and we will show how to meaningfully apply the recent developments in product launches in investor strategy and portfolios. This analysis therefore aims to present an accurate differentiation for the meaningful use of smart beta.

To begin the analysis, a short history and definition of smart beta might be helpful. There are concepts in the literature such as "smart beta", "strategic beta", "beta intelligent", "alternative beta" and "scientific beta", causing added confusion to the already complex investment world. But let's have a look at the two words of the "smart beta" concept in detail.

Beta is a term used in the Capital Asset Pricing Model[7]. It describes a coefficient which measures the sensitivity of a security to the market portfolio itself. The market portfolio has always got a beta of 1. For example, a security with beta of 1.5 responds to a fluctuation of the market portfolio by a factor of 1.5x. Thus, a Beta > 1 indicates a higher market risk as a factor influencing the value of the security. The beta coefficient is part of the one-factor, one-period methods family. The term "factor" is crucial here: the factor is used as an optimization variable.

William Sharpe also coined, along with the launch of the beta concept, the concept of alpha. Beta is categorized as non-diversifiable, measured against a capitalization-weighted market portfolio. Alpha is defined as the residual return, which is not assignable to the market risk (beta).

If one departs from a capitalization-weighted measure of the market portfolio, there remains a need to evaluate a new definition for it, in which comprehensiveness and plausible logic of the market is represented as a reference point by means of a market portfolio. It follows from this that smart beta indices are inadequate in their comparison with market capitalization indices (it is an apples and oranges comparison) and there is a need for new benchmarks. The renowned EDHEC-Risk Institute identified the need for new benchmarks and its research into smart beta referred to Smart Beta 2.0 in exactly this context[8]. In this research, under the term "scientific beta indices", it created a flexible index platform, where currently nearly 3,000 indices are calculated according to different weighting methods, which can be used as potential fair benchmarks for smart beta concepts.

Thanks to increasing computing power, the quantitative analysis of the financial markets is becoming permanently faster and cheaper. Additional factors were isolated and confirmed empirically in the years after Sharpe's CAPM. In their famous Three-Factor Model, Fama/French[9] supplemented Small Cap (SMB) and Value (HML) factors as additional beta coefficients in addition to the market factor. Value has been scientifically documented in the late 70s, although investment gurus like Graham or Buffett put the value factor at the center of their investment strategy decades before. Small Cap was scientifically validated in the early 80s. In 1997 Carhart[10] added the Momentum (MOM) factor to his Four-Factor model, which is one of the most stable risk premiums documented scientifically.

All four factors have in common that they have been validated empirically and isolated through the analysis of the equity markets. As such, they represent risk factors where the market participants can expect to earn a risk premium by holding them. The market portfolio represents the sum of all risk factors.

As is shown historically, the industry focused on the market capitalization-weighted market portfolio indices as valid benchmarks for portfolio strategy guidance. Thanks to the aforementioned multi-factor models, it became possible to systematically segregate the risk premiums of the quantifiable market patterns within the market portfolio so as to transport these premiums into investment products. And, voilà, multi-factor investing was born.

In the 1990s it was Dimensional Fund Advisors (DFA) that was first to launch multi-factor mutual funds, based on the Fama/French model, with substantial economical profit. DFA manages more than $250 billion for mainly institutional investors who rely on multi-factor strategies. Eugene Fama is still involved as a director in an advisory capacity.

The rest of the investment management industry needed 20 years to find a way to promote multi-factor investing to less sophisticated target groups like retail and semi-institutional investors. They gave multi-factor investing a new, trendy and intelligent-sounding name: smart beta.

The campaign of Research Affiliates launched at the end of 2013 shows how the smart beta theme is presented to the investing public. It is positioned as

- investable indices outperforming a target,
- a rule-based, transparent allocation in a broad market portfolio and
- a low-cost combination of the best of the active and passive world.

At first sight this appears quite attractive. A cheaper, more transparent, rule-based active/passive hybrid with a chance of outperformance. What more do you want as an informed investor?

There is certainly no objection to isolating risk factors with economic significance. With an intelligent investment process adding risk factors into the allocation, the risk-return potential set can certainly be better optimized.

But what can an investor in multi-factor strategies realistically expect, and, in contrast, what is promised by industry?

The Magic Money Tree of the Investment Industry?

The promising, monolithic positioning of the smart beta label is the result of a long-standing debate about the advantages and disadvantages of active and passive portfolio management. As discussed previously, for decades it was common to measure the performance of portfolios based on capital-weighted benchmark indices. We all know the devastating success rate of active portfolio management compared to passive strategies; even for short periods only a few active portfolio managers are able to beat this benchmark. So more and more proponents of passive replication of indices saw their views confirmed, as passive strategies became more and more the default setting in the product selection process of investors.

When, after 2008, the disadvantages of cap-weighted benchmark indices were increasingly discussed in the literature, the traditional fund industry began to position their existing strategies as products delivering investable risk premiums. The smart beta label serves the traditional fund providers as a lifeline for an otherwise leaking business model. This fact must be considered by investors when evaluating factors and smart beta.

The disadvantages of market capitalization-weighted indices have, as set forth above, been extensively scientifically analyzed. The recognition of these disadvantages gave birth to the idea that these weaknesses of cap-weighted indices could be alleviated by alternative weighting methodologies. The starting point was simple and naïve weighting methods like 1/N equal weighting, which has evolved over time into a plurality of weighting methods such as "fundamental indexing" (weighting of securities according to different fundamental indicators) or "low-volatility indexing" (stocks with low volatility are weighted higher). There are now a variety of so-called "smart beta" indices, which have also led to an increasing number of smart beta strategies, which have also been made investable.

Despite this huge trend towards alternative weighting schemes, cap-weighted indices still continue to dominate in the asset management industry, even though the underlying assumptions of the Efficient Market Hypothesis[11] and the CAPM[12] are considered falsified in the meantime.

The simple elegance of the CAPM idea that there is a single optimal market portfolio, coupled with the structural underperformance of the "average" active portfolio manager, contributed to the triumph of passive investing (ETFs).

As mentioned earlier, beta is classified as systematic market risk by traditional capital market theory, whereas allocated investors are expected to earn the market return. The securities in the market portfolio are weighted based on the market capitalization of the securities, the so-called cap-weighted index. By definition, each deviation from the market cap weighting is a deviation of passive investing, so the term "beta" in "smart beta" is not really correct. Typically, smart beta indexing strategies are located in the middle, between passive cap-weighted index ETFs and actively managed funds, as these smart beta strategies typically implement a different weighting scheme with a rules-based and transparent investment process. So the investments/weightings in the smart beta strategies are not dependent on the discretionary decisions of the fund manager.

The Ultimate Alpha Machine? Not Really . . .

An index cannot be "smart" on its own – at most, it can be "different". For example, Rob Arnott's "RAFI" fundamental indices were one of the first attempts to provide broad market exposure through an alternate index composition. In this early case, the index weighting factors are determined from fundamental analysis.

Thus a division of second-generation indices into "smart" or "dumb" beta is irrelevant, because there are only different attempts to make observable and quantifiable market patterns investable, so it is correct to talk about "different" or "alternative" betas. This means that smart beta offers and allows investors an alternative form of beta compared to the market portfolio.

So investors should always be careful when indexing strategies are marketed as "smart" and as alpha-generating machines – which they are obviously not, as several risk factors will perform differently over time and will definitely show risk characteristics that differ from classical market-cap weighted indices. Clarity and transparence with regard to the risk structures of different indexing strategies compared to the market-cap weighted alternatives should be made clear, which would help potential investors to evaluate better the risk/return profile of the different smart beta strategies. This clarity would certainly simplify for the investor the difficult task of differentiating between economically significant risk factors and investable smart beta strategies and factors, which are engineered by means of the creative, intellectual gymnastics of financial engineers at product providers and are without economic significance.

As Jason Hsu and Vitali Kalesnik correctly wrote[13]: "We are concerned with the relentless onslaught of shiny, exciting and sexy new factors introduced by bright-eyed, bushy-tailed young financial engineers." With the increasing popularity of multi-factor investing and smart beta, more and more meta-research is being conducted to bring some order into the complex, evolving "factor zoo".

Levi and Welch[14] reviewed 600 (!) risk factors in the broader, popular scientific financial literature. They found in their study that 49% of the factors show no or even negative excess premiums. They finally conclude that for the 600 factors analyzed, the chance to choose a factor with a positive premium is slightly higher than a coin flip. Transaction and management costs have not even been considered in their analysis, so it seems that these are difficult times for investors who hope to choose the right factors in the factor zoo.

So the essential question for the investor is: What risk factors or smart beta strategy can currently be classified as relevant? Fortunately, the vast body of scientific research can give valuable guidance as to how to concentrate on those risk factors which show an observable pattern over longer periods of observations and also have a sound economic grounding. As discussed in the previous chapters, the relevant risk factors and how they can be captured by strategies are outlined in Table 5.1.

TABLE 5.1   Relevant Risk Factors

Factor Exposures	Thesis	Usually measured by
Value	Companies cheaper than their fair value deliver excess returns	Price/Book ratio
Size	Smaller companies deliver excess returns to larger ones	Market capitalization
Momentum	Strong past performers deliver future excess returns	Historical relative performance
Low Volatility	Stable companies with low price fluctuation deliver excess returns to the market	Standard deviation
Quality	Good companies with low debt, high returns and stable earnings deliver excess returns	Degree of debt, high return on equity
Dividend Yield	Companies that pay higher dividends deliver excess returns	Dividend yield

Source: Authors

Researchers reported already in the 1980s a size effect and a value effect in the U.S. stock market: small caps have shown over the long term a systematically higher return compared to large caps[15], and companies with a high book/market value ratio – in other words, value stocks – develop better than stocks with a low book/market value ratio (growth stocks)[16]. These two effects have also been found by follow-up studies to be astonishingly robust. The associated positive return premiums with those risk factors compensate for the higher risk associated with investing in small caps and value stocks. The economic rationale is as follows: small caps and value stocks are particularly exposed to a systematic risk of insolvency. Investors therefore demand a risk premium in the form of a higher yield for the holding of such shares. These findings therefore clearly refute the market efficiency hypothesis and have also been confirmed as reliable and observable in the "real-world" use of market anomalies.

As William Sharpe rightly put it[17]: "Smart Beta strategies are either factor bets (betting on cheap stocks to outperform expensive ones) or an active attempt to beat the market, which would class them as alpha and not beta. If smart beta is really only exploiting others' stupidity, the anomalies it exploits will be eliminated over time. So smart beta is merely an effective strategy for the moment, whose performance will dwindle over time; not a true 'beta'-like exposure to the market."

Investors should ask the following important "false alpha" questions to correctly focus on the economically relevant systematical risk factors:

- From what inefficiency (alpha opportunity), or which market patterns (beta opportunity), does the factor try to benefit?
- How is the inefficiency/market pattern established (theoretically vs. empirically correlation vs. causation, the real economy vs. financial terms)?
- Is the existing inefficiency permanent and can it be captured without high friction costs by products?
- Do they exist globally or regionally?
- Is it replicable or unique?
- Which influence factors are responsible for the stability of the factor?
- Is the product promise of alpha/outperformance compared to a fair benchmark, incorporating correct factor tilts?
- Is an alternative market portfolio used as a benchmark?
- Is it observable which market participants are trying to exploit the market anomaly?
- When is the maximum capacity of the inefficiency of the market pattern reached and start to neutralize?

The basic smart beta criticism indicates that smart beta strategies compared to fair benchmarks – adjusted to the Small Cap and Value factor tilts – often do not produce significant outperformance compared to capital-weighted benchmarks. As more and more investors allocate capital to smart beta strategies, the question of crowding out of attractive risk premiums automatically arises. Investable inefficiencies and market patterns attract investors. With increasing attention, the valuation of the popular risk factor becomes higher, but so also does the inefficiency, and thus future potential returns are reduced at the same time. A very good example is the Low Volatility factor, which gained popularity, following which the respective ETFs increased their assets under management massively. Only time will show if those investors will achieve the risk-adjusted alpha of this risk factor that has been historically observed and now targeted by investors.

Of course, the important part for investors is to judge whether the targeted market anomaly is still profitable after accounting for all implicit and explicit product costs. One of the main strengths of capital-weighted indices is their simple structure and relatively easy conversion to an investable product. Simply put, once invested with the starting weightings, the product runs on like an autopilot. The reinvestment of dividends, corporate actions and index changes falls under the category of things which are quite easy and cost-efficient to manage.

On the other hand, smart beta products are more complex to manage. Rule-bound reallocations, regular rebalancing and liquidity aspects complicate the management. Higher product costs and greater tracking error will result. Investors should ask the following "tracking" questions:

- How liquid is the index/the product underlying?
- How many designated market makers are trading the ETF?
- How is the ETF bid/ask spread evolving over time?
- How is the ETF tracking error/tracking difference evolving over time?
- What derivatives are used by the market maker of the ETF to hedge his book in order to provide liquidity?

One important factor in understanding the outperformance of smart beta strategies is the rebalancing effect, which plays a very important role in that regard. This is a very important explanation for the observed factor zoo, as many tested factors are showing attractive risk-return profiles at first sight, whereas the periodically rebalancing effect is causing these results, even though the factor actually observed is without economic significance. Rob Arnott of Research Affiliates agrees on the "rebalancing alpha"[18]: "The value tilt of our company's products accounts for about a third of the added-value we claim for us, with the rest coming from the rebalancing."

Investors should ask the following "rebalancing" questions:

- How much data snooping is in a factor?
- Is it possible to determine the rebalancing premium of a factor a priori?
- Are the product vendors ready to show backtesting details?

CONCLUSION

With the help of the checklist and questions introduced here, investors should be in a better position to select the relevant indices, strategies and product offerings from the complex "factor zoo" which is constructed by the sales and marketing units of product providers.

Moreover, the critical smart beta findings presented allow us to settle on concrete recommendations for asset allocation choices in the current challenging capital market and investment landscape:

- Select and focus on empirically and academically validated recurring factors.
- Use fair benchmarks to measure fund managers or smart beta strategies, not only capitalization-weighted indices.
- Use rule-based rebalancing as a simple quasi-alpha tool in the investment process.

In our view, for long-term investment success there are simple – but not easy – rules to follow, which are outlined in great detail in the previous sections. We have analyzed the inherent cost structure as the natural enemy of long-term investors, and then moved on to the marketing and sales pitfalls of product engineers trying to maximize their own profits. However, as often, the real enemy to long-term success is in ourselves. We are all human, so behavioral traits accompany us with every step, causing structural underperformance and long-term disappointment. Overconfidence, wrong timing decisions and emotional investing are the main problems, and they explain why investors show massive underperformance even against a naïve buy-and-hold benchmark. Additionally, investors tend to neglect the importance of a strategic asset allocation – and of sticking to it over time rather than rebalancing – and also the importance of allocating important portions of wealth to higher-returning asset classes. In the following part of this chapter, we will focus on how investors can mind the behavioral gap – earning more by avoiding investing errors.

MIND THE BEHAVIORAL GAP – EARNING MORE BY AVOIDING INVESTING ERRORS

Different studies have tried to quantify the so-called "behavioral return gap" arising from different behavioral biases and bad emotional decisions in investment management. Behavioral finance is a relatively new field in science, and tries to combine cognitive psychological and behavioral theory with conventional finance and economics, in order to explain often-observed irrational human behavior. Standard finance theory generally assumes that decision makers are acting like "rational utility maximizers", whereas often the opposite is observed: Emotional or psychological influences cause humans to take unpredictable decisions or to act irrationally.

Unsurprisingly, these emotional decisions in investment management cause a very large underperformance for investors when compared to naïve buy-and-hold strategies, thus offering huge potential for those investors who are aware of these human traits. There is a multitude of different behavioral observations of investment decision behavior, and it is beyond the scope of this book to give a comprehensive overview of this fascinating topic. To name a few, though: overconfidence, myopic loss aversion or the fear of regret are important observations of human behavior which systematically cause underperformance of investor portfolios.

To start with, we want to present an example which is influencing investor behavior. We will then try to quantify the behavioral return gap which is attributable to these investment decision-making errors.

Herding – "The Low Volatility Bubble" Case

This fallacy is certainly one of the most important ones, as there are a lot of good examples showing how this behavioral trait affects investors – for example, the technology bubble, with more and more investors jumping on the bandwagon still comes to mind when discussing herding behavior. The rationale behind this fallacy is that the majority of investors could not possibly be on the wrong side, and that the "trendy" investment strategy or asset class seems to be obviously superior when "rationally" analyzed. A look to the recent smart beta fund flows gives us also a good idea of how a crowded trade ultimately leads to an overvalued investment strategy. Ongoing equity market volatility is leading investors to defensive stocks and investment strategies. It is not surprising that in this difficult market environment so-called Low Volatility strategies are gaining massive investor attraction and hence massive inflows. A recent study from BlackRock shows the cumulative flows into different smart beta risk factors, indicating the huge inflow in the last 12 months to ETFs replicating the Low Volatility factor[19] (see Figure 5.4).

Analyzing this flow chart alongside the historical observed outperformance of the Low Volatility risk factor necessarily leads to the question whether performance-chasing behavior is leading to this flow bubble. Looking at the valuation metrics of low volatility stocks compared to the broad market or other risk factors, valuations are very stretched and very expansive compared to historical valuations. By allocating assets to this "en vogue" investment strategy, investors risk future returns being compressed compared to historical averages, so they should ideally avoid investing in overly "trendy" investment strategies or products.

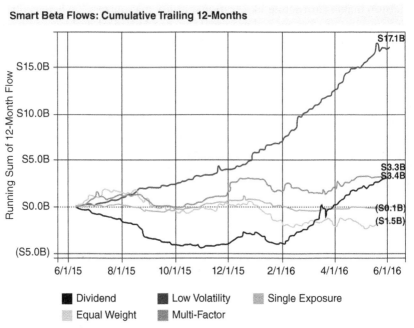

FIGURE 5.4   Smart Beta Flows
Source: Bloomberg, Markit, and BlackRock

Quantifying the Behavioral Return Gap

Estimates from different studies vary between 1% to 3% p.a. underperformance relative to a classical buy-and-hold strategy, which translates into a massive behavioral return gap compounded mid- to long-term.

As an example, the study in Figure 5.5 of Dalbar[20] shows the scope of the timing and selection penalty, which is also compared to the cost penalty.

Unsurprisingly, the average cost penalty of active mutual stock funds vs. a representative fair passive stock index accounts for about 3% p.a., which also explains the massive global run into low-cost efficient ETFs, aiming to effectively reduce this cost gap. The importance of systematically reducing the average cost of investment products was already shown in earlier chapters, as this is the most effective way to improve investor returns.

More surprisingly, the average investor underperforms active stock fund return because of behavioral biases, leading to different costly errors, such as like pro-cyclical investment decisions, herding or too much trading activity (overconfidence).

The important point is that by sticking to a buy-and-hold strategy with regular rebalancing or using rule-based investment strategies to control for

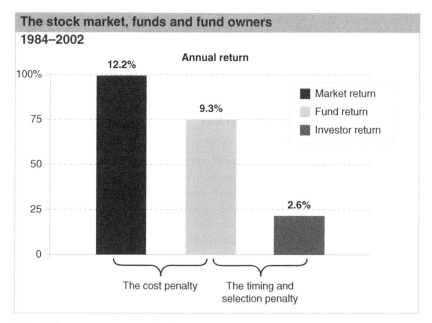

FIGURE 5.5 Cost, Timing and Selection Penalty
Source: © The Vanguard Group, Inc., used with permission

and to mitigate costly behavioral biases, far more value-added can be achieved compared to solely optimizing the average cost structure of investment portfolios.

By allocating an important share to rules-based strategies, the massive behavioral return gap can partly be closed and the average underperformance to fair benchmark indices can be substantially reduced – by earning behavioral alpha.

THE NEXT GENERATION OF ASSET ALLOCATION – RISK FACTOR ALLOCATION APPROACH IN PORTFOLIO CONSTRUCTION[21]

The US economist Harry M. Markowitz did a big favor to the financial industry with his dissertation "Portfolio Selection" (1952). With the Mean-Variance-Optimizer – the centerpiece of the "modern portfolio theory" – he provided a tool that could still be used to make good money with its theoretical foundation and its practical application. Simple enough to teach to students at business schools yet complex enough to impress investors, his model, which was still recognized as a major advance in the understanding of risk and return, formed the starting point for a number of one-factor/ one-period models such as the Capital Asset Pricing Model (CAPM). They all represent the first generation of asset allocation models (from 1950 to 2000). Balanced Portfolios (60/40 portfolio), long-only or buy-and-hold strategies have led to the development of the asset management industry.

Asset Allocation – the Most Important Risk and Return Component

With growing insight into the inadequate diversification effects of the first-generation asset allocation models, institutional investors began to constantly supplement their "classic" equity and bond allocations with additional alternative strategies – for example long/short equity strategies, risk parity or low-volatility strategies. For the purpose of quantitative optimization, multi-factor/multi-period models were used, the theoretical foundations of which date back to the 1970s (arbitrage pricing theory[22]).

But even alternative asset classes and strategies could not escape the trend of increasing correlations in equity market stress phases. If they were still regarded as a source of non-correlation at the beginning of the second generation (around the Millennium), the large growth of hedge funds assets under management led to a mainstream effect and correspondingly increasing correlation with the stock markets[23, 24].

Despite all deficiencies of the MPT, traditional portfolio theory still determines the very important asset allocation decision of most institutional investment processes, impacting the mixture of individual asset classes to implement an optimal policy portfolio. Not least because of the painful market drawdowns during and after the great financial crisis, many institutional investors had to realize that traditional portfolio theory had definitely reached its limits.

During the abrupt withdrawal of liquidity across all asset classes and most markets, the expected diversification potentials could not be reaped. Recent years have seen capital market movements driven mainly by macro and monetary policy, which has resulted in a market scenario of constantly changing equilibrium states – "Risk On" or "Risk Off". Accordingly, there are difficulties in portfolio construction and risk management, particularly as the "new normal" low-interest-rate environment forces investors to continually deteriorate portfolio quality to achieve a constant return yield requirement.

To summarize, the following problem arises for the second generation of asset allocation strategies: Due to the congruent basic assumptions of the first-generation models, risk is artificially reduced to volatility measures alone. Even with the help of more complex mathematical models, implemented by computer-aided algorithms, blind spots were found in the risk-taking. Think of VaR-optimized portfolios as one of the wrong developments.

In addition, rapidly advancing globalization led to a heterogeneity in the definition of asset classes from strategies, structures and geographies, so that diversification based on asset classes did not allow sufficient robustness.

The third generation breaks with the basic assumptions of the first two generations. Its academic foundation began to develop in the 1990s (behavioral finance) and found a context in the combination of neuroscience, evolution and financial econometrics[25]. An full discussion of the third generation would be too lengthy at this point. Let us concentrate instead on an important building block in the current generation: the diversification of risk factors.

To begin with, what is meant by "risk factor"?

Let us try to define it. A risk factor is a measurable, isolable influence factor of an asset class. Individual asset classes can thus be divided into different risk factors, which explain risk, yield and correlation characteristics better than traditional portfolio management approaches. A sufficiently diversified portfolio design across different asset classes can still have high correlation properties in particular situations, since it is moved by the similar or overlapping risk factors. Even if the degree of complexity of the portfolio optimization is increased by the use of risk factors, the resulting advantages and the corresponding reduction of the inherent weaknesses of the traditional portfolio theory is worth the effort of understanding it.

Let us assume an initial categorization of risk factors at the "atomic level". It is possible to divide risk factors into market risk premia, scientific empirical risk premia and alternative/macro/systematic risk premia, as seen in figure 5.6.

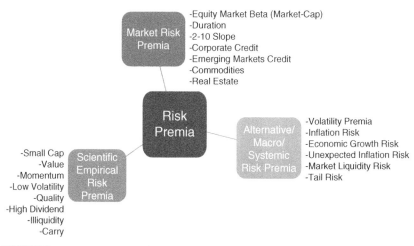

FIGURE 5.6   Categorization of Risk Factors
Source: Kula, Stahn, 2016

The logic behind the risk factor perspective: An investor can expect to earn a risk premium when exposed to a certain isolated risk factor. An implementation of risk factors allocation in portfolio construction shows significantly more robustness as correlations between asset classes are typically higher than correlations between individual risk factors.

Over time, risk factor exposures proved much more stable than correlations between individual asset classes. This can be explained by the fact that typically a large number of asset classes show at least an indirect exposure to the risk factor "stock market". This observation can be seen in market phases of high uncertainty and market upheavals, which then lead to "surprising" price losses for the allegedly poorly-correlated asset classes – to take an example from the great financial crisis in 2008, corporate bonds, high-yield investments and the asset class of diversified hedge funds strategies can be cited.

In times of the "normal" capital market phases, the risk factor "stock market" is slumbering and the good performance results of investments are attributed to the managers' selection and the investment process, even though it is actually partly a compensation for the equity market exposure. Only in extreme situations do these superficially uncorrelated asset classes show their true face and act in a highly correlated manner with equity bets: the diversification does not function when it is most urgently needed.

In a research note by PIMCO[26], this fact was investigated and confirmed. The correlations between risk factors were significantly lower than between traditional asset classes (Figure 5.7). Accordingly, by diversifying the risk factors, significantly more efficient portfolio results could be achieved than with traditional portfolios.

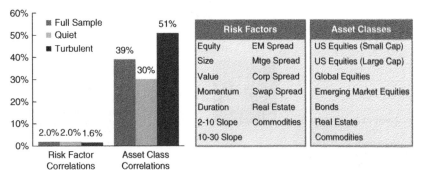

Average Cross-Correlations (March 1994 – December 2009)

FIGURE 5.7   Average Cross-Correlations
Source: www.pimco.com

Most importantly, the finding from this study is that the average correlation of the risk factors in market turbulence does not increase and is therefore significantly more robust than correlations of observed traditional asset classes in stress phases. The average risk factor correlation was stable at about 2% during the regime, while the asset class correlation increased from 30% to 51%.

The proof of the possibility of stable risk factor isolation began with Stephen Ross, the developer of the arbitrage pricing theory (APT), which posits the dependency of stock returns on several risk factors. However, APT does not specify the risk factors to be taken into account, but leaves the selection to the user. In 1993, Eugene Fama and Kenneth French presented a Three-Factor Model[27], in which the expected return on the stock market is dependent on the Size factor and the Value factor in addition to the Market factor already present in the CAPM.

The empirical motivation for these factors was provided by studies from the 1980s, in which researchers reported a size effect and a value effect on the U.S. stock market: Small caps show a systematically higher return in the long term than large caps[28]. Companies with a high book value/market value ratio (value shares) develop better than stocks with low book value/market value ratio (growth shares)[29]. These two effects were also proved to be remarkably robust in follow-up empirical studies. According to Fama and French, the positive return premiums associated with these factors represent a compensation for a higher risk associated with investing in small caps and value stocks: Small caps and value stocks are particularly vulnerable to systemic insolvency risk. Investors would therefore require a risk premium in the form of a higher return to hold such shares.

These findings have thus clearly disproved the market efficiency hypothesis and have been confirmed as robust market anomalies that can also be observed in global capital markets.

From the Use of Individual Risk Factors to a Portfolio Multi-risk Factor Implementation

Through a reinterpretation of diversification, portfolio construction, risk premiums and risk factors in the investment process, an effective management tool is presented for investors here as a portfolio construction tool for asset allocation of the next generation.

Completely new control options for asset allocation are derived with the consistent further development of this idea, which is implemented with a plurality of separable risk factors and premiums in an optimized portfolio. It turns out that, as shown in earlier chapters, besides the well-known Small

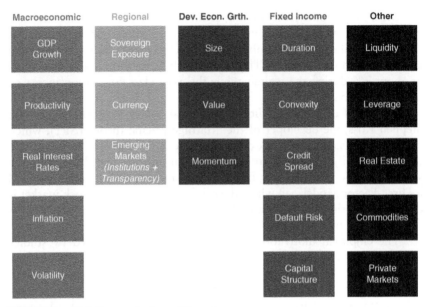

Macroeconomic	Regional	Dev. Econ. Grth.	Fixed Income	Other
GDP Growth	Sovereign Exposure	Size	Duration	Liquidity
Productivity	Currency	Value	Convexity	Leverage
Real Interest Rates	Emerging Markets *(Institutions + Transparency)*	Momentum	Credit Spread	Real Estate
Inflation			Default Risk	Commodities
Volatility			Capital Structure	Private Markets

FIGURE 5.8   Risk Factors in Asset Allocation
Source: Copyright 2013, CFA Institute. Reproduced and republished from the
Investment Risk and Performance Newsletter with permission from CFA Institute.
All rights reserved.

Cap or Value risk factors, there are also a certain number of other real risk
factors which can be used in the context of portfolio construction to improve
the risk-return payoff profile.

Figure 5.8 shows one possible classification of risk factors that can be
used in the context of asset allocation[30].

By leaving the "superficial" view of asset classes within the classical
portfolio construction context and changing the perspective by considering
the key risk drivers, a holistic and much broader view can be implemented
in asset allocation, which can also be adapted to the individual needs of the
investor. The structure shown is only an example and can be adapted and
grouped in accordance with investor or portfolio restrictions. Macroeconomic
factors are the main risk drivers for a variety of asset classes, which can be
"reconstructed" by appropriate combination of these factors.

The challenge in the practical implementation for investors is that not
all risk factors can be approached efficiently and many are not trivially
investable. Often "proxies" must be used by investors who are trying to
come near the targeted risk factor. As an example, the risk factor "volatility"
could be replicated by a long position in the VIX Futures Index or the corresponding ETF – as shown earlier, although product offerings exist, the

efficient investment into and tracking of this risk factor is very difficult to successfully implement.

Despite this practical difficulty, driven by the triumph of passive investments and intelligent indexing product solutions in recent years, investors have significantly extending possibilities available to them in portfolio construction. For example, individual risk factors are already packaged efficiently in smart beta ETFs.

Figure 5.9 shows the main advantages of a relatively simple factor portfolio compared to a traditional portfolio construction, including the associated risk and return statistics[31].

The analysis shows that the simple factor portfolio achieves equity-like return characteristics (5–7% per annum for various periods) with significantly lower volatility than a traditionally optimized investment portfolio. Surprisingly, both portfolios are mutually correlated slightly negative at –0.29, which is also reflected in the "5 Year" results from 2007 to 2011. As we know, this capital market cycle was particularly challenging for investors, encompassing as it does the great financial crisis. The factor portfolio could nonetheless realize a positive performance of 6.74%, within which the volatility factor in particular showed a significant positive contribution to the factor portfolio. The analysis shows that this period has been navigated with about half the volatility of the traditional portfolio and thus

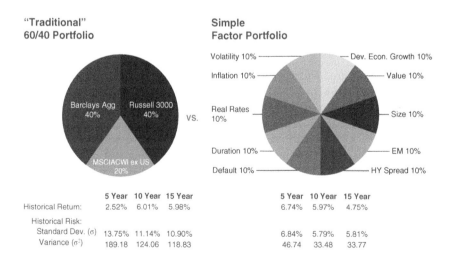

FIGURE 5.9   Traditional vs. Factor Portfolio
Source: Copyright 2013, CFA Institute. Reproduced and republished from the Investment Risk and Performance Newsletter with permission from CFA Institute. All rights reserved.

showed significantly more robustness, both in design and in the risk and return characteristics of the investor portfolio.

Risk factor diversification is an important building block in the third generation of asset allocation strategies. Accordingly, it requires a fundamental readjustment of the investment processes of most investors, who are still constructing their portfolios based on the traditional Markowitz portfolio optimization models, and achieving suboptimal results.

Only extensive research and appropriate communication can speed up this process of understanding. This chapter showed that with an expanded and new view to portfolio construction, traditional optimized portfolio can be significantly improved in their current risk return characteristics by a strategic shift to allocations to granular risk premiums. Moreover, with the rise of efficient investment vehicles, total cost burden can be systematically lowered and the robustness of the portfolio can be increased, independent of different capital market environments.

Through the implementation of a diversified portfolio of risk factors, the portfolio is significantly more robust to future capital market regime changes which are not possible to forecast. With the risk factor-based asset allocation approach, investors get a toolbox and a robust platform to implement corresponding cyclic or macroeconomic views and to better adapt to changing market conditions.

To conclude this chapter, we want to give an outlook on possible future research concerning risk factor portfolio construction, as there is still a lot of research to be done – particularly with regard to the practical implementation for investors.

Important future issues are:

- How stable are historically observed risk factors/premiums? Are they of a cyclical nature?
- The weighting of individual risk factors in the portfolio context is also an important question. Should the investor just equal-weight the relevant risk factors with regular rebalancing? Or should the investor apply quantitative optimization methods, including risk premium estimates, or should they use quantitative, non-predictive optimization processes?
- Despite product offerings in the recent years, the implementation is still cumbersome for some risk factors, as for long/short positions the investor often must use derivatives. Can this situation be improved?
- Which methods can be used for risk premium estimates and how can they be improved?
- From strategy to tactics: Is there a potential value-added from the tactical use of risk premiums?
- Can risk factors be used to improve tail risk hedging?

THE ULTIMATE QUESTION: PASSIVE OR ACTIVE?

With the ongoing massive industry tilt towards passive investment strategies, the question arises: Do active funds have any chance of existence in the near future? It is certainly a provocative question, as the traditional active fund industry is still significantly larger than the ETF industry and the "battle" is far from being decided. Certainly, the structural underperformance of active funds in the last decade together with the equity and bond bull market after the great financial crisis supported the run to cost-efficient and easy-to-understand passive investment products. As capital markets trended upwards, ETFs and other passive products were perfectly positioned as the bull market performance participation was 100%.

As the massive trend towards passive is still running, the market shift towards ETFs will continue until a new equilibrium is found. In the active fund industry, closet benchmark products and "index huggers" charging active fees will be particularly likely to continue to lose ground, as no real value-added is offered to investors compared with passive index products. The active investment management sector is reacting to this industry disruption by repositioning their product landscape and adapting their investment processes. It is of little surprise that the new mantra of active funds is the "high active share" proposition to differentiate them from ETFs. Another evolution to provide differentiation from the passive investment sphere are long-short or market-neutral funds, which are another way of offering investors a different risk-return profile not yet offered by ETFs.

In the heated passive or active debate there is obviously a philosophical component, as most proponents of one or the other strategy are quite fixed in their opinion. We are convinced that the question is not "either/or", but "as well as". We believe in the coexistence of both investment philosophies, as the more assets that are "naïvely" indexed, the more valuable opportunities for active fund managers will arise, improving their potential performance possibilities vs fair benchmarks. Furthermore, with the rise of smart beta products, the traditional definition of active or passive has been altered. With smart beta, investors get access to an investment style which is placed inbetween truly active and truly passive, adding further portfolio construction possibilities for investors. As already shown in the previous chapters, though, it is important to select the right smart beta methodologies, which is not always that easy, since lower transparency and higher complexity are substantially when compared to classical ETFs.

Obviously, in this philosophical passive vs. active debate there is no one right answer for everyone. Thinking of an optimal future portfolio design, the coexistence of classical passive investment vehicles, replication of scientifically well-documented weighting schemes like momentum or value and the addition of high-conviction active funds could be one possible alternative to portfolio construction to optimally use the different product sets and conscious alpha and beta combinations.

Finally, the important question arises as to whether investors can hold their portfolio positions over long time horizons, including drawdown markets. With the massive rise of assets under management with passive investment vehicles, it will be interesting to observe whether investors will hold them even in difficult capital market cycles and whether they stay disciplined when prices get down and keep emotions off the table. As already shown, the behavioral gap arising from bad emotional investing decisions is far outpacing the cost factor or structural underperformance of active funds.

Those investors who can implement and execute a disciplined investment strategy which is not driven by emotional decision making will have a long-term advantage. Holding to the established strategic asset allocation and a well-implemented policy portfolio with regular rebalancing will provide the highest probability of reaching predefined financial goals – independent of whether the products are passive, smart beta or truly active.

NOTES

1. Rawson and Johnson, 2015: 2
2. Vanguard, 2014
3. Kinnel, 2016
4. This part was written and co-authored by Kula/Schuller (2014), "Smart Beta Dekonstruktion"
5. Arnott, Kalesnik, Moghtader and Scholl, 2014; Haugen and Baker, 1991
6. Famous term coined by Cochrane, 2011
7. Sharpe, 1964
8. Amenc N, Goltz F, Martellini L (2013) "Smart Beta 2.0", Edhec-Risk-Institute, http://faculty-research.edhec.com/_medias/fichier/edhec-position-paper-smart-beta-2-0_1378195044229-pdf,
9. Fama and French, 1992
10. Cahart, 1997
11. Fama, 1970
12. Sharpe, 1964
13. Hsu and Kalesnik, 2014
14. Levi and Welch, 2014
15. Banz, 1981
16. DeBondt and Thaler, 1985; Fama and French, 1992
17. Sharpe, 2014
18. Chaves and Arnott, 2012
19. Blackrock ETF Landscape
20. Bogle Financial Markets Research Centre, 2006

21. This part was written and co-authored by Kula/Schuller (2013), "Diversifikation von Risikofaktoren"
22. Ross, 1976
23. Asness and Krail, 2001
24. Anson, 2008
25. Lo, 2004
26. Page, 2011
27. Fama and French, 1992
28. Banz, 1981
29. De Bondt and Thaler, 1985
30. Podkaminer, 2012
31. Podkaminer, 2012

CHAPTER 6

Unchaining Innovation – The Future of Active Investing in Passive Products

When it comes to investing, there are two competing approaches with regard to investment styles. One approach is based on the efficient markets theory, which states that the asset price of a certain security fully reflects all available information about that asset at any time. This leads towards a fair pricing of the asset. Mispricing may occur only on a temporary basis. The other approach argues that despite the existence of real-time data, quantitative computer power and sophisticated research tools, pricing inefficiencies occur in some securities and market segments and certain opportunities can be monetized by exploiting mispriced securities and trading them for a profit.

ALTERNATIVE INVESTING

Hedge funds and so-called alternative asset managers are the guild dedicated to the second of these approaches. These hedge fund managers try to react quickly in times of market weakness and generate stable returns even in bear markets when prices are going south. In this context, alternative investment managers strive to provide market-neutral returns for their clients. Steady returns are what draw investors towards the hedge fund industry. Meanwhile, hedge funds play a critical role in capital formation and are more than ever influential participants in the exchange-traded securities and option markets. Hedge funds in particular are focused on liquid long/short strategies that favor various sector ETFs as versatile trading instruments to gain exposure to their desired industry quickly.

Hedge Funds are Also Facing New Rules

As there is no official definition of what a hedge fund is, most pundits would characterize a hedge fund as a pooled investment vehicle (often structured as a limited partnership), managed by an investment professional (the "general partner") that trades publicly traded securities and/or associated derivatives. Due to the new legislation under the Dodd–Frank Act, many hedge funds and hedge fund advisors are now registered with the Securities and Exchange Commission (SEC). This is not a quality mark per se, though it is a positive move towards increased transparency. On the flip side, the Dodd–Frank Act in particular has created a "paper monster": a guarantee of life-long business for lawyers, compliance advisors and auditing companies. Perhaps a bipartisan initiative in the future may find ways to reduce the regulatory framework back to a more practical level.

Based on figures from data provider Preqin, North America is still the most established region in the hedge fund industry and accounts for the majority (60%) of managers. Nineteen percent of hedge fund managers are based in Europe; of these, more than half (52%) are headquartered in the UK – whether this share remains stable in the post-Brexit world is impossible to predict. Asia-Pacific hedge fund managers constitute 17% of all firms within the industry, with the majority of these based in the financial centers of Hong Kong, Australia and Singapore[1].

Most observers expected a sudden death of hedge funds in the aftermath of the financial crisis, peaking in the Lehman collapse in September 2008. However, it turned out that most of these bets were wrong: A majority of hedge funds are still alive and kicking – despite Dodd–Frank and other new costly compliance and regulatory hurdles. According to research provider HFR, there are currently 8,474 funds, managing roughly $3 trillion in assets[2]. One of the most desired strategies for investors in North America is Equity Long/Short and Equity Market Neutral. In Europe, Global Macro strategies are favored by the majority of investors. Investors based in Asia-Pacific focus on Equity Long/Short strategies most[3]. Despite all survivor strength the hedge fund sector has showed recently, it was easier for them to generate tremendous outperformance in the past then it is today. Investors using simple index tracking products, aka ETFs, often achieved in "ordinary" equity markets like the broad-based S&P 500 Index better or at least equal returns to hedge funds playing in the same asset class. Undoubtedly, one reason for the favorable returns in equity markets was the liquidity-driven bull market, which begun in the year 2009 by the open market operations and interest rate cuts of major central banks.

Some Seek Alternatives to Traditional Alternative Investments

Perhaps of greater significance to many investors than simply the desire for outperformance are the problems that exist with current hedge fund offerings, including the still-hefty fees (including performance fees), a lack of transparency, manager-specific risk, access issues, and, in recent times, increasing correlation to the broad equity markets. Indeed, a few large institutional investors have openly split exactly because of these factors. For example, the California Public Employees' Retirement System (Calpers), a $300 billion retirement giant, announced in 2015 that it will wind down its alternative portfolio to a minimum. Calpers intend to increase its investments into more liquid, less complex and less costly products. Additionally, several flagship hedge fund managers, such as Perry Capital, which was one of the longest-standing hedge fund managers, chose to close down flagship hedge funds as their strategies failed to show value-added in the last years. As money-making opportunities are reduced with the emergence of computer-driven strategies and index funds, the hedge fund industry struggles to persuade investors that hedge funds are worth the high fees they charge. The hedge fund closures in 2016 are the biggest shakeout in the hedge fund industry since the great financial crisis. Another segment facing severe difficulties is the fund of hedge funds businesses. Companies such as Aurora Investment Management have decided to close down operations as clients seek to cut fees to middlemen and to invest directly in hedge funds.

All of these factors have laid the groundwork for so-called "Alternative ETFs" (Table 6.1). In the past, mutual funds have been the go-to wrapper for most alternative investment strategies which have been marketed to the masses. Meanwhile, ETFs have taken over this role very often. Through these exchange-listed passive products, hedge fund replication, inflation-hedging, sophisticated commodities exposures, and other (often fancy) strategies that usually are employed by the alternative investment industry are easily accessible to a broad investor base, including private investors, while also offering institutional investors and high net worth investors new ways to maintain exposure to the alternative asset class.

Selected Alternative ETF Strategies

Most of the products mentioned can be categorized within the following Alternative ETF strategies, which are provided at a glance.

Long/Short (Equity) Long-short strategies which hold equal dollar amounts of both long and short positions are called "market-neutral strategies". However, there are some variations. Some hedge funds will maintain a long

TABLE 6.1 Alternative Exchange-Traded Products at a Glance (listed on a U.S. Exchange)

Ticker	Fund Name	ETF Issuer	TER (Expense Ratio)	AuM	Focus	Weighting Scheme	Active per SEC
VXX	iPath S&P 500 VIX Short-Term Futures ETN	Barclays Capital	0.89%	$1.72B	Volatility	Single Asset	No
QAI	IQ Hedge Multi-Strategy Tracker ETF	IndexIQ	0.96%	$1.18B	Global Macro	Multi-Factor	No
UVXY	ProShares Ultra VIX Short-Term Futures ETF	ProShares	1.32%	$723.35M	Volatility	Single Asset	No
XIV	VelocityShares Daily Inverse VIX Short-Term ETN	Credit Suisse	1.35%	$561.91M	Volatility	Single Asset	No
SVXY	ProShares Short VIX Short-Term Futures ETF	ProShares	1.28%	$347.64M	Volatility	Single Asset	No
TVIX	VelocityShares Daily 2x VIX Short-Term ETN	Credit Suisse	1.65%	$275.42M	Volatility	Single Asset	No
VIXY	ProShares VIX Short-Term Futures ETF	ProShares	0.84%	$221.63M	Volatility	Single Asset	No
WDTI	WisdomTree Managed Futures Strategy Fund	WisdomTree	0.65%	$186.26M	Long/Short	Proprietary	Yes
MNA	IQ Merger Arbitrage ETF	IndexIQ	0.77%	$132.15M	Long/Short	Multi-Factor	No

(Continued)

TABLE 6.1 (*Continued*)

Ticker	Fund Name	ETF Issuer	TER (Expense Ratio)	AuM	Focus	Weighting Scheme	Active per SEC
FTLS	First Trust Long/Short Equity ETF	First Trust	1.47%	$122.39M	Long/Short	Proprietary	Yes
RLY	SPDR SSgA Multi-Asset Real Return ETF	SSgA	0.70%	$86.40M	Global Macro	Proprietary	Yes
HTUS	Hull Tactical US ETF	ETC	0.91%	$84.19M	Global Macro	Proprietary	Yes
ZIV	VelocityShares Daily Inverse VIX Medium-Term ETN	Credit Suisse	1.35%	$75.28M	Volatility	Single Asset	No
VIXM	ProShares VIX Mid-Term Futures ETF	ProShares	0.84%	$63.29M	Volatility	Single Asset	No
JPHF	JPMorgan Diversified Alternatives ETF	JPMorgan	0.85%	$51.89M	Global Macro	Proprietary	Yes
VXZ	iPath S&P 500 VIX Mid-Term Futures ETN	Barclays Capital	0.89%	$49.47M	Volatility	Single Asset	No
DBV	PowerShares DB G10 Currency Harvest Fund	Invesco PowerShares	0.58%	$45.63M	Long/Short	Equal	No
RALS	ProShares RAFI Long/Short ETF	ProShares	0.95%	$39.86M	Long/Short	Fundamental	No

Ticker	Name	Provider	Expense	AUM	Strategy	Type	Multi-Factor
HDG	ProShares Hedge Replication ETF	ProShares	0.95%	$36.24M	Global Macro	Multi-Factor	No
DIVY	Reality Shares DIVS ETF	Reality Shares	0.89%	$33.36M	Long/Short	Proprietary	Yes
XIVH	VelocityShares VIX Short Volatility Hedged ETN	UBS	2.30%	$31.53M	Spreads	Fixed	No
GAA	Cambria Global Asset Allocation ETF	Cambria	0.25%	$27.45M	Global Macro	Proprietary	No
CPI	IQ Real Return ETF	IndexIQ	0.62%	$26.85M	Global Macro	Multi-Factor	No
LSVX	VelocityShares VIX Variable Long/Short ETN	UBS	2.30%	$26.50M	Spreads	Fixed	No
BSWN	VelocityShares VIX Tail Risk ETN	UBS	2.30%	$23.92M	Spreads	Fixed	No
CSLS	Credit Suisse X-Links Long/Short Equity ETN	Credit Suisse	0.95%	$21.47M	Long/Short	Proprietary	No
DYLS	WisdomTree Dynamic Long/Short U.S. Equity Fund	WisdomTree	0.48%	$20.66M	Long/Short	Fundamental	No
ALTS	ProShares Morningstar Alternatives Solution ETF	ProShares	0.95%	$19.79M	Global Macro	Technical	No
VEGA	AdvisorShares STAR Global Buy-Write ETF	AdvisorShares	2.00%	$16.99M	Global Macro	Proprietary	Yes

(Continued)

TABLE 6.1 (*Continued*)

Ticker	Fund Name	ETF Issuer	TER (Expense Ratio)	AuM	Focus	Weighting Scheme	Active per SEC
MATH	AdvisorShares Meidell Tactical Advantage ETF	AdvisorShares	1.48%	$14.32M	Global Macro	Proprietary	Yes
XVZ	iPath S&P 500 Dynamic VIX ETN	Barclays Capital	0.95%	$14.21M	Volatility	Technical	No
QMN	IQ Hedge Market Neutral Tracker ETF	IndexIQ	0.94%	$14.07M	Long/Short	Multi-Factor	No
BTAL	QuantShares US Market Neutral Anti-Beta Fund	FQF Trust	2.15%	$13.72M	Long/Short	Equal	No
VIIX	VelocityShares Daily Long VIX Short-Term ETN	Credit Suisse	0.89%	$12.91M	Volatility	Single Asset	No
MCRO	IQ Hedge Macro Tracker ETF	IndexIQ	1.02%	$10.08M	Global Macro	Multi-Factor	No
GTAA	AdvisorShares Morgan Creek Global Tactical ETF	AdvisorShares	1.61%	$7.61M	Global Macro	Proprietary	Yes
FMF	First Trust Morningstar Managed Futures Strategy Fund	First Trust	1.00%	$7.33M	Long/Short	Proprietary	Yes

Ticker	Name	Provider		AUM	Strategy	Method	
LALT	PowerShares Multi-strategy Alternative Portfolio	Invesco PowerShares	0.97%	$6.93M	Long/Short	Proprietary	Yes
QEH	AdvisorShares QAM Equity Hedge ETF	AdvisorShares	2.03%	$5.49M	Long/Short	Proprietary	Yes
MRGR	ProShares Merger ETF	ProShares	0.75%	$5.40M	Long/Short	Multi-Factor	No
STPP	iPath US Treasury Steepener ETN	Barclays Capital	0.75%	$5.31M	Spreads	Duration	No
QED	IQ Hedge Event-Driven Tracker ETF	IndexIQ	0.99%	$5.05M	Global Macro	Multi-Factor	No
GIVE	AdvisorShares Global Echo ETF	AdvisorShares	1.50%	$4.54M	Global Macro	Proprietary	Yes
RRF	WisdomTree Global Real Return Fund	WisdomTree	0.64%	$4.16M	Global Macro	Proprietary	Yes
FUT	ProShares Managed Futures Strategy ETF	ProShares	0.76%	$4.04M	Long/Short	Proprietary	Yes
DIVA	QuantShares Hedged Dividend Income Fund	FQF Trust	1.59%	$3.86M	Long/Short	Equal	No
VMIN	REX VolMAXX Inverse VIX Weekly Futures Strategy ETF	ETC	1.45%	$3.70M	Volatility	Proprietary	Yes
DYB	WisdomTree Dynamic Bearish U.S. Equity Fund	WisdomTree	0.48%	$3.69M	Long/Short	Fundamental	No

(Continued)

TABLE 6.1 (*Continued*)

Ticker	Fund Name	ETF Issuer	TER (Expense Ratio)	AuM	Focus	Weighting Scheme	Active per SEC
FLAT	iPath US Treasury Flattener ETN	Barclays Capital	0.75%	$3.53M	Spreads	Duration	No
RINF	ProShares Inflation Expectations ETF	ProShares	0.30%	$3.52M	Spreads	Duration	No
VMAX	REX VolMAXX Long VIX Weekly Futures Strategy ETF	ETC	1.25%	$3.40M	Volatility	Proprietary	Yes
FAAR	First Trust Alternative Absolute Return Strategy ETF	First Trust	0.95%	$2.90M	Long/Short	Proprietary	Yes
MOM	QuantShares US Market Neutral Momentum Fund	FQF Trust	2.69%	$2.42M	Long/Short	Equal	No
ICI	iPath Optimized Currency Carry ETN	Barclays Capital	0.65%	$2.39M	Long/Short	Equal	No
SIZ	QuantShares US Market Neutral Size Fund	FQF Trust	2.93%	$2.15M	Long/Short	Equal	No

Ticker	Name	Issuer	Expense Ratio	AUM	Category	Weighting	Leveraged
TVIZ	VelocityShares Daily 2x VIX Medium-Term ETN	Credit Suisse	1.65%	$2.04M	Volatility	Single Asset	No
QLS	IQ Hedge Long/Short Tracker ETF	IndexIQ	1.09%	$1.92M	Long/Short	Multi-Factor	No
CHEP	QuantShares US Market Neutral Value Fund	FQF Trust	2.46%	$1.25M	Long/Short	Equal	No
VIIZ	VelocityShares VIX Medium Term ETN	Credit Suisse	0.89%	$831.42K	Volatility	Single Asset	No
IVOP	iPath Inverse S&P 500 VIX Short-Term Futures ETN	Barclays Capital	0.89%	$510.73K	Volatility	Single Asset	No
XXV	iPath Inverse S&P 500 VIX Short-Term Futures ETN	Barclays Capital	0.89%	$485.03K	Volatility	Single Asset	No

Source: ETF.com

bias, which means that they have some equity market exposure depending on the views of the hedge fund manager, who will alter the beta-positioning over time. Nevertheless, the market beta of a long bias strategy will never be fully invested in equities like an ETF. In contrast, there are also variations of strategies which have a more equity-like exposure, for example the so-called 130/30 strategies. With these strategies, a hedge fund has a 130% long exposure to certain stocks and a 30% short exposure, so it is basically fully invested in the equity market. Strategies such as 120% long and 20% short are also used. Due to the fact that equity markets tend to move up over time, there are only a few hedge funds that have a long-term short bias. Investors should acknowledge that the asset managers/providers of Alternative ETFs linked to Long/Short strategies have a broad discretion in their specific long/short allocation and ongoing stock selection. The individual investment decisions are – as with real hedge funds – in the hands of the ETF's asset managers; there is no strict, predictable rule according to which the ETF is managed.

Global Macro   This hedge fund strategy focuses on investing in securities whose prices fluctuate based on the changes in economic policies and macroeconomic shifts along with the flow of capital around the globe. This opportunistic and discretionary investment style includes currency strategies (the relative value of the US Dollar vs. the Brazilian Real, for example), interest rate trading (tactical bets on different interest rate levels) as well as investments into selected equity, bond and commodity markets, which economic indicators are promising from an investor's perspective.

Volatility   Volatility as an asset class is one of the most advanced investment strategies. There are some ways to use volatility to generate alpha or to utilize certain low-volatility assets (those with lower than average market volatility). Active volatility strategies often play around the volatility curve (aka the volatility term structure), applying especially complex active option strategies to exploit the volatility risk premium for investors. In this context, investors should understand the difference between "realized (historical) volatility" and "implied (expected) volatility". Implied volatility is derived from the option prices. Overall, volatility reflects the dispersion of asset prices. With regard to low-volatility stocks, these are particularly interesting in certain market cycles. Low-volatility stocks typically produce outperformance in periods of market stress for risky assets (bear markets). On the other hand, low-volatility stocks lag in performance when risk assets are in favor (bull markets).

Managed Futures   The alternative asset class of "managed futures" is closely related to commodity trading advisors (CTAs). This designation refers to an alternative manager's registration status with the U.S. Commodity Futures Trading Commission and National Futures Association. However, CTAs may trade financial and foreign exchange futures, not only commodities. Investors using Alternative ETFs with a direct link to managed accounts/ CTA investment style should be aware that it is challenging to measure the success of CTAs by simply using the passive long-only commodity indices mentioned above, such as the Goldman Sachs Commodity Index (GSCI) or the Thomson Reuters Core Commodities CRB Index (CRB), as performance benchmarks. These indices are not appropriate because in practice they include only a small fraction of the futures CTAs trade. Also, these commodity benchmarks do not account for active management or the managers' ability to establish short as well as long positions. As a result, Alternative ETFs linked to a managed futures strategy will usually have a low correlation with traditional benchmarks. To some extent it would make more sense to compare the performance of CTA allocations with absolute return mandates, as investors can also observe industry-standard indices for CTAs such as the SG CTA Index (formerly known as Newedge CTA Index) for performance comparisons.

Alternative ETFs are a perfect case where active strategies could be embedded into a passive product. However, like any sophisticated financial product, it is imperative that investors properly educate themselves about the methodology, index design, risks and payoff profile that the individual Alternative ETF replicates. However, the risks from an Alternative ETF are vastly different from those of a traditional hedge fund, and the advantages can potentially be very powerful.

Advantages of Alternative ETFs

A major issue when investing directly into hedge funds is performance dispersion. Average returns hide an extraordinarily wide range of individual fund performance. Eventually, given the fees charged by managers (the average is slightly below the oft-cited "2 and 20" – 2% of assets and 20% of performance results), picking the right hedge fund or, better, the right hedge fund manager, is still paramount. The only thing more painful than paying a pricey management fee is paying that same fee for poor performance (compared to publicly investable benchmark indices). So essentially there are two hurdles that an investor must clear: manager selection and subsequently access to the sophisticated, hopefully good-performing strategy. Hedge fund replication through ETFs can help solve for both of these problems, while also reducing the fees. On average, ETFs which replicate hedge fund strategies charge slightly below 1% management fee annually. However, the annual fee range within Alternative ETFs ranges from literally nothing (0.25%) up to well above 3%, which is very hefty. One big advantage, or perhaps the biggest advantage, is the omitting of performance fees of alternative strategies wrapped into an ETF. Usually, an alternative asset manager gets rewarded for its superior returns through the performance fee. Essentially, the hedge fund manager is allowed to keep, for example, 10% or 20% of the portfolio's outperformance for itself. This performance fee does not exist with Alternative ETFs – at least not until now.

To put it in a nutshell, the trade-off is that investors using an Alternative ETF will not be placing their money directly with a hedge fund. Such Alternative ETFs are not trying to provide direct hedge fund access, but rather are seeking to synthesize hedge fund returns and use readily available equities, which often include other pre-existing ETFs or futures already listed on the market to replicate hedge fund industry performance. An additional benefit in not being invested with a traditional hedge fund manager could actually be not being tied to lock-ups or "gates". Finally, Alternative ETFs are a way to escape the above-mentioned performance fees.

Hidden Costs and Risks to Watch Out For

Despite the many advantages Alternative ETFs could offer for smart portfolio management, buy-side investors should keep an eye on certain costs – some of them are hidden and are not clearly reflected in annual fund operating expenses. One major item to watch out for is transaction costs. The ETF pays commissions whenever it buys and sells securities. These transactions are summarized as the "portfolio turnover". As one can expect, a higher portfolio turnover rate will ultimately lead to higher transaction costs and may result in higher taxes when ETF units/ETF shares are held in a taxable account. These costs affect the ETF's performance directly. As hedge fund strategies are often associated with active trading, investors should carefully review the portfolio turnover of the selected Alternative ETFs. Detailed information about the portfolio turnover is stated in the prospectus summary or other ETF-specific information. From a risk management perspective, when investing into Alternative ETFs investors should perform sufficient due diligence on the specific index or basket. What exactly does the strategy achieve (or strive to achieve), and which instruments are used to replicate the strategy effectively? For example, investors should request information about how much of the ETF's total assets will be invested in the component securities of the index. Or what about currency effects in global hedge fund strategies like long/short European equities?

Finally, the persistence of the outperformance of the specific Alternative ETF vs. broad indices or similar strategies is something to consider.

Another aspect that investors should bear in mind is the sometimes confusing fact that "liquid alternatives", as Alternative ETFs often named, are anything but liquid. The average AuM of U.S.-listed ETFs linked to an alternative investment strategy is $100 million. However, some of them are much slimmer, having less than $10 million assets. In other words, the liquidity to trade in and out of these passive products is somewhat limited, and this is reflected in a wider bid-ask spread. The difference could be up to 7% under normal market circumstances (see Figure 6.1). On average the bid-ask spread of Alternative ETFs is around 0.45%.

It is clear that Alternative ETFs will not fully usurp the role of traditional hedge funds, including alternative asset strategies, but that is not what they are designed to do. They will serve to further democratize an important, sometimes obscure, asset class, letting many types of investors benefit from the low correlation and steady returns that Alternative ETFs could deliver, often along with drastically reduced costs and greater transparency compared with hedge funds themselves. Also, lock-up periods, which are

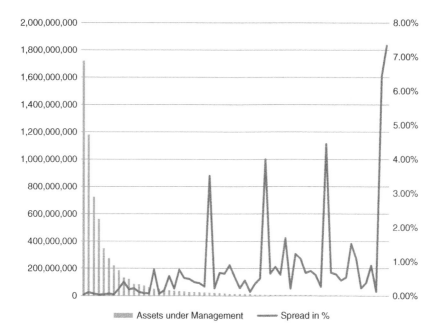

FIGURE 6.1 AuM vs. Spread of Alternative ETFs
Data Source: ETF.com, as of October 30, 2016

common with their real hedge fund peers, are unknown to Alternative ETFs. This means that they could be used as a valuable addition to a modern portfolio.

ENVIRONMENTAL, SOCIAL AND GOVERNANCE (ESG)-BASED INVESTMENTS[4]

The importance of ESG or sustainable investments is steadily increasing. According to the figures presented in the Global Sustainable Investment Review, a total of USD 21.4trn of investments in broad terms is pursuing a socially responsible investing (SRI) approach as of the end of 2014[5]. Europe leads the way with a total of USD 13trn, followed by the U.S. with USD 6.5trn. In Switzerland, SRI assets have exhibited an increase of +169% vs. 2014 and currently stand at CHF 190bn according to the figures published by Swiss Sustainable Finance (SSF) and the Forum Nachhaltige Geldanlage (FNG)[6]. The 2014 figures reveal that the most commonly used portfolio formation process is negative screening, i.e. exclusion of certain business activities. More generally, SRI investments are managed according to one of three principles: (i) exclusion criteria, (ii) best in class, and (iii) minimum value (minimum rating), or a combination of those. While ethical investing became well-known in the 1990s, it is not a new phenomenon and in fact has ancient origins which date back as far as biblical times[7]. While for many years investors had only a choice between different active mutual funds, only very recently, ETFs have started offering passive exposure to SRI-screened equity and fixed-income benchmarks as well.

Doing Good and Doing Well?

The discussion surrounding the added-value of SRI investment styles is still the subject of debate in academic literature. While the advocates of sustainable investing point out that SRI assets generate outperformance, critics of this approach argue the opposite. An early influential paper by Moskowitz[8] finds that stocks with socially responsible attributes exhibit higher expected returns compared to conventional stocks because market participants are not able to correctly price social responsibility effects. Similarly, Hamilton, Jo and Statman[9] argue that investors tend to underestimate the likelihood of negative news about companies that are considered to be controversial with regard to SRI standards and hence these stocks have lower expected returns. In contrast, most empirical studies based on US data suggest that SRI-restricted portfolios provide similar performance to non-screened portfolios[10]. Similarly, Geczy, Stambaugh and Levin[11] find that when the CAPM model is applied, actively managed SRI portfolios deliver almost identical results to unconstrained portfolios. The more recent studies[12] find that SRI-screened portfolios do not deliver superior risk-adjusted returns compared to conventional or low-rated SRI portfolios.

A large number of empirical studies have evaluated the added-value of an SRI screening process based on the return differences between SRI and non-SRI mutual funds. For example, Statman[13] investigates Jensen's alphas and finds support for the hypothesis that risk-adjusted returns of SRI mutual funds are not significantly different from those of conventional mutual funds. Also, Goldreyer and Diltz[14] find no measurable effect on performance by following an ethical investing approach based on ethical mutual funds using an extended sample of equity, bond and balanced funds. Luther, Matatko and Corner[15] compare the returns of UK-based ethical unit trusts to the performance of broad stock universes and find some evidence of outperformance, which they explain by a small-cap bias present in their sample. Other studies[16] also report a small-cap bias in SRI mutual funds. Both studies, after controlling for the size effect, still report an outperformance of SRI mutual funds compared to conventional counterparts. However, DiBartolomeo[17] and Kurtz[18] find that if the KLD 400[19] returns are corrected by the large-cap and growth effects, most of the reported outperformance disappears. Also Renneboog, ter Horst and Zhang[20] find that SRI funds in the U.S., UK and in many continental European and Asia-Pacific countries underperform their domestic benchmarks by between 2.2% to 6.5%. However, with the exception of some countries such as France, Japan and Sweden, the risk-adjusted returns of SRI funds are not statistically different from the performance of conventional funds.

Isolating the SRI Factor

In contrast to most literature which has focused on active SRI portfolios, our analysis concentrates on rules-based index portfolios. As they are constructed by rigorous rules-based and transparent standards, they allow for a comparison between screened and non-screened performance without the shortcomings of the previous studies. In particular, this analysis addresses the shortcomings of previous studies which are often unrelated to the specifics of an SRI approach. In fact, many of the SRI findings are driven by active portfolio management processes. Built on an extended pool of recent literature, this study uses some well-known risk-adjusting measures as well as a single and extended multi-factor regression model to examine whether the SRI screening portfolio formation process delivers a measurable performance impact. The aim of the study is to confirm or reject the claim that SRI-screened portfolios yield inferior performance as they hold a subset of the unconstrained market portfolio and hence, due to this limitation, forgo relevant return opportunities. In addition, we test if a second claim holds true, which had been put forward by Bello, Hong and Kacperczyk, and Stratman and Glushkov[21] – that the limitation of the SRI screening process results in higher risk levels due to constrained diversification characteristics.

To provide meaningful answers, the study uses daily log returns of SRI-screened Total Return Net index constituents of six developed and one broad emerging equity market exposures as well as returns from the largest developed corporate bond market. In order to ensure that the results are comparable across asset classes and regions, the source for all index level data was limited to one single provider, which has a consistent and comprehensive data history available. Currently, in the view of the study authors, only MSCI is in a position to deliver on these data requirements, and hence the research study is based on the MSCI index data for equity and on MSCI/Barclays for bonds. In total, the dataset covers a market capitalization of USD 9.2trn as of May 2016. The daily data history spans from October 1, 2007 for more than half of the analyzed equity exposures. However, for EMU exposure, daily returns are available from May 27, 2010, and for UK and Emerging Markets, from June 1, 2011 onwards. The shortest data sample is available for the bond exposure, where daily return history starts from 30 May, 2013. All index level data used in this analysis end at March 21, 2016. The analysis looks at the data from three different angles. In the first approach, risk-adjusted performance is compared. In the second, we run simple as well as extended regression models. In particular, common equity factors are added, to understand whether SRI performance is driven by systematic risk drivers. Third, valuations to test to what extent there is an inter-dependency between SRI-screened and conventional portfolios driven by market sentiment are looked at.

Table 6.2 provides a first insight and presents descriptive statistics for the data sample divided into SRI and non-SRI portfolios and subdivided by equity and bonds as well as regions. The mean returns for the SRI portfolios have generally been higher than their non-SRI counterparts with the exception of the U.S. The biggest excess mean return is from Emerging Markets SRI, with more than 3.2%, and from UK SRI, with more than 2.3% annualized. Considering the volatilities, it becomes apparent that SRI portfolios have generally lower risk associated with them, the exception being the UK, Japan and Pacific (made up of c. 67% Japan). In the case of Japan, the excess standard deviation is around 1.2% higher for the SRI portfolio on an annualized basis. On a risk-adjusted basis, it is only the U.S. which delivers an inferior risk-reward profile. Emerging Markets reports the best trade-off between mean and risk for the entire data sample.

TABLE 6.2 Descriptive Statistics for SRI and Non-SRI exposures

Equity	SRI					Non-SRI				
	Mean Return p.a.	Std. Dev. p.a.	Maximum Return (d)	Minimum Return (d)	Reward-to-risk	Mean Return p.a.	Std. Dev. p.a.	Maximum Return (d)	Minimum Return (d)	Reward-to-risk
EMU[1]	8.91%	19.13%	4.76%	−5.44%	0.466	7.21%	19.94%	5.16%	−5.48%	0.362
USA	4.67%	21.02%	9.80%	−9.30%	0.222	4.87%	21.70%	11.04%	−9.51%	0.225
UK[1]	7.18%	16.12%	4.13%	−4.93%	0.445	4.83%	15.60%	3.82%	−4.69%	0.309
Japan	−0.20%	25.90%	13.55%	−10.68%	−0.008	−1.02%	24.72%	13.06%	−10.44%	−0.041
Emerging Markets[1]	−1.29%	15.73%	5.22%	−6.35%	−0.082	−4.52%	16.30%	4.82%	−6.52%	−0.277
World	2.59%	18.00%	8.16%	−6.93%	0.144	2.11%	18.63%	9.10%	−7.32%	0.113
Pacific	0.60%	22.07%	9.99%	−9.35%	0.027	−0.22%	21.20%	9.83%	−9.18%	−0.010

Fixed-Income	Mean Return p.a.	Std. Dev. p.a.	Maximum Return (d)	Minimum Return (d)	Reward-to-risk	Mean Return p.a.	Std. Dev. p.a.	Maximum Return (d)	Minimum Return (d)	Reward-to-risk
US Corporates[2]	3.00%	4.58%	0.83%	−1.10%	0.655	2.87%	4.66%	0.86%	−1.11%	0.614

Source: Thomas Merz, MSc., Managing Director, UBS Asset Management, data per March 21, 2016

Notes:
[1]. Index rules include a 5% issuer cap.
[2]. Sustainable thresholds used for bonds slightly differ from the ones used for Equities. For further details on index methodology differences between bonds and equities, see MSCI website: www.msci.com.

183

Generally, the SRI-screened portfolios for both equity as well as bond exposures exhibit better risk-adjusted performance figures compared to their conventional counterparts. Table 6.3 shows (with US equity as the only exception) superior risk-adjusted returns (Treynor ratio, Information ratio, Modified Sharpe ratio) for all analyzed SRI portfolios. The results suggest that the screening process represents a decision-driven selection process which in many cases is able to deliver matching or even superior performance. Our results seem to support the hypothesis put forward by Renneboog, ter Horst and Zhang[22], that SRI portfolios benefit from lower costs, arising from the avoidance or minimization of reputational damage, better management and customer satisfaction that leads to higher sales and revenues and finally transmits into less risky investments with higher risk-adjusted returns.

TABLE 6.3   Risk Adjusted Performance for SRI Exposures

Equity	SRI			Non-SRI
	Treynor Ratio	Inform. Ratio	Mod. Sharpe Ratio	Mod. Sharpe Ratio
EMU[1]	0.018	0.601	0.470	0.362
USA	−0.002	−0.058	0.225	0.224
UK[1]	0.023	0.836	0.452	0.309
Japan	0.008	0.274	−0.008	−0.041
Emerging Markets[1]	0.035	0.755	−0.085	−0.277
World	0.005	0.212	0.145	0.113
Pacific	0.008	0.247	0.027	−0.011
Fixed-Income	Treynor Ratio	Inform. Ratio	Mod. Sharpe Ratio	Mod. Sharpe Ratio
US Corporates[2]	0.001	0.000	0.654	0.612

Source: Thomas Merz, MSc., Managing Director, UBS Asset Management, data per March 21, 2016

Notes:
[1] Index rules include a 5% issuer cap.
[2] Sustainable thresholds used for bonds slightly differ from the ones used for Equities. For further details on index methodology differences between bonds and equities see MSCI website: www.msci.com.

Does the SRI Alpha Exist?

Correspondent with the simple return-per-unit-of-risk measures, SRI-screened portfolios, with the exception of US equity, all have positive alpha estimates while more than half exhibit less market risk compared to conventional portfolios. The alphas range from -0.01% to +2.91% for US and Emerging Markets respectively. However, the alphas reported in Table 6.4 are statistically insignificant using HAC adjusted standard errors whereas all betas are highly significant. In other words, we find that SRI-screened portfolios yield significantly neither better nor worse than conventional portfolios, but in many cases bear slightly lower risk with betas significantly lower than one. Our results are consistent with more recent academic publications which also indicate that investing in SRI equity indices do not entail additional costs which affect returns negatively. For European SRI portfolios in particular, our results are in line with the findings of Garz, Volk and Gilles[23], who also find positive but only slightly significant SRI alphas for European exposures.

Table 6.5 shows the statistics from the extended regression analysis using four additional return drivers in order to refine our model. By introducing some of the most commonly used and well-researched equity factors, we aim to analyze whether there is any systematic equity factor which would drive the SRI returns. As the availability of fully rules-based daily factor returns with a regional break-down is limited to equities, and within equities to the Eurozone and the U.S., we are constrained in applying the extended regression model to all our SRI portfolios. The regression analysis is therefore repeated for only two SRI portfolios: Eurozone and US equities. However, as these two investment regions are seen as the most important exposures, at least for Europe-based investors, the results remain robust and allow for meaningful conclusions.

First, we find that the signs of the reported alphas remain unchanged. For the European portfolio, a positive but insignificant alpha of 1.45% and for the U.S. portfolio a negative alpha of -0.35% annualized is reported. Both betas are significantly smaller than 1, indicating that the risk exposure to the market is reduced. In particular, for the U.S. exposure, this risk is considerably lower, with a beta of 0.89. Only two factor loads from the extended model are significant in the case of the U.S. portfolio. In contrast, adding equity factors in the European case leads to only insignificant factor loadings. In both cases, the reported R^2 figures indicate that the fitting of the model remains very good, and the reported alphas are reliable estimates for the true risk-adjusted excess returns.

While active SRI managers may display bias towards certain sectors, it could be of interest to add sector returns to the regression model to see if

TABLE 6.4 Empirical Results From the 1-factor (CAPM) Model

Exposure	Observ.	1-factor-alpha			$r_{nSRI,t}-r_{f,t}$			Coeff. of det.
	n	α (d)	α (p.a.)	t Stat / p-value	Mkt		t Stat / p-value	Adj. R²
EMU[1]	1518	0.0001	2.04%	1.6225 / 0.1049	0.95012	(***)	-10.8103 / 0.0000	0.981045
USA	2211	0.0000	-0.01%	-0.5027 / 0.6152	0.95697	(***)	-6.5521 / 0.0000	0.975621
UK[1]	1254	0.0001	2.28%	1.4518 / 0.1468	1.01751	(***)	2.798242 / 0.0052	0.969853
Japan	2211	0.0000	0.86%	0.5255 / 0.5993	1.03756	(***)	8.31539 / 0.0000	0.980847
Emerging Markets[1]	1254	0.0001	2.91%	1.4513 / 0.1469	0.93105	(***)	-7.57828 / 0.0000	0.930999
World	2211	0.0000	0.55%	0.0085 / 0.9932	0.95896	(***)	-8.24619 / 0.0000	0.985477
Pacific	2211	0.0000	0.84%	0.2350 / 0.8143	1.02954	(***)	5.986444 / 0.0000	0.978267
US Corporates[2]	703	0.0000	0.19%	-0.1006 / 0.9199	0.98089	(***)	-7.88434 / 0.0000	0.995936

Source: Thomas Merz, MSc., Managing Director, UBS Asset Management, data per March 21, 2016

Notes:

[1] Index rules include a 5% issuer cap.

[2] Sustainable thresholds used for bonds slightly differ from the ones used for Equities. For further details on index methodology differences between bonds and equities see MSCI website: www.msci.com.

TABLE 6.5 Empirical Results From the 5-factor Model

Exposure	Observ. n	5-factor alpha α (d)	α (p.a.)	t Stat	p-value	$r_{nSRI,t}-r_{f,t}$ Mkt	p-value	Beta coefficient 1–4 HML	p-value	LVOL	p-value	QMJ	p-value	TSY	p-value	Coeff. of det. Adj. R^2
EMU1	1393	0.0001	1.45%	1.2962	0.1951	0.95488 (***)	0.0000	−0.0267	0.2695	0.0165	0.4685	−0.0067	0.7983	0.0232	0.2101	0.981019
USA	2062	0.0000	−0.35%	−0.3001	0.7641	0.88714 (***)	0.0000	−0.0855 (**)	0.0103	0.0193	0.4255	−0.0462	0.2061	0.2067 (***)	0.0000	0.976306

Source: Thomas Merz, MSc., Managing Director, UBS Asset Management, data per March 21, 2016

Notes:

[1] Index rules include a 5% issuer cap.

[2] Sustainable thresholds used for bonds slightly differ from the ones used for Equities. For further details on index methodology differences between bonds and equities see MSCI website: www.msci.com.

any of the sectors are systematic drivers of the SRI returns (for this argument see for example Derwall et al. 2005). Since the SRI indices are formed to be sector-neutral (i.e. to keep sector allocation as in the conventional portfolio), there is no need to run such analysis for our dataset.

By comparing the results from both regression models, the study confirms that SRI portfolios yield non-different mean returns compared to conventional portfolios. This holds true for the single factor (beta being the only risk factor) as well for the extended, five-factor model. In both cases both alphas are not significantly different from zero, confirming that the SRI screening process does not deliver significantly different mean returns vis-à-vis conventional portfolios when adjusted by market and equity factor exposure. Furthermore, the results support the argument that the SRI screening process reduces the overall portfolio risk with market risk loadings of below 1 (in the case of the U.S., beta being 0.89). This may be the result of the fact that SRI portfolios restrict the holdings of companies which are involved in controversial activities and hence such stocks are understood to be affected the most when controversial discussions drive market risk and performance.

The Relative Valuation Critics

Following the critics that the observed out-performance of SRI-screened portfolios may be a direct result of the buying (or selling) pressure from the market due to media and press attention, the data sample by looking at relative valuation patterns over the entire sample period is also tested. To test whether SRI returns move concurrently relative to valuations due to over-attention from the buy-side (sell-side), Arnott et al.[24] suggest putting relative valuations in relation to relative performance. They propose comparing rolling windows of multiple periods of the cross-sectional valuation ratios. Extending their framework to a number of commonly used valuations, we find no clear trend in the time series.

Furthermore, the causal relationship between the price innovation and the cross-sectional change in valuations is tested. With the exception only of the UK, only weak co-movement levels with R^2 figures ranging from 0.00 to 0.46 can be found. In case of the UK portfolio, Figure 6.2 reports an R^2 clearly above 0.5. However, we do not believe that the UK result indicates an undermining of the general finding, as the UK is the only portfolio which includes small-cap stocks. As a ratio which includes price information divided over book value, it is surprisingly clear that in the case of small caps such ratios of ratios (relative valuations) are very sensitive to price changes and hence co-move in greater amplitude to overall market sentiment and hence portfolio performance.

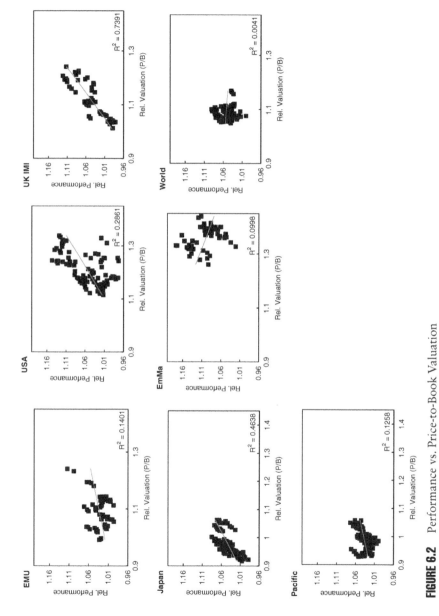

FIGURE 6.2 Performance vs. Price-to-Book Valuation
Source: Thomas Merz, MSc., Managing Director, UBS Asset Management, data per March 21, 2016

In order to limit a selection bias when looking only at a specific valuation ratio, the framework of Arnott et al. was extended, and we repeat the valuation analysis for all commonly used ratios. Indeed, we find that the selection of one single valuation seemed to be arbitrary when deriving a general conclusion regarding the potential co-movement of SRI performance with respective valuations.

As Table 6.6 reveals, in the UK case mentioned previously, three out of five tested valuation ratios report R^2 figures below 0.5. P/CE and PE in particular indicate that there is only a very weak relationship. In our view this illustrates that the choice of the valuation ratios can have a significant influence on the reported results. In particular, we do not find evidence that the performance of SRI portfolios can be explained by the innovation of valuation ratios and as a result of such a dependency, investors would be exposed to the risk of below-average returns as valuations revert to their long-run mean.

CONCLUSION

This chapter focuses on a new data sample of daily SRI-screened equity and bond portfolios across regions. It aims to address some of the controversial discussions around the benefits of investing in SRI-based portfolios

TABLE 6.6 R^2 from the Trend Regression Using Different Valuations

Rel. Valuation	Trend Regression R^2				
	P/B	P/CE	P/E	P/E Fwd	Yld
EMU[1]	0.1401	0.5327	0.0043	0.0704	0.0440
USA	0.2861	0.0328	0.2787	0.0630	0.1855
UK[1]	0.7391	0.1288	0.1482	0.5685	0.4911
Japan	0.4638	0.0383	0.0096	0.0128	0.0935
Emerging Markets[1]	0.0998	0.3737	0.1021	0.0222	0.4717
World	0.0041	0.0396	0.0162	0.1404	0.0005
Pacific	0.1258	0.0060	0.0151	0.0047	0.0116

Source: Thomas Merz, MSc., Managing Director, UBS Asset Management, data per March 21, 2016

Note:
[1] Index rules include a 5% issuer cap.

by using a new sample of daily return data from October 2007 through March 2016. The sample period includes a number of severe market corrections such as the financial crisis, the European Sovereign Crisis, and the implications of large-scale interventions from various central banks around the world and therefore seems to be a relevant sample to test the stated hypothesis. To test the hypothesis as to whether the SRI screening process in isolation adds value to an investor's portfolio, the analysis is limited to fully rules-based, highly transparent SRI-screened portfolios which can be easily added to an existing investment universe through index tracking solutions.

The main finding is that there are insignificant return differences between SRI-screened and conventional (non-screened) portfolios. Evidence wasn't found which would support the findings from a number of previous studies that restricted SRI portfolios leave investors with lower than expected levels of returns and higher levels of risk compared to unrestricted portfolios. In contrast, the results support the hypothesis that investors can expect higher risk-adjusted return levels vis-à-vis conventional portfolios, which confirms similar findings of a number of earlier studies where SRI alphas also were found to be insignificantly different from zero.

By looking at the results from the different regression models, it can be confirmed that SRI-screened portfolios have delivered positive but insignificant alphas vis-à-vis conventional exposures. This holds true for the single factor as well as for the extended, five-factor model, which corrects the alpha estimates for common equity factors. The results hold true also when price indices are considered, i.e. no dividends are reinvested. This indicates that even if non-SRI compliant companies compensate their value proposition for current and/or potential shareholders by increasing the level of dividend distributions, SRI-screened portfolios still deliver the same level of return with a lower level of risk, and hence the benefit of SRI screening remains intact.

The data sample also provided evidence that the return and risk results are robust when challenged with the relative valuation argument. No evidence was found that innovation in valuation ratios are closely linked with the performance of SRI portfolios. This consideration is very relevant because it also confirms that SRI-screened portfolios have produced higher risk-adjusted returns regardless of the cross-sectional change in valuations and hence, the present market sentiment. Based on the relative valuation tests, the results support the hypothesis, that investors can expect similar risk and return characteristics for SRI-screened portfolios out of sample.

CUSTOMIZED INDEXING

As smart beta strategies – as well as non-traditional benchmark indices – are gaining popularity, more and more alpha-generating factors are exploited in research papers. Meanwhile there are a few hundred factors which all claim to generate abnormal (positive) returns. In 2013, the trio of Harvey, Liu and Zhu composed an interesting research paper in which they studied 313 other papers which were focused on cross-sectional return patterns.[25]

Conspicuous in Figure 6.3 is the exponential slope of the number of factors and papers within the latest years. Factor investing, as many index providers call it too, has become quite popular. But with this quantity of factors comes a lot of data mining. Also an outperformance often disappears when the alpha factor has become public. Nevertheless, the sum of exploited factors has helped index issuers to huge growth. As more and more factors and thus different weighting schemes were discovered, the indexing industry developed suitable indices to participate in these factors.

One trend which will continue in the future is customized indexing. Here index providers such as MSCI, S&P or FTSE Russell develop indices for the individual needs of a client. Accordingly, asset managers, pension funds or insurance companies are no longer bound solely to the traditional, pre-assembled indices (and subsequently the ETFs) available on the market. The buy-side, as well as the sell-side of course, can create

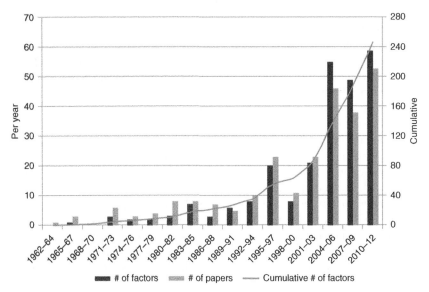

FIGURE 6.3   Increase in Factors and Papers
Source: Harvey, Liu, Zhu (2016)

their own customized index and get exactly the investment strategy or the exposure they want. The ability to implement industry-sector and even single security-level exclusions or inclusions allows investors to construct an index solution that is fully tailored and thus may exhibit a better, investor-focused, risk-return profile. Thanks to the ability to construct an individual benchmark, an investor is no longer forced to allocate its money towards off-the-shelf ETF/index offerings.

According to MSCI's webpage, MSCI is calculating more than 7,000 "customized indices" globally for over 700 clients. Around 70% of the indices can be launched within 48 hours, or at least in less than a week, depending on the simplicity or complexity. From an index provider's perspective, an important aspect of being competitive within the customized index area is how good or bad the modularity of their index offering and operations is. Inflexible, non-modular setups will need much more time and produce more internal costs than flexible, modular and scalable operational models.

However, investors should not necessarily call smart beta indices a customized index. A customized index is merely an individually created investable underlying, or better, an individually reshaped investment benchmark.

Customized Equity Indices

Thanks to the possibility of launching an individually designed index pretty fast and sometimes at relatively low cost nowadays, new investment ideas can be capitalized within a short time – actually in a few days. Also, existing benchmarks can be adjusted towards a more individual approach. In particular, concentration risks or sector overweightings could be bypassed by creating a customized equity index. Great examples of existing indices which are heavily influenced by a small group of (overweighted) stocks are the Nasdaq 100 Index and the Swiss Market Index (SMI). Both equity benchmarks are based on market capitalization which weight constituents based on the market value at which the stocks are currently trading. Hence an overexposure towards a few stocks is inevitable. However, equal-weighted indices could effectively avoid the risk of overly concentrated positions in highly valued stocks, which could easily occur in market cap-weighted indices. In the Nasdaq 100 Index, two stocks (Apple and Alphabet, the holding company of Google) count for 10%. Moreover, ten stocks represent nearly 50% of the index (see figure 6.4). One of the world's most concentrated equity benchmark is the Swiss Market Index. Three stocks count for 58% of the total index, and the famous consumer staples company Nestlé alone represents 22% or almost one quarter of the whole Swiss equity benchmark (see Figure 6.5). An equal-weighted index could reduce this concentration risk successfully.

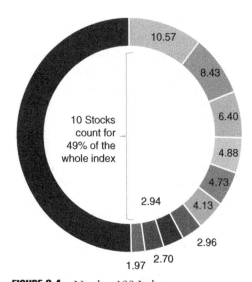

FIGURE 6.4 Nasdaq 100 Index
Data Source: Nasdaq, as of November 18, 2016

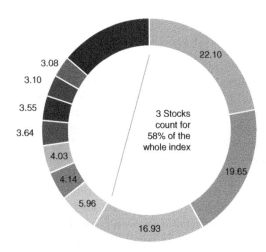

FIGURE 6.5 Swiss Market Index
Data Source: Bloomberg, Markit and BlackRock, as of November 18, 2016

Trend Plays

Further upcoming trends will be monetized by smart people within shorter time frames. The smaller and faster a company is, the higher the possibility of being the first mover, as decisions don't have to be accepted by various committees. However, customized indices on thematic investments face the risk of having no more than a "flavor of the month" appearance – and face no or tiny inflows after the specific investment trend is over. However, there are also some great examples of brilliant market timing. A perfect example is the U.S.-listed ETF (HACK) tracking the ISE Cyber Security Index. The index is effectively a customized basket of cyber security stocks. The index has been created in conjunction with PureFunds' founder Andrew Chanin, since he wanted to offer investors something which capitalizes on the increasing threats of cybercrime. What could be more fitting than putting some cyber security stocks together into an index? Just twelve days after the ETF started trading on the NYSE, entertainment giant Sony had to declare that hackers had stolen a huge amount of sensible client data – among them social security numbers. The following cyber security debate provided HACK with millions of dollars of net inflows. As of October 31, 2016 the fund's AuM is still at US$749 million, which reflects a gross management fee (0.75% TER) of roughly US$5.6 million – a huge success for a customized equity index, focused on a niche but trendy sector.

Customized Fixed-Income Indices

Also in the bond markets, customized indices and tailored benchmarks have become more and more fashionable. This can be a rewarding strategy as an ordinary fixed-income index is weighted by outstanding debt. This means that the more debt a company or country issues, the higher its weight in a bond index becomes. Shouldn't it be the other way round? Greece's debt crisis, which began in the year 2010, triggered a rethinking of traditional bond indices. In the light of deteriorating credit quality, portfolio managers and large institutional investors including sovereign wealth funds have been looking for alternative routes to tailor their sovereign debt exposures in order to avoid allocation to unstable or unwanted debt exposures. An example of how an off-the-shelf index and its ETF may influence the portfolio's concentration risk is the iShares Global Government Bond ETF. This exchange-traded fund tracks the performance of the Citigroup G7 Index. The two absolute most indebted countries globally, the United States and Japan, account for roughly 65% of the index. This is a classic concentration risk towards two debtor nations that many investors aren't aware of. Risk is not reduced even if the investors allocate money towards Government bonds – but increased due to focus on just two nation's debt securities.

Here is the opportunity for customized (smart beta) indices to deliver added-value. One established and easy strategy to reduce the pro-cyclicality and concentration risk is GDP weighting. This approach defines a country's weight in an index by its gross domestic product's growth and so offers a smarter way because it is more tied to a country's economic fundamentals. As emerging markets are usually growing faster than the well-established developed markets, they usually have a higher allocation in a GDP-weighted strategy. They also often (but not always) have lower debt levels and thus lower leverage. Another pro is the fact that concentrating on GDP growth is more forward-looking than debt-weighting. No one can say if the debt markets in the past will be the important markets in the future. A GDP-weighted customized index can also be a good complementary strategy to a classic pro-cyclical fixed-income investment as bond prices are usually moving in the inverse direction to GDP growth. So if a country's economy is expanding, an investment will be taken counter-cyclical and provide value.

As an example, Research Affiliates, a well-known index engineering company, uses more than one valuation measure to define its index allocation. For them, a country's ability to repay debt is most important. This measure is highly correlated with a country's economic size, measured by population, GDP, energy consumption and rescaled land area.[26]

Based on the corporate bond indices, the relevant factors are different to the global sovereign bond indices. For the Citi RAFI World Corporate Investment-Grade Bond Index, cash flow and adjusted assets have been chosen as the basis for the fundamental size of a company's debt service capacity. Cash flow is a direct measure of the funds available to service debt. Adjusted assets are a measure of the value supporting the contingent claim underlying the long term debt issues. Relative to capitalization-weighted indices, cash flow weighting generally tilts an index towards higher debt coverage, and adjusted assets weighting lowers an index's aggregate leverage.[27] Thanks to the possibilities with customized indices, certain regions or debtors (indicated by debt ratios, for example) can also be excluded in the individually designed index. Also, depending on built-in rules-based rebalancing cycles, the index constituents could be adjusted in certain frequencies. This might be necessary especially when debt levels are changing (certain issuers increasing their debt, for example). In this way, the investor's assets are always only exposed to debt securities that fit into the predefined criteria. In customized fixed-income strategies, it is as important as in customized equities indices to understand the weighting scheme and know the figures of the index. Besides the top constituents, in customized bond indices it is essential to have a look at the duration, credit risk and country/sector allocation of the desired strategy.

More recently, in spring 2016 for example, the turmoil in U.S. energy bonds are a good example of sector exposures that investors wish to avoid under certain circumstances – or play specifically as part of the satellite, alpha-generating investments. Hence a customized U.S. energy bond index would have made sense for investors who want to get specific exposure to a sector when it is distressed and therefore significantly discounted. On the other side, customized fixed-income sector indices are a brilliant opportunity to exclude certain (predefined) industries like defense, gambling or deep-sea drilling. Remembering the Deep Horizon oil spill, a blunt disaster caused by energy companies BP and Transocean, it might be appropriate for some investors, especially pension trusts and large endowments, to stay away from securities of certain risk-bearing or unethical sectors. A customized index could be designed to avoid such sectors strictly.

Customized Commodities Indices

As the indexing industry is focusing on equities and fixed-income, one important asset class must not be missed out – commodities. However, the world of commodities indices is somewhat more complex. As already mentioned at the beginning of this book, most commodity indices and their associated ETFs are exposed to future contracts. A future contract has an expiration date. Hence it must be replaced from time to time. This means the curve risk is inherent: this risk is caused by replacing and re-weighting the commodity futures that comprise the specific index. The replacement will generate a profit or loss to the investor, the so-called "roll return" that will be reflected in the level of the indices. This return will be affected if the prices of the relevant longer-dated contracts are higher (or lower) than the prices of the shorter-dated contracts. If the prices of the relevant longer-dated contracts are more expensive than the prices of the shorter-dated contracts, then the roll return will generally be negative, and the so-called "contango" will occur (as mentioned previously). Conversely, if the prices of the relevant longer-dated contracts are cheaper than the prices of the shorter-dated contracts then the roll return will generally be positive ("backwardation"). The contango/backwardation effect will affect the performance of the commodity index accordingly: in a positive or negative way, whenever the underlying futures are replaced.

Another relevant topic when it comes to commodities indices is the bias towards a specific commodity or commodity group – energy, for example. Prominent broad-based benchmarks such as the S&P Goldman Sachs Commodity Index include over 56% exposure to energy commodities. WTI Crude as single commodity exposure influences the price movements pretty largely, with a weight of 22.8%. The second largest index constituent is Brent Crude with 16.4%. This strong bias is favorable for the performance contribution if energy performs well but a disaster if the price for crude oil suffers. A customized index, for example with equal-weighted commodities, could be an appropriate way to reduce such obvious risks. Additionally, investors have the possibility to design a customized index, which deviates from the classic futures roll mechanism.

Also, in commodities there are some opportunities to gather an advanced risk-adjusted return compared to a market capitalization weighted index. One possibility is the adjustment of the roll date and contract compared to the Goldman Sachs Commodity Index (GSCI). Another popular investment strategy is the optimization of the futures curve, which means reducing the losses based on contango and increasing the profits from backwardation. The WisdomTree Enhanced Commodity UCITS ETF (WCOA) is an example of this particular smart beta approach. It tracks the Optimized Roll Commodity Total Return index and lowers the costs of holding commodities long term. Another example is Ossiam, a French ETF issuer, part of Natixis Global Asset Management. The company has launched a risk-weighted smart beta commodity ETF. The Ossiam Risk Weighted Enhanced Commodity ex Grains ETF uses the components of the GSCI, but weights them based on their historical volatility over the last year, which means that commodities with a lower volatility get a higher weighting in the index. This reduces the high allocation to the energy sector in the index and calls to mind the minimum volatility approach in equity smart beta strategies.

NOTES

1. 2016 Preqin Global Hedge Fund Report
2. Financial Times, 2016
3. Credit Suisse Mid-Year Survey of Hedge Fund Investor Sentiment, Summer 2016
4. This section is contributed by Thomas Merz, Managing Director, UBS Asset Management
5. Alliance, G. S. I. Global Sustainable Investment Review 2014, February 2015, www.gsi-alliance.org. The report includes professionally managed assets in all the regions covered by Global Sustainable Investment Association member organizations, incl. public and private investments that consider environmental, social and governance (ESG) factors in portfolio selection and management
6. SSF 2015 Annual Report (www.sustainablefinance.ch) and Sustainable Investments in Switzerland (Excerpt from the Sustainable Investment Market Report 2016, http://www.forum-ng.org/de/fng/aktivitaeten/836-ueberdurchschnittliche-zuwaechse-bei-nachhaltigen-geldanlagen-in-deutschland-oesterreich-und-der-schweiz.html)
7. Bauer, Koedijk and Otten, 2005
8. Moskowitz, 1972
9. Hamilton, Jo and Statman, 1993
10. See for example Diltz, 1995, Guerard, 1997 and Sauer, 1997 for early references
11. Geczy, Stambaugh and Levin, 2005
12. Among others, Derwall, Koedijk and ter Horst, 2011 and Auer and Schuhmacher, 2016
13. Statman, 2000

14. Goldreyer and Diltz, 1999
15. Luther, Matatko and Corner, 1992
16. Luther and Matatko, 1994 and Mallin, Saadouni and Briston, 1995
17. DiBartolomeo, 1996
18. Kurtz, 1997
19. Domini 400 Social Index was launched in May 1990. Today, MSCI KLD 400 Social Index is part of the MSCI index family, index details available via: https://www.msci.com/documents/10199/904492e6-527e-4d64-9904-c710bf1533c6
20. Renneboog, ter Horst and Zhang, 2008
21. Bello, 2005, Hong and Kacperczyk, 2009 and Stratman and Glushkov, 2009
22. Renneboog, ter Horst and Zhang, 2006 and 2008
23. Garz, Volk and Gilles, 2002
24. Arnott et al., 2016
25. Harvey, Liu and Zhu, 2014
26. Research Affiliates, Index Methodology of the Citi RAFI Sovereign Developed Markets Bond Index Series
27. Research Affiliates, Index Methodology, https://www.yieldbook.com/f/m/pdf/citi_indices/Citi_RAFI_corp_20140404_v11.pdf

Glossary

12B-1 Fee This is an annually charged fee that the holders of mutual funds have to pay indirectly to the fund company for their marketing and sales activities. The fee is usually paid to the broker for selling the fund shares to investors. The fee is automatically charged from the fund's assets. The fee is not limited by the SEC but under FINRA rules it cannot exceed 0.75% of a fund's average net assets per year.

Active Management The process of discretionary selecting securities with the purpose of trying to outperform a benchmark index. Active portfolio managers use economic data, investment research, market forecasts and other indicators to help them make their investment decisions.

Alpha A statistical measure of performance. Alpha reflects the amount by which a mutual fund or portfolio outperforms or underperforms. Positive alpha means a portfolio's performance was higher compared to its corresponding benchmark index. Negative alpha means a portfolio's performance was lower compared to its index.

Ask Price The price at which a security is offered for sale, which is effectively a fund's NAV (for no-load funds). The opposite of the ask price is the bid price.

Asset Allocation The process of apportioning investments among various asset classes, such as stocks, bonds, commodities, real estate, collectibles and cash equivalents. Asset allocation affects both the risk and return of investors, and is often used as a core strategy in basic financial planning.

Asset Class Refers to the categorization of an asset. Representative asset classes include equities, bonds, commodities, etc.

Authorized Participants This term refers to large financial institutions, such as specialist firms and market makers, which are involved in the creation and redemption activity of ETF shares.

Basis Point Measurement used to quote bonds. One basis point is equal to 0.01%, or one one-hundredth of one percent. 100 basis points is equal to 1%, whereas 50 basis points would equal one half percent, or 0.50%.

Basket A unit or group of securities. The grouping of securities within an ETF is sometimes referred to as a basket.

Benchmark A benchmark is a yardstick or standard for measuring the performance of an investment. For example, the Barclays Capital U.S. Aggregate Bond index is a popular benchmark for judging the performance of diversified taxable bond mutual funds. The goal of most money managers and investors is to outperform their respective benchmark.

Beta Beta is a volatility measurement of a stock mutual fund or ETF versus a comparable benchmark like the S&P 500 stock index. A stock fund or ETF with a higher beta than the S&P 500 will rise or fall to a greater degree. In contrast, a stock fund or ETF with a low beta will rise or fall less.

Bid-Ask Spread The bid-ask spread is essentially the price difference between the highest price that a buyer is willing to pay for an asset (bid price) and the lowest price that a seller is willing to accept to sell it (ask price).

Blue Chips Blue chip stocks are regarded as leading companies with high market capitalizations and with world-class products and services, universally recognizable brands and run by top-notch management teams.

Bond A debt instrument issued by corporations and governments to raise capital. Interest on the outstanding debt is paid to bondholders at specific intervals, with the principal amount of the loan paid on the bond maturity date.

Breakpoints Mutual funds with front-end loads, or a sales charge, enable investors to reduce front-end sales charges as the amount of that investment increases to certain levels called "breakpoints". Each prospectus will have details on the breakpoints used to reduce the front-end sales charge.

Call Option A call option gives its owner the right (not the obligation) to buy a predetermined quantity of stock or commodities from the seller at a specified price (strike price) within a certain time frame (expiration date).

Chicago Board Options Exchange (CBOE) Founded in 1973, the CBOE changed options trading by creating standardized listed stock options. Prior to this time, the trading of options was largely unregulated. The CBOE lists options on interest rates, individual stocks and various market indexes. The exchange is located in downtown Chicago, IL.

Closed-End Fund Closed-end funds issue a fixed number of shares through an initial public offering and often use leverage to magnify their performance. Closed-end funds are bought and sold just like stocks and their share price often trades at a noticeable discount or premium to the fund's net asset value.

Closet Index Fund An actively managed fund that closely mimics the volatility and performance of an index fund.

Commission Transaction fee paid to a broker for executing a securities trade. Commission amounts vary and are often dependent on the size of trade, the frequency of trades and sometimes the size of the brokerage account. Discount brokers tend to charge lower commissions for trades versus full service brokers.

Commodity Indexes Indexes that measure either the price or performance of physical commodities, or the price of commodities as represented by the price of futures contracts listed on commodity exchanges.

Contrarian Describes an investor that believes and does the exact opposite of what the majority of investors are doing at any given moment. For example, contrarians might perceive value in a stock or industry sector that is out of favor or has performed poorly. While many investors are inclined to avoid unpopular investments, contrarians are likely to invest in these areas with the expectation of an eventual rebound or change in market sentiment.

Counterparty Risk   Counterparty risk is the risk that an institution defaults and fails to pay on a credit derivative, a credit default swap, insurance contract, a trade or a another financial transaction. ETFs that use swaps or derivatives may be exposed to counterparty risk. ETNs too are subject to counterparty risk because they rely on the creditworthiness of the issuing financial institution.

Creation Unit   The smallest block of shares in an exchange-traded fund that can be purchased or redeemed directly from the fund company at net asset value. Creation units are usually transacted in 50,000 share increments, making them large dollar transactions limited to large institutions and other authorized participants. Instead of receiving cash, the seller of a creation unit would receive a basket of securities that corresponds to the portfolio holdings in a particular ETF. This "in-kind" transfer process is unique to ETF's and does not create tax consequences for the seller.

Custodian   A financial institution that safeguards the investor's securities and other assets.

Deferred Sales Charge   A sales charge deducted from an investment for exiting early, or before the sales charge ceases to exist. Mutual fund class B and C shares often carry a deferred sales charge. Also called back-end load, CDSC or contingent deferred sales charge.

Discount to NAV   A mutual fund, closed-end fund or ETF whose share price is lower than the fund's NAV. The occurrence of significant premiums or discounts with ETFs is rare, whereas with closed-end funds it is common.

Dividend   Distribution of earnings paid out to shareholders. With mutual funds and ETFs, dividends can be a result of capital gains, interest income or dividends paid to the fund itself by securities within the portfolio. Dividends are often paid quarterly, but the frequency can be less and is determined by fund management.

Dividend Yield   The distribution rate of a fund calculated by dividing the amount of the dividends per share by the per share market price of the fund. For example, a fund price of $20 that pays a $2 dividend per year has a 10% dividend yield.

Dow Jones Industrial Average (DJIA)   The DJIA is a widely followed index that is used as a barometer of stock market performance. This stock index is based upon 30 major companies, or components in diversified industries, such as banking, consumer staples, retail, healthcare and technology.

Efficient Market Hypothesis (EMH)   The Efficient Market Hypothesis (EMH) dissuades investors from using fundamental research to find undervalued or mispriced securities. The central idea is that market prices already reflect the full knowledge of investors, which makes it impossible to outperform the market.

Emerging Markets   Refers to the economy or capital markets of developing nations, which are often new, unestablished or have a limited history.

Exchange-Traded Commodity (ETC)   Commodity ETFs (ETCs) invest in commodities, such as precious metals and/or commodities futures. Among the first commodity ETFs were gold exchange-traded funds, which have been offered in a number of countries. In Europe, ETF Securities is pioneer in the commodity ETC space.

Exchange-Traded Fund (ETF) ETFs or exchange-traded funds are low-cost index funds that trade like stocks. ETFs offer intraday liquidity, meaning that they can be bought or sold when the stock market is open for trading. Generally, ETFs are very tax-efficient and have lower annual expenses compared to closed-end funds and active mutual funds. ETFs cover a broad spectrum of assets including stocks, bonds, currencies, real estate and commodities. ETFs can be sold short, leveraged with margin, hedged with call/put options or bought and held.

Exchange-Traded Note (ETN) ETNs or exchange-traded notes are unsecured debt securities that pay a return linked to the performance of a single security or index. ETNs do not usually pay a dividend or annual coupon and they have maturity dates that can range up to 30 years. ETNs held to maturity pay the return of the note's underlying index minus its annual expense ratio. ETNs are subject to counterparty risk, meaning that the creditworthiness of the financial issuer can impact the note's final return and value.

Exchange-Traded Product (ETP) A type of security that is derivatively priced and which trades intraday on a national securities exchange. Exchange-traded products are derivatively priced, where the value is derived from other investment instruments such as a commodity, currency, share price or interest rate. Generally, exchange-traded products are benchmarked to stocks, commodities or indices or they can be actively managed funds. Exchange-traded products include ETFs, exchange-traded vehicles (ETVs), ETNs and certificates.

Expense Ratio The expense ratio of a mutual fund or ETF covers the cost of investment management, legal and administrative expenses, 12b-1 marketing fees and other associated expenses. The expense ratio does not include performance fees and the cost of acquiring a fund, such as commissions or sales loads, and it is expressed as a percentage of the fund's average daily net assets.

FCA The Financial Conduct Authority is the London-headquartered conduct regulator for more than 56,000 financial services firms and financial markets in the United Kingdom and the prudential regulator for over 24,000 of those firms.

FINRA The Financial Industry Regulatory Authority (FINRA) is a self-regulatory organization that oversees the market regulation of all securities firms doing business in the United States. FINRA was created in 2007 through the consolidation of the National Association of Securities Dealers (NASD) with the member regulation, enforcement and arbitration divisions of the New York Stock Exchange.

Front-End Load A sales commission (other than a 12-1b fee) charged at the time of purchase of mutual funds and other investment units.

Fundamental Indexing Fundamental indexing uses a company's fundamentals such as sales, profits, book value, revenues and dividends to determine its weighting within an index. Some fundamental indexes use a multi-factor approach whereas others use one key factor.

Fund Flows Describes the money flow into or out of mutual funds and ETFs.

Fund of Funds Investment strategy that seeks to diversify risk exposure and manager style among various fund managers. Potential pitfalls include a lack of transparency and an added layer of fees. This strategy is popular with hedge fund investors looking to diversify risk among various fund groups.

Fund Overlap Fund overlap refers to the duplication in owning two or more ETFs or mutual funds that have the same identical securities and/or underlying investment strategy. Investors are effectively paying twice for double work. They pay one fund company to execute an investment strategy and then they pay again to a competing fund to do the exact same work.

Grantor Trust This type of fund structure distributes dividends directly to shareholders and allows investors to retain their voting rights on the underlying securities within the fund. The original fund components of the index remain fixed and this ETF structure is not registered under the SEC Investment Company Act of 1940. Merrill Lynch's HOLDRs follow this format.

Growth and Income Fund A mutual fund, closed-end fund or ETF with both the growth of capital and income as the primary investment objective.

Growth Fund A mutual fund, closed-end fund or ETF with the growth of capital as the primary investment objective.

Hedging A strategy used to reduce financial risk or the possibility of loss. For example, an investor owning 100 shares of an S&P 500 stock fund could hedge that long position by owning a short position or put options on the S&P 500 Index.

Income Fund A mutual fund, closed-end fund or ETF that has generating income as the primary investment objective. Income can be derived from various sources, including interest payments, dividends and capital gains.

Index A statistical measure used to track the aggregate performance of stock, bond and commodities markets. Widely followed indexes include those developed and managed by Standard & Poor's, Dow Jones Indices, the NYSE, Nasdaq, Russell, MSCI or STOXX and FTSE Russell.

Index Fund A type of mutual fund or ETF that attempts to match the performance of a stock, bond or commodity index. Index funds are sometimes referred to as passive funds and are notorious for their tax efficiency and low fees. Some index funds follow traditional market cap indexes whereas others follow an equal weight or fundamental indexing approach.

Indexing Investment strategy that seeks to match the exact performance of a specific market or benchmark index.

Index Options Calls and puts on stock or bond indexes. Index options allow investors to trade a particular market sector or index of securities, without having to make individual purchases of each security in that sector. Index options are listed on various exchanges, including the American, New York and Chicago Board Options Exchange.

Inverse ETFs (please see Short ETFs)

Investment Company Act of 1940 The U.S. Investment Company Act of 1940 regulates the organization of companies, including mutual funds that engage primarily in investing and trading in securities. The Act requires these companies to disclose their financial condition and investment policies to investors on a regular and timely basis.

Investment-Grade   Bonds whose issuers are rated AAA to BBB for safety and ability to repay principal by Standard & Poor's, Fitch Ratings or Moody's Investors Service.

Investment Style   Indicates the approach of an investment manager in selecting securities. For example, a certain manager may be value-oriented by emphasizing companies with low P/E or book-to-value ratios, whereas another may emphasize earnings and profit growth.

Large Cap   A large company or large-cap stock generally refers to companies with a market capitalization or size over $5 billion.

Leverage   Margin and use of option contracts are forms of leverage which allow investors to enhance their returns without adding to their investments.

Leveraged ETFs   The main objective of leveraged ETFs is to deliver magnified performance of a particular stock, bond or commodity index. Most leveraged ETFs attempt to duplicate daily index returns by two or three times. Short leveraged ETFs aim for daily index returns that move in the opposite direction, but with magnified performance of two or three times.

Liquidity   Liquidity refers to the ability to convert an asset to cash without substantially affecting its price. Assets that are quickly converted to cash have good liquidity, whereas those that take time are less liquid. The liquidity of an ETF is best determined by the liquidity of the securities in its underlying stock, bond or commodity index along with the trading volume and assets under management of the ETF itself. General market conditions are another secondary factor which can influence an ETF's liquidity.

Load Fund   A type of mutual fund that charges a sales fee either when fund shares are bought (front-end load) or sold (back-end load).

Market Capitalization   The market capitalization of a corporation is the measurement of the company's stock market value based upon the company's number of outstanding shares multiplied by its current share price.

Mid-Cap   A mid-sized company or mid-cap stock generally refers to companies with a market capitalization or size between $1 billion and $5 billion.

MSCI   MSCI calculates and distributes index and company-level data and also licenses the MSCI indexes to third parties for the purposes of creating mutual funds, ETFs, OTC derivatives and other financial products.

Municipal Bond   Municipal bonds or "munis" are debt issued by city, state and local governments to finance various projects. Bond proceeds are typically used by local governments to construct or maintain highways, hospitals and schools. The interest income paid by municipal bonds is free from federal income tax and in many cases exempt from state and local taxes as well.

NASDAQ   National Association of Securities Dealers Automated Quotations is a computerized system that quotes securities traded over the counter and on other exchanges.

Net Asset Value (NAV)   Represents the per share price of a mutual fund. With closed-end funds and ETFs, the true NAV is not always reflected in the share price of the security because it may trade at a premium or discount to the NAV.

The calculation of the NAV is the fund's total net assets divided by the number of shares outstanding, minus fees and expenses.

Open-End Fund   See Mutual Fund.

Open-End Index Fund   This type of fund structure reinvests dividends the date of receipt and pays them out via a quarterly cash distribution. This ETF structure is also permitted to use derivatives and loan securities and is registered under the SEC Investment Company Act of 1940. ETFs that utilize this legal structure include iShares and the Select Sector SPDRs.

Over the Counter (OTC)   Over-the-counter trading is conducted by market makers in the OTC Bulletin Board (OTCBB) and Pink Sheets securities using interdealer quote services like the Pink Quote and the OTCBB. OTC stocks are not usually listed or traded on a stock exchange, although exchange-listed stocks can be traded in the OTC market.

Passive Management   A market strategy that involves selecting a benchmark index to assure investment performance is the same as the underlying index. Passive investing assures that an investor will not underperform (or outperform) a market index. Passive management is the opposite of active management.

Performance Drag   A reduction of portfolio performance due to various factors. An example of performance drag occurs when gains within a portfolio are offset by various expenses, such as management fees, transaction costs and taxes. These expenses create a drag or negative effect on the portfolio's performance.

Portfolio Turnover   Portfolio turnover measures the frequency by which securities within a mutual fund or ETF are bought and sold. Turnover is determined by the dollar value of buys or sells (whichever is less) during a year divided by the total assets in the fund. For example, a mutual fund with $200 million in assets that has $100 million of sales and $100 million worth of purchases (using the same proceeds) during the year would have a 50% turnover rate, indicating an average holding period of two years. A portfolio turnover of 100% signifies that a fund manager has sold the fund's entire portfolio and bought new holdings during the course of a year. High portfolio turnover translates into higher investment costs, whereas low portfolio turnover is better because it lessens the impact of trading and tax-related expenses.

Premium to NAV   A mutual fund, closed-end fund or ETF whose share price is higher than the fund's NAV. The occurrence of significant premiums or discounts with ETFs is rare, whereas with closed-end funds it is common.

Prospectus   Required by securities laws and issued by mutual fund companies and ETFs, the prospectus is a legal document that discloses the investment objectives of the fund, operating history, fund management, management fees, portfolio holdings and other related financial data. Brokers are required to give a prospectus to investors before they invest.

Put Option   A put option gives its owner the right (not obligation) to sell a predetermined quantity of stock or commodities at a specified price (strike price) within a certain time frame (expiration date).

Redemption   A redemption is the return of an investor's principal in a fixed-income security, such as a bond, or the sale of units in a mutual fund. Fund shares will be redeemed at the NAV. A redemption in a fund could be associated with a fee.

RIA An abbreviation for Registered Investment Advisor. This person is registered either with the state/states where they do business or the SEC and is licensed to act as discretionary and/or non-discretionary asset manager. The threshold for a SEC registration of a RIA is $100 million in assets under management. RIAs with assets below that level shall be registered with the state in which they are active.

R-Squared R-squared measures the correlation of a fund's movement in comparison to its corresponding benchmark. An R-squared score of 1.00 would indicate a perfect correlation, whereas a score of 0.00 indicates no correlation. Whereas correlation measures the link between any two securities, R-squared measures one security against a set benchmark or index.

Sector Rotation An investment strategy that uses elements of market timing to identify industry sectors of the economy ready to outperform. Conversely, a sector rotation strategy would likely avoid or underweight industry sectors that are expected to lag the rest of the market.

Securities and Exchange Commission (SEC) A federal agency created by the Securities Exchange Act of 1934 with the primary mission of protecting investors and maintaining the integrity of the securities markets. The SEC has five Commissioners who are appointed by the President of the United States with the advice and consent of the Senate. Their terms last five years and are staggered so that one Commissioner's term ends on June 5 of each year.

Share Classes Some mutual funds use multiple share classes for the same underlying portfolio. For example, investors that buy A shares pay an upfront sales charge to enter a fund, whereas a class B share would defer the sales charge. Some mutual fund families like Vanguard offer their ETFs as an additional share class of existing index mutual funds.

Sharpe Ratio A measure of a fund's historical returns adjusted for risk or volatility, that is the average return earned in excess of the risk-free rate per unit of volatility. The calculation is fund return minus the return on 3-month Treasury bills divided by the fund standard deviation.

Short ETFs The main objective of short ETFs is to deliver inverse or opposite performance to a particular stock, bond or commodity index. Most short ETFs attempt to duplicate daily index returns in the opposite direction. Some short ETFs aim for daily index returns in the opposite direction but with leverage or magnified performance.

Small Cap A small company or small cap stock generally refers to companies with a market capitalization between $250 million and $1 billion.

Smart Beta This is an investment style where the investor passively follows an index designed to take advantage of perceived systematic biases or inefficiencies in the market. A smart beta index is a modified version (for example, U.S. Equities Minimum Volatility Index) of a common benchmark index (for example, the S&P 500 Index). Smart beta-inspired indices are also known as factor indices.

Style Box The investment style box is a visual tool that classifies mutual funds and ETFs by the size (large, mid or small) of stocks that a fund holds along with the investment style of stocks (value, growth or blend) that it holds. The style box has nine investment categories or styles and was developed by Morningstar.

Style Drift Style drift happens when a fund diverts from its prospectus-defined investment strategy to pursue another course.

Target Date Fund A type of mutual fund or ETF that automatically adjusts its mix of stocks, bonds and other assets based upon a specified year or target date. Typically, a target date fund will reduce its exposure to stocks as it approaches its planned target date and maintain a fixed allocation for the remainder of time.

Ticker Symbol The lettering system used to identify a stock, mutual fund or ETF on an exchange. Also called trading symbols.

Total Return Total return is the amount of value an investor earns from a security over a specific period, typically one year, when all distributions like interests and dividends are reinvested. Total return is expressed as a percentage of the amount invested.

Treasury Inflation Protected Securities (TIPS) TIPS are U.S. government debt indexed to inflation. The principal of a TIPS either increases with inflation or decreases with deflation, as measured by the Consumer Price Index. At maturity you are paid the adjusted principal or original principal, whichever is greater. TIPS pay interest twice a year, at a fixed rate. The rate is applied to the adjusted principal; so, like the principal, interest payments rise with inflation and fall with deflation.

Unit Investment Trust This type of fund structure does not reinvest dividends in the fund and pays them out via a quarterly cash distribution. In order to comply with diversification rules, this ETF structure will sometimes deviate from the exact composition of a benchmark index. This type of fund is registered under the SEC Investment Company Act of 1940. The Dow DIAMONDS (DIA), PowerShares QQQ (QQQQ), and the S&P 500 SPDRs (SPY) follow this product format.

Volatility Volatility is determined by the price movement (rise or fall) of a security. Securities that experience sharp increases or declines within a short time frame are considered more volatile than those that do not (see Beta)

Volume Total number of shares or contracts traded on a security. Volume data is tracked and reported daily by major stock exchanges around the world.

Year-To-Date (YTD) The period beginning at the start of the calendar year up until the most current date.

Yield Curve A graph that illustrates the relationship between the yields of bonds with the same credit quality, but with varying maturities. A positive yield curve means short-term interest rates are lower versus long term rates. A negative yield curve is just the opposite, whereas a flat yield curve shows little variance in the yields of short-term bonds and long term bonds.

Zero Coupon Bond A zero coupon bond is bought at a discounted price to its face value and the principal is repaid at the bond's maturity date. Unlike conventional bonds which make semi-annual payments, zero coupon bonds do not make periodic interest payments. U.S. Treasury bills, U.S. savings bonds and any other bond that has been stripped of its coupons are all examples of zero coupon bonds. Investors earn a return from zero coupon bonds after compounding interest is paid at maturity plus the difference between the discounted price of the zero bond and its par or redemption value.

References

Anson, M. (2008) The beta continuum: From classic beta to bulk beta. *Journal of Portfolio Management*, 34(2), 53–64.

Arnott, R., Kalesnik, V., Moghtader, P. and Scholl, C. (2014) Beyond cap weight: The empirical evidence for a diversified beta. *Journal of Indexes*, Jan/Feb, 16–29.

Arnott, R., Beck, N., Kalesnik, V. and West, J. (2016) How Can 'Smart Beta' Go Horribly Wrong?

Asness, C., Krail, R. and Liew, J. (2001) Do hedge funds hedge? *Journal of Portfolio Management*, 28(1), 28–32.

Auer, B. R. and Schuhmacher, F. (2015) Do socially (ir)responsible investments pay? New evidence from international ESG data. *The Quarterly Review of Economics and Finance*, 59(C), 51–62.

Banz, R. W. (1981) The relationship between return and market value of common stocks. *Journal of Financial Economics*, 9(1), 3–18.

Bauer, R., Koedijk, K. and Otten, R. (2005) International evidence on ethical mutual fund performance and investment style. *Journal of Banking and Finance*, 29(7), 1751–1767.

Bello, Z. Y. (2005) Socially responsible investing and portfolio diversification. *Journal of Financial Research*, 28(1), 41–57.

Bienkowski, N. (2013) 10 Years On. The Gold ETF that Spawned a $200 Billion Industry. *Alchemist*, 7, 14–17.

Blocher, J. A. and Whaley, R. E. (2015) Passive Investing: The Role of Securities Lending. Owen Graduate School of Management, Vanderbilt University.

Bogle Financial Markets Research Centre (2006) Mutual funds: Trading practices and abuses that harm investors. Hearing of Senate, November 3, 2003. https://www.vanguard.com/bogle_site/sp20031103_2.html

Cahart, M. M. (1997) On persistence in mutual fund performance. *The Journal of Finance*, 52(1), 57–82.

Chaves, D. B. and Arnott, R. D. (2012) Rebalancing and the value effect. *Journal of Portfolio Management*, 38(4), 59–74. https://papers.ssrn.com/sol3/papers.cfm?abstract_id=1982735.

Cochrane, J. H. (2011) Presidential address: Discount rates. *Journal of Finance*, 66(4), 1047–1108.

Cogent Research (2016) The Pull of Active Management – Examining the Use of Active vs. Passive Strategies in the Institutional Marketplace.

De Bondt, W. F. M. and Thaler, R. (1985) Does the stock market overreact? *The Journal of Finance*, 40(3), Papers and Proceedings of the Forty-Third Annual

Meeting American Finance Association, Dallas, Texas, December 28–30, 1984, 793–805.

Derwall, J., Guenster, N., Bauer, R. and Koedijk, K. (2005) The eco-efficiency premium puzzle. *Financial Analysts Journal*, 61(2), 51–63.

Derwall, J., Koedijk, K. and ter Horst, J. (2011) A tale of values-driven and profit-seeking social investors. *Journal of Banking and Finance*, 35(8), 2137–2147.

DiBartolomeo, D. (1996). Explaining and controlling the returns on socially screened US equity portfolios. Presentation to New York Society of Security Analysts, September 10.

Dillon Eustace (2009) Exchange Traded Funds and the UCITS Framework. Dublin.

Diltz, J. D. (1995) Does social screening affect portfolio performance? *The Journal of Investing*, 4(1), 64–69.

Dow Jones Indexes (2011) Introduction to the Dow Jones Volatility Risk Control Indexes. https://www.djindexes.com/mdsidx/downloads/analytics_and_research/Dow_Jones_Volatility_Risk_Control_Indexes_White_Paper.pdf.

Fama, E. (1970) Efficient capital markets: A review of theory and empirical work. *Journal of Finance*, 25, S383–417.

Fama, E. and French, K. (1992) The cross-section of expected stock returns. *Journal of Finance*, 47(2), 427–465.

Fama, E. and French, K. (1993) Common risk factors in the returns on stocks and bonds. *Journal of Financial Economics*, 33(1), 3–56.

Financial Times (2016) Hedge funds: Overpriced, underperforming. May 24. https://www.ft.com/content/9bd1150e-1b76-11e6-b286-cddde55ca122.

Garcia-Zarate, J. (2016) Conceptual simplicity of physical replication has won over investors. FT Adviser, October 17. https://www.ftadviser.com/opinion/2016/10/17/conceptual-simplicity-of-physical-replication-has-won-over-investors/.

Garz, H., Volk, C. and Gilles, M. (2002) More Gain than Pain, SRI: Sustainability Pays Off. WestLB Panmure.

Geczy, C., Stambaugh, R. F. and Levin, D. (2005) Investing in socially responsible mutual funds. Available at SSRN 416380.

Giese, G. (2012) Optimal design of risk control strategy indexes.

Global Sustainable Investment Alliance (2015) Global Sustainable Investment Review 2014.

Goldreyer, E. F. and Diltz, J. D. (1999) The performance of socially responsible mutual funds: incorporating sociopolitical information in portfolio selection. *Managerial Finance*, 25(1), 23–36.

Guerard, J. B. (1997) Is there a cost to being socially responsible in investing? *The Journal of Investing*, 6(2), 11–18.

Hamilton, S., Jo, H. and Statman, M. (1993) Doing well while doing good? The investment performance of socially responsible mutual funds. *Financial Analysts Journal*, 49(6), 62–66.

Harvey, C. R., Liu, Y. and Zhu, H. (2014) … and the cross-section of expected returns. *The Review of Financial Studies*, 29(1), 5–68. https://faculty.fuqua.duke.edu/~charvey/Research/Published_Papers/P118_and_the_cross.PDF.

Haugen, R. and Baker, N. (1991) The efficient market inefficiency of capitalization-weighted stock portfolios. *Journal of Portfolio Management*, 17, 35–40.

Hong, H. and Kacperczyk, M. (2009) The price of sin: The effects of social norms on markets. *Journal of Financial Economics*, 93(1), 15–36.

Hsu, J. and Kalesnik, V. (2014) Finding smart beta in the factor zoo. https://www .researchaffiliates.com/en_us/publications/articles/223_finding_smart_beta_in_ the_factor_zoo.html.

Jones, B. (2012) Rethinking Portfolio Construction and Risk Mangement. Deutsche Bank.

Kinnel, R. (2016) Predictive power of fees: Why mutual fund fees are so important. Morningstar, May.

Kula, A. (2015) Optimized Indexing combined with Risk Overlay: Analysis and Empirical Test of Margrabe's Exchange Option. http://papers.ssrn.com/sol3/ papers.cfm?abstract_id=2657190.

Kula, G. and Stahn, S. (2015) Next generation of indexing: Combining optimized indexing with dynamic beta management. http://papers.ssrn.com/sol3/papers .cfm?abstract_id=2513407.

Kurtz, L. (1997) No effect, or no net effect? Studies on socially responsible investing. *The Journal of Investing*, 6(4), 37–49.

Levi, Y. and Welch, I. (2014) Long-term capital budgeting. http://papers.ssrn.com/ sol3/papers.cfm?abstract_id=2327807.

Lo, A. W. (2014) The adaptive markets hypothesis: Market efficiency from an evolutionary perspective. *Journal of Portfolio Management*, 30(1), 15–29.

Luther, R. G. and Matatko, J. (1994) The performance of ethical unit trusts: choosing an appropriate benchmark. *The British Accounting Review*, 26(1), 77–89.

Luther, R. G., Matatko, J. and Corner, D. C. (1992) The investment performance of UK "ethical" Unit Trusts. *Accounting, Auditing & Accountability Journal*, 5(4).

Mallin, C. A., Saadouni, B. and Briston, R. J. (1995) The financial performance of ethical investment funds. *Journal of Business Finance & Accounting*, 22(4), 483–496.

Johnson, B., Bioy, H. and Boyadzhiev, D. (2016) Assessing the true cost of strategic-beta ETFs. *Morningstar Manager Research*, February. http://media.morningstar .com/uk/MEDIA/ETF/AssessingtheTrueCostofStrategicBetaETFs.pdf.

Moskowitz, M. (1972) Choosing socially responsible stocks. *Business and Society Review*, 1(1), 71–75.

Page, S. (2011) The Myth of Diversification: Risk. Factors vs. Asset Classes. PIMCO.

Podkaminer, E. L. (2012) Risk factors as building blocks for portfolio diversification: The chemistry of asset allocation. CFA Institute.

Renneboog, L., ter Horst, J. and Zhang, C. (2006) Is ethical money financially smart? Finance Working Paper, No. 117/2006, European Corporate Governance Institute, Brussels.

Renneboog, L., ter Horst, J. and Zhang, C. (2008) The price of ethics and stakeholder governance: The performance of socially responsible mutual funds. *Journal of Corporate Finance*, 14(3), 302–322.

Rawson, M. and Johnson, B. (2015) Fee study: Investors are driving expense ratios down. Morningstar. https://news.morningstar.com/pdfs/2015_fee_study.pdf.

Ross, S. (1976) The arbitrage theory of capital asset pricing. *Journal of Economic Theory*, 13(3), 341–360.

Russell Investments (2014) Smart Beta Guidebook, An Overview of Russell Smart Beta Indexes.

Sauer, D. A. (1997) The impact of social-responsibility screens on investment performance: Evidence from the Domini 400 Social Index and Domini Equity Mutual Fund. *Review of Financial Economics*, 6(2), 137–149.

Sharpe, W. (1964) Capital asset prices: A theory of market equilibrium under conditions of risk. *Journal of Finance*, 19(3), 425–442.

Sharpe, W. (2014) Is "smart beta" smart enough to last? Financial Times. https://www.ft.com/content/808189b8-f0a9-11e3-8f3d-00144feabdc0.

Statman, M. (2000) Socially responsible mutual funds (corrected). *Financial Analysts Journal*, 56(3), 30–39.

Statman, M. and Glushkov, D. (2009) The wages of social responsibility. *Financial Analysts Journal*, 65(4), 33–46.

Stoneberg, J. and Smith, B. (2016) Getting Smart About Beta. Invesco White Paper Series on the Active/Passive Debate.

Swiss Sustainable Finance (2016) Swiss Sustainable Finance Annual Report 2015. Zurich.

Titman, J. (1993) Returns to buying winners and selling losers: Implications for stock market efficiency. *Journal of Finance*, 48(1), 65–91.

Vanguard (2012) Joined at the hip: ETF and index development. Vanguard Research, July.

Vanguard (2014) Costs and charges: Their key role in successful investing. Vanguard Research, March. https://www.vanguard.co.uk/documents/portal/company/costs-charges-the-vanguard-way.pdf.

Index

Printed and bound by CPI Group (UK) Ltd, Croydon, CR0 4YY

06/07/2023

03233374-0002